# The Lord's Prayer

# The Lord's Prayer

*A Text in Tradition*

Kenneth W. Stevenson

Fortress Press
Minneapolis

THE LORD'S PRAYER
A Text in Tradition

Fortress Press edition 2004

Cover image: *The Worshippers*, Ghent Altarpiece, Jan van Eyck

ISBN: 0-8006-3650-3

Printed and bound in Great Britain by Biddles Ltd,
www.biddles.co.uk

08 07 06 05 04 1 2 3 4 5 6 7 8 9 10

# Contents

# Preface and Acknowledgements

'As our Saviour taught us . . .' It is these words, or something like them, that usually introduce the best-known and best-loved prayer in the Christian repertoire, with its simple but far-reaching claims about God's name, kingdom and will, and his sustenance, forgiveness and providence. No other prayer is introduced in quite the same way, with its origins in the New Testament and the teaching of Jesus of Nazareth. Yet the prayer has never stood still. Its text has continued to be a matter of debate. The way it has been interpreted has varied from one tradition and century to another. Its shape and content have been matters of dispute, as witness the question of whether it is made up of six or seven petitions, and whether the doxology is the best way to end it. Its position in public worship has been hotly debated, as at the Reformation, when some radical Christians gave up using it altogether. And in recent times, its Jewish setting has revealed a rich hinterland of reflection on the prayer's central themes. That the prayer began life as one taught by a rabbi to his followers opens up new vistas, including the possibility that it is not the private property of the Church but the possession of the whole human race.

In an earlier book (*Abba Father: Understanding and Using the Lord's Prayer*, Canterbury Press, 2000), I attempted to look at some of these questions in a preliminary way. But a longer and more detailed study beckoned from the perspectives of biblical, historical and liturgical theology – of which the ensuing pages are the result. We begin (Chapter 1) with questions of method and scope and end (Chapter 9) with points of analysis, as well as the abiding questions that history is unlikely – fortunately! – to settle. The main part is a walk through history: Chapter 2 looks at the biblical, Jewish and early evidence; Chapters 3 and 4 take in the patristic East and West, in each case confining the liturgical details to a separate, concluding section; Chapter 5 takes up the later East, while Chapter 6 provides a comprehensive treatment of the medieval West, with an increasing focus on the prayer in English that pervades the rest of the book; while Chapter 7 examines the later Middle Ages, Reformation and Counter-Reformation in all their dissonance, Chapter 8 takes us into the modern period and beyond, with an emerging consensus on the prayer's place and function in public worship, its continuing tradition of interpretation and its unresolved issues of translation and meaning.

I am, as always, grateful to the many people who have generously helped me with advice, comment and encouragement: Julie Anderson, John Baldovin, Joop van Banning, Paul Bradshaw, Sebastian Brock, David Brown, Michelle Brown, Colin Buchanan, Julian Elphick-Smith, Gillian Evans, David Ford, Elisabeth Glenthøj, Graham Gould, Benedict Green, Dan Hardy, Peter Heath, John Hillawi, William Horbury, Leslie Houlden, Michael Jackson, Edward Kessler, Martin Kitchen, Ann Loades, Andrew Louth, Jean Maslin, Ashley Null, James Priory, Geoffrey Rowell, Robert Sanday, Bryan Spinks, Graham Stanton, Elisabeth Stevenson, Robert Taft, Christian Thodberg, Robert Thomson, Andrew Tremlett, Geoffrey Wainwright, John Walsh, Benedicta Ward, John Webster and Rowan Williams; Rob James responded to some recondite calls for photocopying; Quarr Abbey, on the Isle of Wight, provided space to pray and think as well as their fine library, Abbot Cuthbert and Brother Duncan always appearing at the ready; to Christine Smith and SCM Press my thanks for their confidence in the project, and also to my Portsmouth colleagues, Mervyn Banting, David Brindley, Peter Hancock, Alex Hughes, Michael Jordan and Christopher Lowson – they allowed me three months' study leave in early 2003, the high point of which was the hospitality extended to Sarah and myself by the Anglican Centre in Rome, and Richard

Garrard kindly arranging for an invitation to give a lecture with the same title as this book at the Gregorian University. My greatest debt of gratitude goes to Sarah, who lived alongside this book with rather more patience than I deserve.

In what follows, I have tried to allow the various strands of evidence, literary, theological, homiletical and liturgical, to speak for themselves. Not that the story is invariably clear, especially in the early centuries, nor that the overall picture is particularly tidy, which it is certainly not. It may help the reader to know at this stage that, because of the array of authors and sources, and the (relatively) short and easily accessed material involved, we have kept cross-references to a minimum, so that when a comparative source is mentioned in the text, bold type in the index will lead directly to where that particular source is discussed in full.

Forty-five years ago, Edmund Ivens, Rector of St Anne's, Dunbar, pointed out in my confirmation preparation that the two opening words of the Lord's Prayer belonged to everyone – and not just to the priest. His teaching lies behind this book, which is dedicated to his memory, and to all who faithfully teach the People of God how to use this unique prayer and savour its rich meanings. What I hope will emerge from this study, which is as much about interpretation as about use, is a conviction that the Lord's Prayer, so far from being fixed in stone, is a living text which keeps finding new climates and new terrain in order to be 'the prayer of the Lord' – in any age.

Kenneth Stevenson
Bishopsgrove
Fareham

30 July 2003
Feast of St Peter Chrysologus

# 1

# Scope and Method

## Introduction

> Last night, going to bed alone, I suddenly found myself (I was taking off my waistcoat) reciting the Lord's Prayer, in a loud, emphatic voice – a thing I had not done for many years – with deep urgency and profound and disturbed emotion. While I went on I grew more composed; as if it had been empty and craving and were being replenished, my soul grew still; every word had a strange fullness of meaning that astonished and delighted me. It was late; I had sat up reading; I was sleepy; but as I stood in the middle of the floor half undressed saying the prayer over and over, meaning after meaning sprang from it; overcoming me again with joyful surprise; and I realized that simple petition was always universal and always inexhaustible, and day by day sanctified human life.[1]

So wrote the poet Edwin Muir in his autobiography. The day was 1 March 1939 and the circumstances were special. For a start, Muir's wife was seriously ill, but apart from that, Europe was slowly plunging into war for the second time in the same century. A double-pronged anxiety was therefore pressing on him, as he found himself reciting the Lord's Prayer when he undressed that night. He does not tell us who taught him the prayer, but it was a familiar text which he may have known for his baptism, which (we subsequently learn) took place when he was three years old. On this particular occasion, he knows that he is saying it louder than usual. The words, so familiar, take on a new intensity of meaning. That intensity strikes him in a

1

particular way, because he comes to realize the richness of the prayer, which interlocks with his need to repeat it 'over and over again'. And it is through the intensity of the occasion, as well as his repeated recitation of the prayer, that he comes to recognize its purpose in a new way – to sanctify human life 'day by day'.

The 'Our Father', the 'Paternoster', the 'Lord's Prayer' is the central prayer of the Christian faith. But uniquely among all other prayers, it has a directly scriptural base, so that it can with some justification be called 'the canonical prayer' – in spite of the many variations of text and usage which we shall encounter across the cultures and centuries. As we shall see, the texts that have been used by the churches down the ages have tended to be a slightly edited version of what we read in Matthew 6:9–13, an example if ever one was needed of polishing Scripture in order to suit liturgical needs. The prayer is located in Scripture, the longer version at the very heart of the Sermon on the Mount, the shorter version in the centre of Jesus' ministry in Luke 11:2–4. The sixteenth-century Reformer John Calvin sees it primarily as a quotation from Scripture, as a guide to prayer rather than a liturgical text, whereas the seventeenth-century preacher Lancelot Andrewes, in a series of sermons published in 1611, describes *this* prayer as 'the prayer of charity' and all others as 'the prayer of nature'.[2] Perhaps that is a somewhat exaggerated way of making the point, but it marks the contrast which the vast majority of Christians have recognized. It was Cyprian of Carthage in the middle of the third century who is the first-known person to use the title *dominica oratio* – the *Lord's* Prayer – in his short discourse upon it.

What enabled Muir to turn to these words in a time of personal and national need was the fact that a standard text was corporately known and used by a community. And that lies at the heart of what the Lord's Prayer is about – the prayer of a community, taken from the New Testament, where it appears in two versions (Matthew 6:9–13 and Luke 11:2–4) but also located in the Christian tradition by virtue of the threefold needs of translation, use and interpretation, and in the context of worship that is both communal and individual. It is these perspectives that will come up again and again in the course of this study, the process of what might be called text in context. As we shall discover, interpretations of the Lord's Prayer vary a great deal according to context. The work of scholarship is never far from the surface, and the questions of interpretation in such a richly ambiguous prayer form an essential part of the story.

## The evidence

The literary evidence is – potentially – as vast as the number of treatises, sermons, addresses and expositions that have come down to us. They tend to combine various features, which include guides to worship and prayer, explanations of the biblical text, and ethical instruction in the Christian faith.

The earliest tradition was probably based on *catechesis*, the first example of which is Tertullian. Instruction for new Christians was obviously essential, and to base teaching about prayer and discipleship on the Lord's Prayer proved to be of lasting significance, flowering in the fourth and fifth centuries in such writers as Ambrose in the West and Theodore of Mopsuestia in the East. Catechesis moves into a formal question-and-answer mode exemplified in the eleventh century with Bruno of Würzburg, which develops into a 'catechism' style at the Reformation.

*Preaching* on the Lord's Prayer is also a persistent tradition. From the evidence that has come down to us, baptismal preaching overlaps with catechesis, as witness the short homilies of Augustine and Peter Chrysologus in the fifth century, for the benefit of those about to be baptized. Less baptismal and more devotional is the set of homilies by Gregory of Nyssa in the late fourth century. It is not always easy to delineate between different styles, but Augustine's exposition of the Sermon on the Mount (394), perhaps based on preaching, is more exegetical, and the Lord's Prayer is encountered in its biblical context. This is also what happens with John Chrysostom, as well as Martin Luther – who probably preached on the Lord's Prayer more than anyone else known to us. There is, too, the rich series of sermons preached by Thomas Aquinas in Lent 1273, back home in his native Kingdom of Naples, the year before he died.

*Exposition* of the prayer, in a verse-by-verse fashion, carefully applied to the Christian life, is also discernible in these writers. Perhaps it reaches its peak, as far as length is concerned, in the mid-twelfth century with Abbot Frowin of Engelberg. A simpler approach is taken by Anselm of Laon earlier in that century. An equally devotional (but theologically different) approach is to be found at the Reformation in John Calvin's *Institutes of the Christian Religion* (1536).

Another area of overlap between the Middle Ages and the Reformation is the *paraphrase*, where an individual writer composes an extended meditation based on the Lord's Prayer, which is no longer an exposition, but a prayer in its own right. There is an early eleventh-century Anglo-Saxon example, as well as those attributed to Francis de Sales and Francis of Assisi. This tradition survived the Reformation, to the extent that John Calvin wanted a lengthy paraphrase to form the basis of the intercession at the Sunday morning service. The devotional paraphrase tradition (for private devotional use) lived on in such writers as Jeremy Taylor and Thomas Wilson, distinguished seventeenth- and eighteenth-century Anglican bishops.

The Reformation also produced *metrical versions* of the Lord's Prayer, particularly in Martin Luther's 'Vater Unser im Himmelreich' (1539), probably composed for use with the Catechism. The prayer could thus be sung by the whole congregation. The tradition continued into the eighteenth century with John Wesley in England, and into nineteenth-century Denmark with N. F. S. Grundtvig.

In some of these writings, allegorical interpretation develops, particularly in *numerology*. Augustine honed this approach, and divided the prayer into seven petitions, applying the sevenfold structure to the first seven Beatitudes (Matthew 5:3–9), as well as to the sevenfold gifts of the Spirit (Isaiah 11:2). This became fashionable in the later West, and an assumed way of dealing with the prayer, sometimes extended to include the seven vices (deadly sins), the seven words from the cross, and even the orders of the Church. It was rejected by John Calvin at the Reformation, who went further and insisted that Augustine's sixth and seventh petitions (temptation and evil) be combined, and that the doxology (never part of Latin devotion, but used in most of the East) be added as the proper conclusion to the prayer.

The *structure* of the prayer is therefore constantly addressed. Augustine, influenced by Tertullian, dominates the West, with a Platonist view of 'three heavenly' (name, kingdom, will) and 'four earthly' (bread, forgiveness, temptation, evil). But this was modified in the early twelfth century as the petition for bread was increasingly seen as both heavenly and earthly. Aristotelian influence shifted the balance for the thirteenth century so that the prayer was seen in its entirety as a quest for the ultimate good, God himself. Martin Luther adapted this inheritance, taking the view that the prayer is made up of three spiritual petitions (name, kingdom, will), one natural (daily bread) and three for deliverance (sin, temptation, evil). But Eastern writers from the fourth century onwards regarded the prayer as consisting of six petitions, temptation and evil forming a single petition. As we shall see, this ties in with modern biblical scholarship.

Another interpretation is *liturgical*, where writers and preachers deal with the Lord's Prayer as part of the liturgy. The germ of this approach is to be seen in the homilies of the late fourth and early fifth centuries attributed to Cyril of Jerusalem. They explain the liturgy to those who have recently been baptized, and who have only just attended the eucharist for the first time, since the non-baptized were often sent out at the end of the Service of the Word. The liturgical approach was taken further in the sixth century at Constantinople with Patriarch Germanus, and in a more elaborate way with writers such as Amalar of Metz in the West in the ninth, with liturgical teaching intended for the whole people of God, not just for the newly baptized. In a more complex liturgy, everything needed an explanation as to why it was where it was, and the Lord's Prayer was no exception.

But what of the actual *use* of the Lord's Prayer in the liturgy? Baptismal homilies point to its centrality for the newly initiated, so that, for example, John Chrysostom can draw attention to the recitation of the prayer immediately after coming up from the font. By one of those twists of history, the same position is adopted by Thomas Cranmer in the Second Prayer Book in 1552, except that it is to be recited by all, and not just by the new Christian. Writers such as Ambrose and Augustine (in the West) and John Chrysostom and the author of the Jerusalem *Mystagogic Catecheses* (in the East) only provide evidence for the prayer's place in the eucharist from the late fourth century onwards, and between the eucharistic prayer and the communion. But two devices come to be used, as if to highlight the uniqueness of the prayer. One is to introduce it with a special formula (perhaps also to help the congregation join in saying the opening words, 'Our Father'). Another is to append a short prayer (called an embolism) taking up the theme of deliverance from evil ('deliver us, Lord'), with which the prayer ended. No other liturgical prayer is given such treatment, and it is a sure sign that there was a need to heighten its importance. At the Reformation, the embolism was abolished, as the doxology, 'For thine is the kingdom', gradually took over, with its stress on God's glory alone.

Different ways of *reciting* the Lord's Prayer also emerge from the evidence. Roman usage, retained for the superior in the *Rule of St Benedict* at the main morning and evening offices of Lauds and Vespers, was for the celebrant alone to recite the prayer at Mass. This practice persisted right up until the changes made after the Second Vatican Council in the Roman Missal of 1970. In early medieval Spain a variant of this practice developed, where the priest recited each petition, and the congregation responded with an 'Amen'. The more general custom was that everyone should join in. In both the medieval West and in the East, the Lord's Prayer also came to be associated with the use of the rosary, with the result that it was frequently repeated, a practice taken over in the West as a penance in connection with private confession. The Reformation reaction against such 'vain repetitions' was to restrict the use of the prayer, and to teach vehemently about it, and to isolate it in public liturgy, so that it could stand out with some prominence. This explains Luther's insistence that it is not *our* prayer, based on human effort, but *Christ's* prayer for us and with us now. On the other hand, the reaction of the Baptists in the 'Radical Reformation', the early Independents, was to refrain from using the prayer at all, and to regard it as a guide as to how to pray, and not a text to be said without understanding (or sincerity).

A further ingredient is what might be called the *secular* use of the prayer. A context that may be religious but which could stand on the edges of the community of faith. While Dante's 'Purgatory' has a profoundly religious base, it is not exactly a churchly context; and yet the early thirteenth-century Italian poet uses the Lord's Prayer as a basis for meditating on deliverance from evil. Beyond the edge of faith are the reflections of the twentieth-century Italian Jewish writer Primo Levi, for whom the experience of living in a concentration camp meant that 'daily bread' took on a meaning that pitched survival beyond what one could easily imagine.

Preaching always has a particular context, as witness F. D. Maurice's sermons delivered in London in the spring of 1848 while the revoluntionary barricades were going up in Paris, Helmut Thielicke in Stuttgart during the air raids at the end of the Second World War, and Alexander Schmemann's addresses broadcast into the Soviet Union from the USA, where he was a distinguished Russian Orthodox teacher. But taken together, all these overlapping approaches and uses provide a rich field of enquiry and comparison.

## Biblical, literary and liturgical scholarship

Biblical and liturgical scholarship have been going on for centuries, as the many works on the Lord's Prayer demonstrate, as witness Jerome's work on the Latin text of the Gospels and his commentary on Matthew, both written in the late fourth century. Many of the writers we shall be looking at will further corroborate this fact. But a number of scholars from recent times have left their imprint on the task of probing into the origins and meaning of the prayer. A number deserve mention at this stage.

First, Ernst Lohmeyer's *The Lord's Prayer*, originally published posthumously in German in 1952, appeared in English translation in 1965.[3] Lohmeyer was a German Lutheran scholar who disappeared at the hands of the Soviets at the end of the Second World War. The special features of his work are his attention to the Semitic background of the two texts of the prayer, and his detailed knowledge of early Christian literature; he spans biblical and patristic scholarship. His theory that the Lucan version of the text is originally from a 'northern' (Galilean) dialect of Aramaic and that Matthew's version is from a 'southern' (Jerusalem) dialect has not stood the test of time. Like many other twentieth-century writers, Lohmeyer stresses the eschatological background of the prayer – the inauguration of the kingdom of God.

The German Lutheran scholar Joachim Jeremias's *The Prayers of Jesus* was originally published in German in 1966, and appeared in English in the following year. Less patristic than Lohmeyer, Jeremias stresses yet more strongly the eschatological setting of the prayer, is convinced about its Semitic origins and interprets the opening word, 'Abba', as what a child informally calls their father. Such a view has been nuanced by James Barr, not so much in what Jeremias maintained, but in how it came to be used by others to imply a child's use of a term like 'Daddy'; 'abba' is, rather, an adult's intimate address to their father.[4]

Jean Carmignac's massive study, modestly entitled *Recherches sur le Notre Père*, was published in 1969.[5] Carmignac was a French Roman Catholic biblical scholar who specialized in the Dead Sea Scrolls. His theory that the Lord's Prayer was originally composed in Hebrew (the sacred language of Jewish religion) and not Aramaic (the language Jesus spoke with his disciples) has not gained widespread acceptance. But his knowledge of the literature, not just patristic but medieval and in the period since, is the most comprehensive that has appeared so far.

As far as the text of Matthew's Gospel is concerned, three particular studies stand out. One is Ulrich Luz's commentary, the first part of which was published in German in 1985, and in

English in 1989.[6] Luz's approach has been described as part of the *Wirkungsgeschichte* ('history of influence') school. This is of special importance when dealing with the Lord's Prayer as a whole, which he regards as the very centre of the Sermon on the Mount, because it becomes impossible to drive a wedge between a biblical scholarship intended to unearth 'the original meaning' of the prayer, and a historical scholarship intended to explain and critique how Christians have interpreted it. The scope of Luz's work, embracing both historical and liturgical perspectives, is an important tool in our study. Second, there is the detailed commentary by W. D. Davies and Dale C. Allison, the first volume of which was published in 1988. Davies and Allison pay careful attention to the Semitic background, particularly to Jewish prayer, but less to questions of history of interpretation.[7] The other study is Graham Stanton's *A Gospel for a New People: Studies in Matthew*, which was published in 1992. Stanton's impressive scholarship in this particular instance serves to underline the place of the Lord's Prayer as not only an integral part of the Sermon on the Mount, but also relating to the whole of Matthew's Gospel as well.[8]

A text-critical approach is taken by D. C. Parker, whose *Living Text of the Gospels*, published in 1997, contains a significant study of the Lord's Prayer.[9] Parker argues for a more relaxed attitude to its 'canonical' aspect than has been taken before. This means seeing translation as an inalienable part of an ongoing (and never-ending) process of interpretation, in which the text emerges as having something of a life of its own. Parker's overall thesis goes a long way towards understanding what we might call the 'Post-New Testament' life of the Lord's Prayer's text, not only in itself, but in homiletical interpretation and liturgical use – which are very much part of this study. As we shall show, the text of the Lord's Prayer, so debated among (for example) Anglophone Christians today, was unstable from the very beginning. Our study finds a (partial) echo in Bruce Metzger's interest in the history of the Bible, in its versions and translations.[10]

This line of enquiry, however, is about much more, and is no argument for some kind of free-for-all, in which the prayer can mean anything. It explains the notion of 'textuality', which is about the relationship of one text with another, as well as the relationship between a text and its interpretation. *Literary theory*, so far from being some kind of wooden threat to the nature of the text as prayer, liberates the text from being a form of 'textualism', i.e. an exercise of sticking rigidly to the text for its own sake.[11] As writers such as Barbara Johnson and Jonathan Culler have shown, literary theory can open up new avenues of understanding. When applied to the Lord's Prayer, these could include the emphasis in formalism that looks at what is happening to the prayer in a particular tradition of interpretation (e.g. Augustine's sevenfold scheme); the new-criticism quest for the prayer as an aesthetic entity in itself, not an historic document under someone's control (e.g. the allegorical interpretation of the prayer representing one of the three days of Christ's burial in the medieval mass); phenomenology's approach to the prayer text and the faithful together, making it into a praying experience (e.g. the newly baptized turning it into the very first words on arising from the font, as in the Armenian rite); or structuralism's stress on meaning as produced not by the text on its own but by the text with its 'reader response' (e.g. the medieval and Reformation paraphrase tradition).

Another significant contribution of a literary kind but in the tradition of biblical criticism, has been made by Benedict Green in his *Matthew, Poet of the Beatitudes*.[12] Green uses an array of scholarship and an ear for language to show how the Lord's Prayer is the 'centre-piece' of the Sermon on the Mount. For Green, Matthew is a Hebraic versifier who wrote the prayer in Greek, and he argues for its preeminence over Luke on the basis of a literary form which consists of three 'aspirations' (name, kingdom, will) and three petitions (dread, forgiveness, protection). As we shall see, questions of structure relate directly to interpretation, and affect the way the prayer is understood in use as well.

When it comes to *liturgical studies*, however, we note a considerable shift in recent years in the way early evidence is approached. In contrast to a generation that was more confident about putting forward patterns and shapes as to how liturgy evolved, Paul Bradshaw has been responsible for introducing a note of healthy scepticism. In his *Search for the Origins of Christian Worship*,[13] published in 1992, and reprinted in a revised edition in 2001, Bradshaw has shown that it is no longer possible to look at the first four centuries as a time of broadly similar styles and speeds of development. As we shall see, this is borne out by the evidence (or lack of it!) for exactly how the Lord's Prayer was used in those early centuries. Although we can note certain lines of evolution, notably the early triumph of Matthew's version (but in an edited form), and significant treatises on the subject by Tertullian, Cyprian and Origen, there is little directly to go on until we reach the fourth century, tempting though it is to read back what we *do* have into that earlier period. It is to him that we owe the need to stress 'text in context' in dealing with liturgical evidence.

Bradshaw builds on the 'comparative' method of liturgical studies, pioneered earlier in the twentieth century by Anton Baumstark, but honed considerably by Robert Taft. This approach leads to a more cautious handling of the evidence, with a dose of what is sometimes called 'the hermeneutics of suspicion'.[14] Instead of trying to build a uniform picture from what might be one isolated piece of evidence, we should either try to see other corresponding trends elsewhere, like the data for the prayer in the eucharist in the late fourth century, or accept the possibility of sporadic (and therefore untypical) practice, such as Chrysostom's reference to the newly baptized reciting the prayer after baptism in Constantinople in 399. What Taft contributes to our quest is a way of looking at liturgical 'units', groups of prayers and liturgical material, and how these evolved together, so that an individual prayer is not looked at on its own. When it comes to the Lord's Prayer, it is important, therefore, to see exactly where it is located, and what surrounds it, as, for example, in how it is introduced and concluded; as we shall see, this provides evidence for a common 'unit' in the eucharist in the later patristic East and West.

There are also two other important studies. The first is by Ingemar Furberg,[15] in 1968, on the Lord's Prayer in the eucharist up to the time of the Lutheran Reformation, which pays as much attention to the medieval as to the patristic writers. The other is by Maria-Barbara Von Stritzky in 1989, on the prayer in the first three centuries in the wider context of Christian writing, which is cautious about placing too much weight on the little evidence we have for the liturgy.[16]

Perhaps the most significant of all developments is the increased attention paid to the *Jewish* setting of Christian worship. The number of articles and studies on this area began to build up through the twentieth century, perhaps one of the single most pioneering being Oesterley's *The Jewish Background of the Christian Liturgy*, published in 1925.[17] Although only a few pages are devoted to the Lord's Prayer, Oesterley draws together enough to demonstrate significant parallels for virtually every part of the prayer. It could no longer be regarded as, in text at least, an entirely fresh set of ideas; unique, yes, but still the product of its setting. Nearly fifty years later came another pioneering work, when in 1974 M. Brocke, Jakob Petuchowski and W. Strolz edited a collection of essays which resulted from a conference held in Freiburg-im-Breisgau, Germany, in 1973, and which were published in English in 1978.[18] This work is important because it gathers together scholars from different fields, and provides a proper treatment of a number of Jewish prayer-texts with a striking resemblance to the Lord's Prayer. Although as long ago as the seventeenth century the Dutch scholar Hugo Grotius argued for a Jewish origin to the prayer, against the tide of many centuries of opinion, it was not until the twentieth century that this side of the question has been really pressed. The area of Jewish–Christian liturgy in general has been the subject of important work by Bradshaw and Laurence Hoffman, as well as a series of essays edited recently by Albert Gerhards, Andrea Doeker and Peter Ebenbauer. Edward Kessler has also championed Jewish–Christian studies not only in relation to the common origins of the two faiths, but with regard to the need for better understanding between us.[19] On that score alone, the

Lord's Prayer emerges as a Jewish prayer, taught by a rabbi to his disciples, which happened to become the central prayer of the Christian faith in consequence, the Jewish setting being an essential part of the story. (It is for this reason that we should speak of Jewish 'setting' rather than 'background'.)

## Issues of interpretation

Over and above the different kinds of evidence, there remain two key factors. One is the ambiguity of the words of the prayer itself, which allows different writers and preachers to pull in sometimes contrasting directions, often investing the prayer with their own theological areas of interest. The other is more complex and relates to more than ambiguity; real differences over what some parts of the prayer mean. Perhaps reflecting the fact that prayers directly for ourselves are harder to apply *to* ourselves than prayers about God *tout seul*, these are mainly confined to the second part of the Lord's Prayer, and concern almost every word in it, whether praying for bread, forgiveness or protection.

- When we speak of 'Our', is it only for the initiated, the baptized, or has it a broader thrust? Is it – at least potentially – to be applied to the whole human race?

- When we speak of God as 'Father', is this as adopted children, or as creator, or both – interpretations shared among many writers? The creator God is 'our' when applied to a wider perspective than the Christian community, the 'adoptive' Father is (arguably) the 'our' of the baptized only. And what of the feminist critique, which instinctively objects to the language of patriarchy?

- When we speak of God's name being 'hallowed', is this in lives dedicated to his service, or a baptized people, or in sacramental worship, as many expositions suggest, or is it by God himself, an eschatological prayer, as modern exegetes suggests?

- When we speak of the kingdom, is this the kingdom as experienced in the here and now, or is it the final kingdom, or is it both? Interpretations of eschatology have a direct bearing on this matter, and there is a tendency, for example, in writers living under the threat of martyrdom, such as Cyprian, to look to the final kingdom, whereas others, such as Augustine, include the triumph of God's grace bestowed in the sacrament of baptism as an experience of that kingdom. Later medieval writers speak of the Church as the kingdom, whereas both Luther and Calvin stress the role of the Spirit in the lives of Christians in that kingdom, which is God's alone.

- When we speak of the doing of the will, to what extent is it irresistible? Here, such writers as Calvin, with a distinction between the 'two wills' of God, permissive and eternal, differ from late medieval writers such as Frowin of Engelberg in the twelfth century, who emphasized free will, graciously guided and corrected by God.

- And when we use the words 'on earth as in heaven', does this apply only to the doing of the will, as modern exegetes suggest, or does it also apply to the coming of the kingdom and the hallowing of the name? Although this view has gained support among biblical scholars in the last hundred years, on linguistic grounds, it was first suggested by Origen in the third century, but taken up by only a few interpreters thereafter.

When we turn to the second part of the prayer, even more difficulties begin to emerge.

- Is the bread exclusively material, as Gregory of Nyssa insisted, or is it also eucharistic, as Tertullian and the North African tradition asserted? And what of the meaning of *epiousios*? Does this mean 'for the coming (day)', or does it mean the bread we need 'to survive'? Here, the Latin translation *quotidianum* is ambiguous, because what we need each day is also what we need in order to survive, whereas the Greek writers tend to interpret it as necessary bread, spiritual or material (or both), made explicit in the fifth-century Syriac translation, 'the bread of our need'.

- When we speak of forgiveness, how strong is that word 'as'? Does it place a real burden on us, in a causative sense, as Gregory of Nyssa taught? Does it refer to penance, as Thomas Aquinas taught? Or is the forgiveness that God alone gives on an entirely different plane, as Calvin clearly taught? And to what extent do writers develop the theme of 'debt'?

- When we pray against temptation, what exactly does it mean? Is it the experience of being tested in this life, or is it the final temptation, the eschatological testing, to be separated from God? Can God really 'lead' us, as the New Testament implies? Or is there a simpler meaning behind the Greek, which partly conceals an Aramaic turn of phrase, meaning 'don't let us be tempted', as Carmignac has suggested?[20] And over against such a solution, which offers what the prayer might have meant in its original milieu, is the wealth of genuine Christian experience of what it is like to be tested in this life not to be taken seriously as part of that 'living text'?

- When we pray to be delivered from evil, is this a personal force, as Tertullian, Cyprian, John Chrysostom and subsequent Eastern tradition held? Or is it more comprehensive, and therefore impersonal, as Augustine taught, followed by the patristic and medieval West? The Greek New Testament has the definite article, whereas Latin knows of no such prefix – which explains this divide as an example of 'living text'. And is this petition a separate one from the preceding, as Augustine and the patristic and medieval West have generally held? Or is it really part of the preceding petition about temptation, as many Eastern writers believed, and as Calvin held, followed by many others, including Karl Barth?

- Finally, what is the place of the doxology? First appearing in the *Didache*, it is a fourth century addition to some Greek manuscripts of Matthew's Gospel. It was used by John Chrysostom and became part of Eastern liturgical tradition, where a doxology is in any case a more general way of concluding other kinds of prayer. Calvin regarded it as integral to the prayer, influencing Reformation practice, but it was never part of the Latin tradition, until ecumenical pressure after the Second Vatican Council.

These are some of the questions that will recur in the study that follows. It will not lead to a uniform, credible exercise in what the prayer 'originally meant'. It will, instead, lead to somewhat less tidy terrain, in which the prayer lives in many different places, and grows in many different directions, although much of the common liturgical evidence points to a position towards the end of daily prayer and near communion at the eucharist, but with no established place at baptism, probably because of the tradition of catechesis. Whatever use is made of it, in worship, devotion or study, the text can not do without its context. It is not a question of *what* it means, but *how* it means. As David Tracy has suggested in relation to textual interpretation, what we are dealing with is a profound 'excess of meaning'.[21]

# 2

# From the Bible to the Third Century

## Biblical and Jewish background

### Introduction

Comparing and contrasting are the best means of finding out more about how a prayer has evolved.[1] But when it comes to the Lord's Prayer, we have both more and less to go on. There are the two Gospel texts, not substantially different, but different enough to spark off an ongoing (and unresolved) debate as to whether Luke's version (Luke 11:2–4), being the shorter, is the earlier, or whether, because Luke shows signs that the language has been polished, Matthew's version is in fact the earlier (Matthew 6:9–13).[2] Then we have the text of the prayer as it appears in the *Didache* ('Teaching'),[3] an early Christian manual, probably from Syria, perhaps from Antioch, variously dated around the turn of the first century and into the second, and therefore within the lifetime of some of the later books of the New Testament, where it is placed between baptism and eucharist, indicating a context to do with both initiation and daily prayer. Whereas the prayer comes in the public context of the Sermon on the Mount in Matthew, and it is prescribed by Jesus to the disciples to distinguish them from John the Baptist's followers in Luke, the *Didache* has Matthew's version, with some slight changes, but its function is for Christians to use as a mark of their identity. These are 'foundational' texts, because they provide the New Testament background. They also show us what may be an 'editorial process' of the Christian community already at work, if not between the texts in Matthew and Luke, then assuredly in the *Didache* version.

The next stage is to look at the two Gospel texts in relation to the Gospels themselves, and to see how they reflect the priorities of each of the two evangelists concerned, and those of the other evangelists. Such a process shows how rooted in the gospel preaching the Lord's Prayer is – a fact repeatedly observed by subsequent commentators, starting with Tertullian, the first known author to write about the prayer, who described it as 'a summary of the gospel'.[4] There are questions, too, about the origin and exegesis of these texts.

But there is an equally significant stage without which the setting of the prayer is not wholly understood, and that concerns its essentially Jewish character. This means looking into two areas; the first is the Old Testament, where there are significant parallels. The second is the tradition of Jewish prayer which contains even more impressive parallels. And the thrust of this part of our investigation will serve to show how *Jewish* the prayer is. This has been underestimated in the past, in the early centuries because of the struggle between Christians and Jews themselves, and in later centuries through the unfortunate legacy of anti-Semitism. It is not enough to say that the Jewish nature of the prayer is a modern invention just because it has been neglected for so long.

Then we move into the three earliest discourses on the prayer. First, there is Tertullian himself, who left his influence on another North African, Cyprian of Carthage, writing later in the third century. Both these show signs of having been used for instruction purposes, and may well have formed the background to baptismal catechesis; and, as we shall see, they also demonstrate how unstable the text of the prayer was. The third author, Origen, takes us to the East, and to a different style and a greater length, which is more to do with instruction in prayer and the spiritual life. Finally, we shall survey the (sporadic) references to the prayer from other authors in these centuries. From this, a picture will emerge of a prayer whose text was unstable, which was used and known and was the basis for instruction; but there is little evidence, as yet, for use in public worship.

The table of texts set out opposite is from Leslie Houlden's

## *The Gospel and* Didache *texts*

| Line | Matthew 6:9–13 | Luke 11:2–4 | *Didache* 8.2 | John |
|------|----------------|-------------|---------------|------|
| 1 | Our Father who is in the heavens | Father | Our Father who is in heaven | 17:1, 3 17:11, 21, 24–25 |
| 2 | may your name be hallowed | may your name be hallowed | may your name be hallowed | 17:11–12 17:26 |
| 3 | May your kingdom come. | May your kingdom come. | May your kingdom come. | 17:1–2 |
| 4 | May your will come to pass as in heaven also on earth. | | May your will come to pass as in heaven also on earth. | 17:4 |
| 5 | Our bread for the morrow (?) give us today | Our bread for the morrow (?) give us each day | Our bread for the morrow (?) give us today | 6:32–35 |
| 6 | and forgive us our debts as we also have forgiven our debtors | and forgive us our sins for we also forgive everyone indebted to us; | and forgive us our debt as we also forgive our debtors; | 17:17 |
| 7 | and do not lead us into test, | and do not lead us into test. | and do not lead us into test, | 17:11–15 |
| 8 | but rescue us from the evil one (?). | | but rescue us from the evil one (?). | 17:15 |
| 9 | | | for yours is the power and the glory for ever. Amen. | |

article in *The Anchor Bible Dictionary*, with two slight adjustments (altering 'art' to 'is' in line 1, and adding the (authentic) doxology to the *Didache* text).[5] It is clear from the outset what are the differences between the three versions: Luke does not have 'our' before 'Father' or the reference to heaven in line 1; he has neither the petition for the doing of the will nor for deliverance from evil (lines 4 and 8); he stresses the 'daily' character of the bread (line 5); and the prayer for forgiveness uses two words for sin, trespasses (a more direct word in Greek) and debts (more acceptably Hebraic as an image for sin, and therefore used both times by Matthew), and places mutual forgiveness in the present tense. The *Didache* has a singular heaven at line 1, probably to harmonize with 'heaven' at line 4; singular 'debt'; and the present tense, as Luke, at line 6 (but whereas Luke has the koinē Greek, *aphiomen*, *Didache* has the classical, *aphiemen*).

What are we to make of these differences? Origen suggested that Jesus gave the prayer to the disciples on two separate occasions – showing, in a quaint manner, some kind of answer to those who were baffled by two texts, so broadly the same, and yet significantly different.[6] But the differences can be explained by recourse to the individual Gospels themselves. Luke often refers to God as Father and no more (Luke 22:42; 23:34, 46). Matthew, on the other hand, likes to refer to God as 'our', 'my' and 'your' (Matthew 5:16; 6:4; 26:42), and with the adjective 'heavenly', as well as balancing heaven and earth on several occasions (Matthew 6:19–20, 25, 28; 16:19; 18:18 and 28:18). Luke does not include line 4, the doing of the will; but there is a central scene in the birth-narrative, a special feature of this Gospel, where Mary surrenders herself before the angel Gabriel to God's will at the annunciation (Luke 1:38). On the other hand, the explicit doing of God's will in discipleship is also a feature of Matthew (Matthew 7:21; 12:50; 18:14; 26:42). Matthew's stress on mutual forgiveness as already having taken place (line 6) follows his emphasis on forgiveness as an essential part of discipleship (Matthew 16:27; 18:23–25); indeed, he goes on to follow the Lord's Prayer with a call to forgiveness (Matthew 6:14–15). Luke's stress on 'daily' (line 5), on the other hand, is echoed in the daily taking up of the cross which was expressed only two chapters earlier (Luke 9:23). He uses the Greek word for sin, with its image of missing the mark (from archery), as well as 'debt', from Matthew. Luke does not have line 8, the petition against evil; but Matthew mentions evil no fewer than twenty-four times, and the (personal) devil twice (Matthew 13:19 and 38). The presence of a doxology at the end of the *Didache* text is not a surprise; there are other doxologies at the conclusion of prayers elsewhere in this document, and to end with a doxology would be in line with Jewish liturgical custom, to the extent that no-one would think of ending a prayer without one. It is interesting to note that the *Didache* does not include 'kingdom', whereas all three occur (but with *kratos* instead of *dunamis*) at 1 Peter 4:11.

The setting of the prayer in each Gospel is also significant. Stanton, among others, has highlighted that it comes in the centre of the Sermon on the Mount, coming immediately after instructions on prayer (including the need to be brief, Matthew 6:7), and leading straight into teaching about forgiveness. Opinions about the Lucan version vary between Christopher Evans, who tends to see it not quite fitting into its context, Raymond Brown, who regards it as following naturally on from the 'one needful thing', from the story of Martha and Mary (Luke 10:42) and Benedict Green, who (less convincingly) suggests a liturgical milieu, 'daily' bread referring to communion, and the omission of evil explained by baptismal usage (the new Christian once cleansed, supposedly does not need to pray against evil).[7]

The internal shape of the prayer is in two sections, the first being petitions, in the aorist imperative (i.e. immediate) in the Greek, and in the second part, the prayer is about our needs, with the verbs altering. Underneath the obvious differences, there is still the sense of the short, rhyming character of the prayer, which is part of its essential genius. Matthew retains the aorist imperative in the second part, whereas Luke uses the present, implying a continuing process, and perhaps also showing a less eschatological view, i.e. 'keep providing us each day with bread'.

With the bread petition we come across the first real crux. Does *epiousios* come from *epi* and *einai* ('to be'), i.e. the bread that is daily, which is how it is rendered in the old Latin version, *quotidianum*, or does it mean 'the bread that we need'? Alternatively, does *epiousios* come from *epi* and *ienai* ('to go'), and therefore means 'the bread of the coming day', i.e. tomorrow? The (lost) *Gospel of the Nazarenes*, written in either Aramaic or Syriac, and dating from the second century, used the word *mahar* (of tomorrow), according to Jerome, an indication perhaps of an early eschatological interpretation of the prayer. Subsequent interpretation explores these possibilities, but contemporary scholarship tends towards the latter interpretation.[8]

The other main crux concerns temptation. The word *peirasmos* has a variety of meanings, from 'testing' (the eschatological view) to 'suffering' (and therefore in daily discipleship). The verb is clearly 'do not lead', an aorist subjunctive, which with the negative in the Greek of the time is equivalent to an aorist imperative; the 'Old Latin' version renders this *ne nos inducas* ('do not lead us'), but there were variants, the mark of the Church struggling with the problem of suffering. There are obvious signs of this elsewhere in the New Testament, such as Paul's conviction that the faithful disciple would not be tempted beyond what they can endure (1 Corinthians 10:13), a theme taken up again (cf. James 1:12 and Revelation 3:10), and in contrast to the view that Jesus himself was tempted like us in every way, but without sinning (Hebrews 4:15). Interpretations of this part of the prayer therefore vary, and although Augustine was clear that the two petitions about temptation and evil should be separated, a number of biblical scholars see the latter almost as Matthew's explanation of the former, or, as Tom Wright succinctly puts it, 'by giving us this prayer, Jesus invites us to walk ahead into the darkness, and discover that it, too, belongs to God'.[9]

But what of the two Gospels in which the prayer does not appear at all? Although we are not suggesting Mark knew of the prayer, there are echoes of its content in his Gospel. Jesus addresses God as 'Abba' in Gethsemane (Mark 14:36); at the very beginning, there is the proclamation of the coming kingdom (Mark 1:14–15), as the Baptist teaches, but this is expressed in the parables (e.g. the sower, Mark 4:1–20); and in Gethsemane, Jesus wrestles with the Father's will (Mark 14:32–42), which also echoes lines 7 and 8, temptation and deliverance from evil. The prayer for bread (line 5) could be seen in the two miracles of the loaves (Mark 6:33–49; 8:1–9); and food is a recurrent theme in Mark's Gospel, as is also the theme of forgiveness (e.g. Mark 11:25–26, where it is in the context of praying). These echoes provide for every single petition, with the exception of the hallowing of the name. But this does not mean that the community of Mark's Gospel knew the prayer; all it means is that the teaching that is embedded in the prayer also occurs in that Gospel.

The Fourth Gospel provides more than Mark, as the table set out above indicates; the striking feature is that all of it, with the exception of the petition for bread (line 5), comes from the 'High Priestly Prayer' of Jesus (John 17). Its opening prays, 'Father, the hour has come' (John 17:1), and it refers to heaven as the place where Jesus was with the Father, and to which he is to return (John 17:11, 21, 24–25). Jesus prays that the disciples be kept in the Father's name (John 17:11); and he prays for the coming of the kingdom by asking the Father to glorify the Son, since he is being given power over all flesh (John 17:1–2). The petition for doing the will (line 4) is echoed by Jesus when he speaks of having done all that the Father gave him to do (John 17:4). Forgiveness may possibly be seen in the prayer for the disciples to be sanctified in the truth (John 17:17); and the context and atmosphere of temptation and deliverance is spread over a number of verses, especially where he prays for the protection and deliverance of his followers (John 17:11–15).

While Mark's brevity may explain the absence of the prayer in that Gospel, the case for John is affected by its length. There is, for example, no narrative of the institution of the eucharist in John, only the washing of the disciples' feet (John 13:1–11). Yet eucharistic imagery and allusion are to be found in the Fourth Gospel (e.g. John 6:35). The community of John probably did not know the Lord's Prayer, but they knew its teaching as prayer from John 17. On the other hand, when we ask that question of the Pauline epistles, we are left with two references to crying 'Abba, Father' (Romans 8:14–16; Galatians 4:6), which could conceivably be some kind of shorthand for the prayer; what is surprising is that Paul does not therefore mention it anywhere. Indeed, the earliest version of the prayer could well have begun, 'Abba', an accepted way of addressing God in prayer, which is how the Lord's Prayer begins, in both the Matthew and Luke versions. The *Didache*'s use of Matthew could be early proof of the Church's preference for this text instead of Luke, or it may reflect the Didachist's knowledge of parts of Matthew's Gospel, although van de Sandt and Flusser have recently argued for its independence even from Matthew.[10] It is not our purpose to adjudicate between the theories concerning the origin of the Matthean and Lucan texts, and what may lie behind them. It is the Matthew version, modified in various ways, that becomes the Church's prayer, and probably at a very early stage, with variants in both its use and its transmission. The *Didache*'s insistence that this is the prayer that distinguishes Christians from 'hypocrites' (i.e. pious Jews) is yet one more indication of the Lord's Prayer as *the* prayer of the Church.

## Jewish setting

We have seen how the Lord's Prayer is a prayer with the atmosphere and teaching of the Gospels embedded in every single syllable. The same is also true both for the Old Testament and for the rich Jewish prayer tradition which scholars such as Karlheinz Müller would want to claim the 'Our Father' to be part of.[11] Indeed, 'Father' is generally used as a name for God with the suffix 'our' in Rabbinic literature. Although Jewish piety would not address God as 'Abba', it certainly addresses God as Father (Hosea 11:1; Isaiah 63:16; 1 Chronicles 29:10; Psalm 89:27). The hallowing of the name of God, which Jews would say was not a typical expression in the New Testament, is paralleled in texts which refer to the sanctification of the people as a response to the manifestation of divine holiness (2 Samuel 6:2; Jeremiah 7:11; Ezekiel 36:23; Leviticus 11:45). The coming of the kingdom relates to God's rule with justice (Ezekiel 20:33; Psalms 46:7; 121:5). The doing of the will pervades the piety of the Psalter, where, as in much interpretation of the Lord's Prayer at this point, there is a rich ambiguity that embraces God's will as both that with which we struggle in order to make sense of our lives as well as the final revelation of his will at the end (e.g. Psalm 119: 27, 30, 32, 33; Isaiah 46:9).

The prayer moves towards what Jews describe as the human partner of the covenant. Daily bread immediately evokes the manna in the wilderness (Exodus 16:15; Numbers 11:6; Deuteronomy 8:3). To ask for daily food, eaten in company with others after thanks have been offered, is a profoundly Hebraic activity. The Old Testament knows first and foremost the forgiveness of God (Exodus 32:32; Psalms 6:2; 18:38; 130:2), but with less stress on mutuality, except when preached about (Leviticus 19:18). Protection from temptation is supremely enacted in the *akedah*, the offering of Isaac by Abraham (Genesis 22:1–19), although there are other examples of the faithful being tested (Exodus 16:4; Deuteronomy 8:2; Judges 2:22). Deliverance from evil is also a recurring theme (1 Samuel 12:10; Psalm 33:19), though Jewish piety would tend to link the two petitions together – as many Eastern writers, and Calvin at the Reformation. And the doxology (cf. 1 Chronicles 29:11–12) is so rooted in Jewish prayer tradition that it is from this milieu that it arose in the *Didache* tradition.

When it comes to actual Jewish prayer, we are able to compare like with like, and move beyond parallels of thought and theology. The *Shema* (Deuteronomy 6:4–5) tells us to love the Lord with all our heart, soul and strength; fundamental to Jewish piety, Birger Gerhardsson takes the view that its threefold character, which Jesus would have known from an early age, lies behind much more of the New Testament than has so far been recognized.[12] That could suggest a correspondence with the Lord's Prayer: the heart may be there in the hallowing of the name and daily bread; the soul in the coming of the kingdom and the gift of forgiveness; and strength in doing the will and protection from temptation and evil. Even if such a view is thought schematic, the threefold focus of the *Shema* still parallels the threefold structure of both parts of the prayer.

But we are on more explicit ground with the *Kaddish*, which the French biblical scholar J.-B. Frey as long ago as 1915 compared with the Lord's Prayer.[13] Although it is mentioned at the beginning of the seventh century in relation to Palestinian synagogue usage, the earliest complete text of the *Kaddish* appears in *Seder Tefillot*, which is a prayer book compiled in the middle of the ninth century for the Sura Academy in Babylonia, where a congregational 'Amen' follows each petition. Working on the basis of its antiquity, and the resistance of at least some of the rabbis to rigidly set forms of prayer, we are able to push the date of origin for the *Kaddish* to an earlier date as Heinemann has argued.[14] Here is the ninth-century text:

Exalted and sanctified be His great Name.
In the world which He created according to His will, may He establish His kingdom in your lifetime, and in the lifetime of the entire House of Israel, speedily and soon.
May His great Name be blessed for ever and to all eternity.
Praised, glorified, exalted, extolled, revered, highly honoured, and adored is the Name of the Holy One, blessed be He beyond all the blessings, hymns, praises, and consolations that are ever uttered in the world.

Known as the 'Half-Kaddish', to distinguish it from the 'Full Kaddish', which contains some additions, both have been part of daily Jewish prayer-services for a very long time, the former being recited before the *Amidah* (the 'Eighteen Benedictions'), and the latter after it. And unlike Scripture itself, but like Christian liturgy, the *Kaddish* has come down to us as versions, different traditions and liturgical uses of small insertions. (The *Kaddish* for the departed has a special addition at the end.) The parallels with the first part of the Lord's Prayer – the name, the kingdom, the will – are obvious. They are more than linguistic, for they penetrate into the lifeblood of the Lord's Prayer and demonstrate its Jewish setting in a tradition inspired by certain norms but allowed to develop according to different needs and circumstances. (The practice of the intercalated 'Amens' we shall come across again in the (Spanish) Visigothic liturgy.)

Two other Jewish prayers contain parallels. One is the *Amidah* (the so-called 'Eighteen' Benedictions, although there are in fact nineteen), part of the daily synagogue service; the other is the *Abhinu Malkenu* ('Our Father, our King!'), a festal prayer.[15] In both, similar themes occur to the three which are easily identified in the *Kaddish*. There are others as well, in addition to the repeated reference to God as Father in the *Abhinu Malkenu*, such as the provision of blessings, the gift of forgiveness, and protection from ills.

These ancient Jewish texts take us into a world of faith-experience expressed in prayer that is paralleled in the Christian experience of praying the Lord's Prayer. William Barclay draws out the importance of its Jewish setting, and includes a discussion of Rabbinic views on the content and motivations for prayer, such as that it should primarily be about mercy, not fixed claims, and that it should be concentrated.[16] The Lord's Prayer qualifies on these (and other) counts. The major point of difference with much Jewish prayer (the *Shema* and the *Kaddish* excepted) is that it is so short, which reflects Jesus' own injunction against long-windedness (Matthew 6:7). It also shows that *his* prayer, rooted as it clearly was in the piety of his upbringing, is in that sense distinct. But it is still fundamentally a Jewish prayer, taught by a rabbi to his followers; indeed, when the *Didache* enjoins that it should be prayed thrice daily, there is a direct echo of the Old Testament custom, continued in Rabbinic tradition, and taken over in the New Testament, to pray three times each day (Daniel 6:10; Psalm 55:17, cf. Acts 2:15; 10:3, 16).[17]

What can be made of our discussion so far? The Lord's Prayer is not a fixed text, but lives in an already existing tradition, slowly evolving in the manner that Jewish scholars have noted of the venerable prayers of their tradition as well. Both the New Testament contexts provide a focus on teaching. In Matthew, in the Sermon on the Mount, the prayer summarizes the teaching itself, but Jesus only gives the prayer as a guide, not as an exact prescription. In Luke it comes when the disciples observe him praying on his own, a special feature of the third evangelist (cf. Luke 3:21; 5:16; 6:12; 9:18, 28; 22:41), and they ask him to teach them how to pray. But nothing is known of any liturgical use of the Lucan version in antiquity, beyond the fact that it appears in a Gospel with more explicit liturgical material than the others in the canticles of the birth-narratives (cf. Luke 1:46–55, 68–79; 2:14, 29–32). And while the meaning of the prayer presents its challenges (How eschatological was it intended to be? Is Luke's stress on bread 'each day' a sign of the Church settling down into history? And what exactly is the test from which we pray to be protected?), it is of sufficient importance to appear in full in the earliest Church Order, the *Didache*, and to be prayed in the same way as by devout Jews, three times daily. It is, therefore, not only fundamentally a *Gospel* prayer, but it is at heart a very *Jewish* prayer, so that it stands at the two points – of arrival and departure – which make the New Testament what it is. Many of the themes of the prayer – the name, the kingdom, the will, as well as sustenance, forgiveness and divine providence – are central to the ongoing traditions of Rabbinic Judaism.[18] Christians wanted to pray along these lines, and to express their identity by it, but there appears already to have been an acceptance, as in Jewish tradition, that versions would vary, within its established rhythms.

## The second and third centuries

### Tertullian

The earliest known discussion on the Lord's Prayer is by Tertullian (*c*.160–*c*.225), in North Africa, and it takes the form of a short discourse on prayer in general, which deals with attitudes, set times and other questions, but at whose heart lies a treatment of the prayer, clause by clause. It is supposed to have been written between 200 and 206, and therefore before he became a Montanist.[19] All three of the discourses on the prayer from this early period emanate from North Africa: Tertullian and Cyprian came from the western and Roman part, whereas Origen came from Alexandria, although his treatise dates from the Palestinian stage of his ministry. Tertullian's discourse is preceded by one on Baptism, and followed by one on Repentance and a further discourse addressed to those who might be martyred; all this sets his work in the context of early Christian suffering.

Some years ago, Geoffrey Lampe contributed an article to a collection of essays in honour of Gordon Rupp on a number of patristic commentaries on the first part of the Lord's Prayer, in which he draws attention to the brevity and influence of Tertullian's discourse.[20] Cyprian and Augustine, among others, knew and used it. Well into the fourth century, Hilary of Poitiers noted that it dates from his Catholic rather than Montanist time, and maintained that it was so good that he had no need to include a treatment of his own in his commentary on Matthew's Gospel.[21]

Tertullian begins (in chapter 1) by drawing attention to the fact that this is a 'new form of prayer', and therefore quite different from anything any other religion (Jewish included) ever taught; this is a familiar slant in early Christian writers. Seeing the prayer in the context of Jesus' teaching in Matthew's Gospel, he stresses the need to pray in secret, to pray in faith, and to pray briefly – which leads him to the oft-quoted description of the Lord's Prayer as a summary of the gospel ('breviarium totius evangelii'). The next seven short chapters deal with the opening, and the six petitions of the prayer. As far as the first clause is concerned (ch. 2), Tertullian concentrates on two aspects of fatherhood, first that he is our God, and we are his children (quoting John 1:12, often cited at this point in subsequent writings), and, second, that our mother, the Church, is not passed by. It is worth noting in this, the earliest discourse of the prayer, that motherhood is seen as important, but located in the Church, not the Godhead.

Tertullian focuses the hallowing of the name (ch. 3) first of all on Christ, 'for the Son is now the Father's new name', yet again pointing to the uniqueness of the Christian faith. It is not the task of the Christian to wish God well, he says, with a touch of irony, but to offer worship to Him, quoting the *Sanctus* (Isaiah 6:3; Revelation 4:8), in which context we are 'candidates for angelhood'. Hallowing is also about this life, too, for 'we pray . . . that (the Name) may be hallowed *in us* who are in Him, as well as all others for whom the grace of God is still waiting' – 'in us' meaning 'in all'. When it comes to the next clause, we come across a significant textual variant, which will have reflected Tertullian's own liturgical practice, his congregations included: the doing of the will precedes, rather than follows, the petition for the coming of the kingdom. Reading between the lines, one can guess what lies behind this inversion, for Tertullian seems aware of changing something he has inherited – but obviously feels able to do so. Just as we have prayed that the name may be hallowed in all, so now we pray that God's will may be done in all (ch. 4); we are 'heaven' and 'earth' (another insight which is used by later writers, but without the inversion). Like Cyprian who followed him here, Tertullian translates the petition simply as 'your will be done in the heavens and in earth' (*fiat voluntas tuo in caelis et in terra*), but he pluralizes 'heaven', presumably to harmonize with the prayer's opening. It does not quite express the delicacy of the Greek, with its stress on deliberate correspondence between heaven and earth; perhaps Tertullian's Latin version of the prayer reflected his own straight and ordinary style. Doing the will means following Christ's teaching, 'in preaching, working, in enduring'. For Tertullian, one of the most supreme ways of fulfilling God's will is to die for the Christian faith, which evokes the Gethsemane scene (Luke 22:42). This now leads into the petition for the kingdom coming 'in us' (ch. 5); we should not pray, as Tertullian maintains some do, for the 'protraction' of this age, but that 'your reign be hastened'; and he makes an eloquent reference to 'the souls of the martyrs beneath the altar'. For Tertullian, the kingdom is the result of doing the will.

Having prayed about heavenly things, the name, the will, the kingdom, Tertullian now looks at 'earthly necessities'; a distinction which Augustine is to make more explicit. When we pray for daily bread (ch. 6), he comes straight out with another text that recurs at this point, Jesus as the Bread of Life (John 6:35), which Tertullian takes to mean that we are praying to remain for ever in his Body, and not to be divided from it. That means the 'religious remembrance', the eucharist, is a physical as well as a spiritual reality. For by God's generosity not only are we provided for, but we should provide for others, hence giving bread to the person who knocks on our doors late at night (Luke 11:5–9). For Tertullian, the bread is both heavenly (eucharistic) and earthly (food), which once more Augustine takes up. Having contemplated the generosity of God, we now look to his mercy, in the prayer for forgiveness (ch. 7). 'A petition for pardon is a full confession, because those who beg for pardon fully admit their guilt.' Debt is about guilt (Matthew 18:21–35), and debts should be remitted (Matthew 18:21–22). Finally, Tertullian deals with temptation and deliverance from evil in the same section (ch. 8), unlike Augustine, who saw them as distinct and separate. 'Lead us not into temptation' he immediately interprets as 'suffer us not to be led into it, by him (of course) who tempts'. Here we come across the first example of a long tradition of wrestling with the meaning of this petition. If we ask not to be led into temptation, then, says Tertullian, we are asking God not to 'suffer us' to be led into it, God being (ultimately) the agent of the temptation. And he draws on the *Akedah*, Abraham with Isaac on the mountain (Genesis 22:1–19). Temptation, though permitted by God, is by the devil, the same process Jesus warned against in Gethsemane (Luke 22:40). That is why the final clause where he reads 'take us away' (*devehe*), not 'deliver us' (*libera*), 'is consonant and interprets the sense of' temptation.

Tertullian goes on to recapitulate the meaning of the prayer under its main headings – Father, Name, Will, Kingdom, Bread, Forgiveness, Protection. The prayer 'ascends, by its own prerogative, into heaven, commending to the Father what the Son has taught' (ch. 9), and he recommends that this is the prayer on which all others should be based (ch. 10). In the remaining sections, he deals with anger, disturbance of mind, washing hands, taking off cloaks, sitting after prayer (implying a standing posture), raising hands, the kiss of peace as a new custom, a way of concluding prayer with others, and other matters such as time and place, ending with a powerful defence of the power of prayer.

What we have here is a glimpse of how some early Christians viewed the Lord's Prayer. The text, reflecting one of the 'Old Latin' versions of the New Testament, is not fixed, hence the change in the order. And it requires not only explanation, as in the case of daily bread, but paraphrase, as in the case of temptation. Scripture is brought in to assist in the process, and we are left in no doubt as to the centrality of the prayer, whether on one's own or in company with others, in the ordinary life of the Christian, as a summary of the gospel.

## Cyprian

Cyprian was a citizen of Carthage, and was baptized in maturity in 246. Ordained Bishop of Carthage in 247, he was executed during the persecution of the Emperor Decius on 14 September 258, and was immediately venerated as a martyr. This inevitably gave his writings a certain authority, the treatise on the Lord's Prayer (the first to be unambiguously entitled *De Dominica Oratione*) written in 252 included.[22] The context of Cyprian's treatment is more overtly baptismal than Tertullian's, the work of a bishop for his own flock; and it is clear that, in addition to the five instances of almost direct quotation from Tertullian,[23] Cyprian's focus is more on the community itself. Of the thirty-six chapters, nearly all are devoted explicitly to the prayer; he adopts a style that was followed by subsequent preachers, consisting of a general introduction, a verse-by-verse exposition, and a final exhortatory section. It is no surprise that the atmosphere of persecution should come through, as he encourages his fellow Christians to be faithful in their discipleship.

The first seven chapters discuss the meaning and purpose of prayer, following the gospel precepts (ch. 1); the opening words of the following chapter, 'among the rest of his saving advice and divine precepts with which (Jesus) teaches people about salvation, he also gave us a form of praying', echo the introductory words to the Lord's Prayer which were later brought into the Roman rite and are in general use in many churches today.[24] There is the need for proper forms, not 'ill-assorted words' (ch. 4), and the importance of praying from the heart (chs 4 and 5). Four chapters deal with the opening address to the heavenly Father.

> We do not say, My Father Who art in heaven, nor Give me this day my bread, nor does each one ask that his own debt only be remitted, nor does he request for himself alone that he may not be led into temptation and may be delivered from the evil one. Prayer with us is public and common; and when we pray we do not pray for one but for the whole people, because we the whole people are one. (ch. 8)

Here Cyprian develops Tertullian's view of the unity of the Body of Christ; he refers to 'this compendium of heavenly teaching', and, in the first of several allusions to baptism, speaks of 'the very first words of his (new) birth that he has renounced his earthly and fleshly father' (ch. 9). For baptism renews us through the birth of spiritual grace and makes us God's children (ch. 10), which means behaving like them (ch. 11) – bringing out the ethical imperative of discipleship that was implicit in Tertullian.

The hallowing of the name is prayed for by 'we who have been hallowed in baptism', and the 'daily' praying of this prayer has a relationship with our growth in the baptismal life – a feature Augustine draws out more explicitly. We pray that the kingdom may be 'made present in us', for Christ is the kingdom, which is not what the Jews teach (ch. 13). Doing the will is to try to be 'an heir with Christ' (ch. 15), another baptismal allusion, because 'we are ourselves earth and heaven; and in both – that is, in body and in spirit – we pray that God's will may be done' (ch. 16). And developing Tertullian's theme of evangelism, in his handling of the hallowing of the name, Cyprian goes on to say that 'we pray for those who are still earth and who have not begun to be heavenly' (ch. 17).

Daily bread Cyprian regards (unlike Tertullian), unequivocally as the eucharist: 'we ask that this bread should be given to us daily, that we who are in Christ, and daily receive the Eucharist for the food of salvation, may not . . . be separated from Christ's body' (ch. 18). We are not to take any thought for tomorrow (Matthew 6:34), another text that is to become popular here, because generosity and simplicity of life are the ways of following Christ (ch. 20); this may reflect the experience of living in the aftermath of the plague two years earlier. Again, following Tertullian, he links this petition with the next; 'after the supply of food, pardon for sin is also asked for', with a warning that we need both to be forgiven by God and to forgive others if we are to receive eternal life (ch. 22). Forgiveness is seen as 'the greater sacrifice', which leads to 'peace and brotherly concord' (ch. 23). Cyprian actually adopts Tertullian's paraphrase, 'suffer us not to be led into temptation' (*et ne patiaris nos induci in temptationem*) as the text of the prayer itself, and echoing Tertullian's view of the will of God, he says that 'the adversary can do nothing against us unless God has previously permitted it'. Our 'fear, devotion and obedience' should therefore be directed to God, so that temptation does not overtake us (ch. 25), since temptation is a warning about our own infirmity and weakness (ch. 26). He sees the final petition as separate but still linked; 'when we say, deliver us from evil, there remains nothing further which ought to be asked'; and evil he interprets, following Tertullian, as the devil (ch. 27). In the remaining chapters, Cyprian discusses other matters related to prayer, which include references to the opening dialogue for the eucharistic prayer ('Lift up your hearts') and, like Tertullian, standing as the posture for prayer (ch. 31); as well as the practice of praying at set hours during the day (ch. 34), not ceasing to pray during the night (ch. 36).

Given the fact that he had a rhetorical training, it is no surprise that Cyprian's Latin is more literary than Tertullian's. He writes at greater length and provides a more developed treatment of the prayer than his master. Unlike Tertullian, he does not divide the prayer into 'heavenly' and 'earthly' petitions. It is a more sacramental discourse, with its references to baptism and the eucharist; there is a more worldly focus, with his allusions to the need for generosity and forgiveness; and his use of Tertullian's paraphrase of the petition about temptation as the text is another indication of how unstable the text of the Lord's Prayer was. We are beginning to grasp, too, a tradition of imaginative interpretation of the gospel prayer, which already had a life of its own within the community of faith. And he is the first person that we know who referred to this prayer as *dominica oratio* – the Lord's Prayer.

### Origen (c.185–c.254)

In 233 or 234, Origen was asked by two friends, Ambrosius and Tatiana, to resolve their difficulties as to why they should pray at all.[25] By that time, Origen was well established at Caesarea, Palestine, where he had built up a theological school, and had a considerable reputation as a preacher and interpreter of the Scriptures. He had left Alexandria, after a distinguished career in 215, because of political difficulties, not endearing himself to the church authorities back home for accepting an invitation to preach in Palestine even though he was a deacon and not a bishop (nor a presbyter). Like Cyprian, he suffered under the persecution of Decius, but is reputed to have died in prison. Subsequent generations regarded him as theologically suspect; this was partly because of his love of allegory and his apparent subordination of Christ to God, which some believed to contain the germs of Arianism. He was also criticized for teaching that the soul could progress without divine grace. This may explain why the treatise *On Prayer* was not translated into Latin, like many other of his works. It comes in two parts, the first dealing with prayer in general (chapters 1–17), the second with the Lord's Prayer (chapters 18–34) which could have been used in baptismal instruction. More extensive than anything we have met so far, it breathes the atmosphere of Platonism; for example, Origen has no time for any way of looking at the prayer in terms of a 'heavenly' first part followed by an 'earthly' second part, addressed to human needs; it is a *proseuchē*, a prayer which can only be addressed to God the Father, which embraces what we would call theological as well as devotional approaches.

Like the biblical scholar he demonstrates himself to be elsewhere, Origen begins by drawing attention to the two versions in the New Testament, suggesting that Jesus gave them on two separate occasions (18.3). And like Tertullian and Cyprian, he contrasts the prayer of the Church (the 'true synagogue') with Jewish worship (20.1); Jesus' warning about brevity (Matthew 6:7) inspires Origen to warn that Christians should not babble when they pray (21.1). He then turns to each petition of the prayer. Unable to find any examples of addressing God as Father in the Old Testament (22.1), he interprets this in Christian terms as our sonship, which gives us a moral obligation to live up to our calling (22.3). God's place 'in heaven' is not be understood spatially (23.1; a 'degrading notion', 23.3), yet the incarnation enables us to contemplate his heavenly reality (23.3), as we follow Christ.

The hallowing of the name, Origen interprets as our growth in knowledge of God, the One who shows Himself who He is (24.2), and he uses allegory to illustrate what appears to be a view of growth in knowledge that is akin to *anamnesis* in Platonism: 'anyone that clarifies the things that pertain to God recalls these things rather than learns them, even though he seems to hear from someone, or thinks that he discovers the mysteries of worship' (24.3). The petition for the kingdom is based on the view that the kingdom is already in our midst (Luke 17:20–21): 'he who prays for the coming of the kingdom of God rightly prays that the kingdom of God might be established, and bear fruit and be perfected in himself' (25.1) – a perfection that results from knowledge. The saint who acknowledges God dwells in the presence of God. Such a view spills over, logically, into the doing of the will, where it is our task to pray to do that will in order that we might be like those in heaven. 'When this will of God is done by us on earth as it is in heaven, then we shall be like them that are in heaven' (26.1). To pray in this way is to be a 'co-worker' with God (26.4), for heaven is Christ and earth is the Church (26.3). 'He who does the will of God and does not disobey His saving and spiritual laws, is heaven' (26.6).

When it comes to bread, Origen resolutely follows his Platonist principles. Interpreting *epiousios* as if *ousios* comes from *eimi* – 'I am', he regards the bread not as 'daily', but 'supersubstantial', as it is translated, using Jerome's term,[26] the bread that we need for our existence. Origen therefore rejects the view of those who 'understand from this that we are committed to pray for material bread' (27.1). 'What is more nourishing for the soul than the Word?' he asks (27.3). He uses a number of Scripture texts (especially from John 6). *Epiousios* in his view is a word 'invented by the Evangelists' (27.7) because of its uniqueness, its reference to incorporeal, unchanging nature; so 'the supersubstantial bread is that which is most adapted to the rational nature and is akin to its very substance, bringing to the soul health and well-being and strength, and giving to him that eats of it a share of its own immortality. For the Word of God is immortal' (27.9). 'This day' means the present age each day, and not the age to come (27.13).

Forgiveness is about using our body 'in such a way as not to waste its substance in our love of pleasure; and we owe it to our soul to look after it carefully' (28.2), for we have 'obligations (meaning debts) to the whole world and all the angels and the whole human race' (28.3). Origen regards the whole of human life as temptation (29.1), a wrestling (29.2), even if he has attained reason (28.5); we must try 'not to yield when we are tempted' (29.9). Yet God does permit temptation (29.11), so that we can grow in knowledge, since there are many gifts for the soul which we do not immediately recognize (29.17). Origen links temptation and deliverance together, and interprets evil personally as the devil – both features that we shall come across repeatedly in the East. God delivers us from the devil 'when we overcome him through taking a courageous stand in face of whatever befalls us . . . when we are afflicted, we are not through

God's help distressed' (30.1). We may be tempted, but our prayer is that we should not be engulfed by it. The remaining chapters resemble Cyprian's concluding material; they concern disposition, posture, place, facing east, and the importance of vigilance. For him, the Church is the right place for this prayer, but unlike Cyprian he gives us no hint as to what goes on there.

Origen's treatise is the first in the Christian tradition to speak of prayer as contemplating God rather than as a way of achieving material benefits. He is therefore the starting-point of a tradition of interpretation that is not baptismal or liturgical or ethical in its focus. Central to his treatment is his interpretation of the term *epiousios* as what Jerome was to translate as 'supersubstantial', thus turning the prayer for bread into a petition for *the* Bread that is incorporeal in itself, the Word of God. We are far away from Tertullian and Cyprian, instructing their faithful in the meaning of prayer in terms of the basics of the gospel, in which, for example, the bread is both spiritual (including eucharistic) and material, for survival. Origen's approach is more sophisticated, more elaborate; and it has a unified focus, for prayer is about contemplation, about enabling us to become more heavenly-minded. Forgiveness and temptation are not about relationships in the community and possible martyrdom – they are about the progress of the soul towards a richer understanding of God. There is conflict, but it is an essentially inner struggle.

## Other sources

Apart from these three treatises, all we have to go on in this early period are a few echoes – and, considering the importance subsequently attached to the prayer, they are sparse in number. In his Letter to the Philippians, Polycarp (*c*.60–*c*.135) quotes the petitions for forgiveness and against temptation, using the Matthew text; and Irenaeus (*c*.130–*c*.200) alludes to the petition for forgiveness as well in the *Adversus Haereses*.[27] Clement of Alexandria (*c*.150–*c*.215) gives us a little more in his various works: he quotes the opening, the kingdom on earth as in heaven, the petition for forgiveness, as well as the hallowing of the name.[28] Dionysius of Alexandria (†*c*.264) gives us a gloss on the temptation-prayer along the lines of Tertullian and Cyprian, that it means 'allow us not to fall into temptation'.[29] But what is surprising is that there is nothing about the prayer anywhere else; nothing among the Apostolic Fathers, nor in the *Apostolic Tradition*, nor in the *Didascalia Apostolorum*; nor do we find any reference to the prayer, for example, in the paschal homily of Melito of Sardis (†*c*.190).[30]

The main liturgical parallel available to us is in the *Apocryphal Acts of Thomas*, which probably come from the early third century, in Edessa, Syria. They are taken more seriously than in the past, for example in the development of the baptism and marriage rites, and they were also known to Epiphanius as well as Augustine.[31] In the Twelfth Act of St Thomas, the apostle (twin brother of Jesus) ends up preaching in a prison; at the end of which he stands up and recites the Lord's Prayer. Matthew's version of the text is followed, but with two differences: first, the petition for daily bread is omitted in the Greek version, but the Syriac version includes it in the form, 'give us the constant bread of the day', and, second, the Lucan version is used of the petition for forgiveness (with trespasses as well as debtors, Luke 11:4). Both these variations are significant. The absence of the bread petition may be an error, but in view of the difficulties in relation to this verse (heralded by Origen's interpretation) we must hold open the possibility that it has been omitted, even though the Greek version is not always as reliable as the Syriac. The adoption of the Lucan version shows a linguistic dexterity – Luke is more 'literary' than Matthew. But whatever the motivation for these variants, they demonstrate textual instability for a prayer; and, most important of all, they bring the prayer into the public domain of early Christian worship.

## Conclusion

- The story so far is about the development of a text, or rather, of texts, in a culture that had no printing technology in a religious milieu (Jewish) that had its own prayer-traditions with common themes, but whose content was not fixed in stone. The Jewish setting is the most important contribution of the twentieth century's own experience to our understanding of the prayer – not just in Old Testament parallels (important as they are in exploding myths about the unprecedented character of the prayer's content), but in the themes, style and atmosphere of such prayers as the *Kaddish* and *'Abhinu Malkenu*. The two versions of the prayer in the New Testament reflect the style of each Gospel-writer; and for reasons to do with that Gospel's popularity (and the apostolic status given to its author), Matthew's version was taken over as the basis for transmission of the prayer in antiquity. The *Didache* provides the first specifically 'liturgical' text in Greek, in the context of common life, and the need to pray regularly, adding a doxology – something we shall encounter in the East from the fourth century onwards.

• Was the Lord's Prayer first written in Aramaic or Greek? The touchstone appears to be *epiousios* – whether it translates a word like *mahar* in the Gospel of the Nazarenes, as Jerome records, and some modern scholars such as Jeremias believe, or whether it is an essentially Greek term, coined by Matthew in his poetic artistry, as Green maintains. We favour the former view, but in the end, it makes little difference for the purposes of our study, as the history of interpretation and use unfolds. Similarly, scholars are divided on whether the prayer has a dominical origin, which H. D. Betz accepts to be the case.[32]

• The three third-century authors provide treatises from which we can note the prayer's facility to slip into different theological styles – Origen's Platonism contrasting with Tertullian's more basic, instructional approach. But we can also see, particularly in Cyprian, a growing *baptismal* consciousness, with his language of hallowing and new birth; as the episcopal author of a treatise on baptism[33] for the instruction of new

Christians as well as those who have been disciples for a long time, he had pastoral challenges different from Origen.

- Then there are questions about the text of the prayer. Origen uses Matthew's Greek version, but Tertullian changes the order of the kingdom and will petitions, giving 'in earth and in heaven' and 'take us away from evil'. Origen interprets *epiousios*, not as 'of today', but as 'supersubstantial', which (as we shall see) Jerome uses for the Vulgate text of the New Testament. Here it was to lie, in the face of the older Latin versions already embedded in liturgical usage (Tertullian and Cyprian) which preferred *quotidianum*. But the Gospel of the Nazarenes has *mahar*, 'of tomorrow', which is echoed in subsequent Coptic manuscripts of Matthew.[34] Between Tertullian and Cyprian we can identify a similar process in relation to the temptation petition. Tertullian provides his own interpretation ('suffer us not to be led') immediately after the standard text ('lead us not'), which Cyprian adopts as his translation. Augustine was aware of this North African tradition, and we shall see him wrestling with the same issue. All three of them interpret 'evil' as the devil – a tradition which Augustine broadens, with long-term consequences. But the textual questions are to remain, particularly in relation to the meaning of temptation, which Origen tried to get around in another way; whereas the two Latin Fathers could not conceive of God as the direct agent of temptation, Origen saw God's role with the tempted disciple as the provider of strength not to give up.

- But what of the use of the prayer? The evidence that we have is not considerable. The main third-century liturgical source comes from the *Acts of Thomas*, at the end of public preaching, hardly a private context; and whereas Tertullian, Cyprian and Origen regard it as a prayer of considerable importance, we do not read anything about it in Clement of Alexandria's *Stromateis* VII – which is supposed to be about the meaning of prayer. (A similar surprise is often expressed in the tardiness with which the institution narrative, another part of Scripture,

41

was to make an entry into the eucharistic prayer.)[35] Perhaps the key lies in the background, rather than the foreground; all three of our third-century authors exhort Christians to pray regularly, to stand when they pray, with arms outstretched, facing east, and to base their prayers on what Jesus himself taught. My own view, for what it is worth, is that this was the prayer's main purpose, which may also help to explain its textual instability. It starts life where it began, not in an official liturgy, but as a popular prayer, if not spoken word for word by Jesus himself, then embodying his teaching about prayer. (Other features, such as the interpretation of Cyprian may point to a daily communion in Africa.) As part of a growing popular piety, the prayer was soon to make an entrance into the official services of the Church, and the most likely route for that transition was probably catechesis – the baptismal hallowing Cyprian held so dear.

# 3

# The Patristic East

There has been a tendency in the past to exaggerate the considerable changes that took place in the Church in the fourth century and to contrast an earlier, informal and persecuted Church with a later, structured and 'established' one. But what took place at the time of the Emperor Constantine changed the Church, in its position in relation to the rest of society, internal organization, architecture – and liturgy.[1] The amount of material that we have on the Lord's Prayer suggests separate treatment of East and West. This is a practical measure: Augustine was known in the East, Jerome spent most of his life in Syria and Palestine, and there are distinctly common features among the writers we shall be looking at both in this chapter, and later on. Cyril of Jerusalem and Ambrose of Milan both have their names associated with post-baptismal catechesis on the Lord's Prayer; and John Chrysostom and Augustine give us homilies on what Augustine was the first to call 'The Sermon on the Mount'. Ephrem, moreover, takes us straight into the world of Syriac-speaking Christianity, and Elishe provides an important example of Armenian Christianity – the first Christian kingdom.

The evidence is now greater than it was. We shall see trends in the East to find significant positions for the prayer in public worship, such as by the candidate immediately after baptism, between the eucharistic prayer and communion at the eucharist, and at the end (or the beginning) at daily prayer. The standard Greek liturgical text is Matthew 6:9–13, with the classical form of the verb for 'your kingdom' *come* (*elthetō*, instead of *elthatō*), and the change from aorist (*aphēkamen*) to present tense (*aphiemen*) so that it reads 'as we forgive'. The Syriac varies from the Old Syriac version, with 'constant bread', as we shall see in Ephrem and Elishe, to the *Peshitta* version compiled in the fifth century, which has 'bread of our need', as we shall see in Theodore and Narsai.

## Main authors

### Ephrem the Syrian (c.306–373)

Ephrem was born near the beginning of the fourth century, probably at Nisibis, in Syria. A deacon, he was a prolific writer, mainly in verse and in the Syriac language. After Nisibis was ceded to the Persians in 363, he moved to Edessa, where the bulk of his work is supposed to have been written. Among them is a commentary[2] on Tatian's 'Diatessaron', a version of the four Gospels written in Syriac by the second-century apologist, which has been lost.

In contrast to the rest of his work, Ephrem's treatment of the Lord's Prayer is brief and to the point. We call God father because we are no longer slaves, and he is our heavenly father, because we have earthly fathers as well, and because he is everywhere. We hallow his name, unlike the blasphemers, who do not believe, echoing Romans 2:24, a text that will come up again in connection with this particular clause. He sees the coming of the kingdom and the doing of the will as consequences of the hallowing of the name. 'Give us our constant bread of the day', says Ephrem, following Luke 11:3, which he interprets in material terms; 'this "bread of the day" indicates necessity', he says, in a way that points forward to the *Peshitta* version of the following century, 'the bread of our need'. We shall see ordinary need more strongly put forward by Gregory of Nyssa. Forgiveness has to be mutual, echoing Jesus' own teaching (Matthew 18:35). Perseverance through temptation is seen as 'a reward', a victory of the spirit over the flesh (Matthew 26:41); for if we are unable to bear it, 'we might lose all fear of God', which he regards as being delivered into the hands of evil. This short commentary takes us into a long tradition of biblical commentary that reflects the situation of the Church at the time; no longer slaves, living among the faithless, relying on daily survival as a gift of God, while trying to forgive and to resist temptation, in faith.

## *The* Mystagogic Catecheses *attributed to Cyril of Jerusalem*

Cyril was Bishop of Jerusalem from 349 until his death in 387, when he was succeeded by John of Jerusalem. It was a troubled episcopate, since he was banished from his see on two occasions on suspicion (from two different quarters) of heresy; in the end, Gregory of Nyssa was sent to report on the Jerusalem church in 379, which pronounced a favourable verdict on Cyril. He is most famous for the sets of baptismal catecheses that have come down to us and which were delivered before Easter. Although those given before Lent (the 'pro-Catechesis'), and the eighteen during Lent and Holy Saturday (the 'Catechesis') are regarded as authentic and dated from early on in his episcopate, the 'Mystagogic' Catecheses, delivered in Easter week, are generally regarded as coming from a much later time, and some have even suggested that they are not Cyril's work but belong to John, his successor. This view was first put forward by W. J. Swaans in 1942, although both C. Beukers and E. J. Yarnold (supported by Bradshaw) regard them as late Cyril, a view also held by A. Doval. Juliette Day, however, has argued a strong case for post-Cyril authorship as late as the early fifth century, on the grounds of language, theology and the details of the baptismal liturgy itself. They deal with the eucharistic liturgy, which the newly baptized has only just witnessed for the first time, and the fifth of these concerns the Lord's Prayer. Nothing is said about baptism; Egeria, for example, the nun from the Atlantic coast of Spain (or possibly Gaul) who gives a full account of her visit to Jerusalem in the early 380s, tells us nothing about this, except that Cyril did teach the candidates – and others – about certain aspects of the Christian faith.[3]

The liturgical milieu of the teaching in the Mystagogic

Catecheses comes across immediately. Catechesis 5 has just dealt with the intercessions in the eucharistic prayer and goes on to explain what happens at the distribution of communion. The term 'mystagogy' means leading through a mystery, which is an appropriate way of referring to teaching about worship, particularly when it applies to the central 'mysteries' of the Christian faith, baptism and eucharist, by invitation, by challenge, by imaginative use of Scripture, and by helping new Christians to make connections between what they were seeing done and said in liturgy and their daily lives; in some places no-one was able to attend the second part of the eucharist until they were baptized, though this so-called 'discipline of the secret' does not seem to have been applied universally. The style of these catecheses is brief, going through the prayer clause by clause.[4] We call God our heavenly Father, because we are his adopted children, and are a 'heaven', because we bear his likeness – an important theme in mystagogy, because of its stress on imitation. Hallowing the name is applied against blasphemers, those who do not know God; this parallels the references in Tertullian and Cyprian, and also Ephrem, to the work of mission. To pray for the coming of the kingdom is 'the mark of a pure soul without reserve'. Angels are central to the next petition, which he takes to mean: 'as in the angels your will is done, so on earth be it done in me, O Lord'.

The preacher interprets *epiousios* in a similar way to Origen; ordinary bread is not *epiousios*, because it is not for the soul, but this bread is for the 'substance' (*ousia*) of the soul. Over forgiveness, 'we make a bargain with God', a theme we shall encounter in Augustine and Peter Chrysologus, stressing mutual forgiveness: 'beware, then, lest, on account of slight and trifling transgressions against you, you debar yourself from God's forgiveness of your most grievous sins'. This mystagogy comes in short, punchy paragraphs, but by far the longest is devoted, unsurprisingly, to temptation, which resembles Origen's treatment: it is about being tested, and not being overwhelmed by it. It leads on to interpreting deliverance from evil as the consequence of being really tempted, because it is 'our adversary, the devil' – the personal force of evil the newly baptized have just renounced.

Finally, the prayer concludes with 'Amen' as the way of 'setting a seal' on it; there is no evidence for a doxology.[5]

The question of the original date of these Catecheses is significant, for they give evidence of the use of the Lord's Prayer in the eucharist. If they come from later on, in the time of Cyril's successor, it is possible to assume that it was during his time that it was introduced into the eucharist. The treatment is, understandably, baptismal – the audience he is addressing.

## Gregory of Nyssa (c.330–c.395)

Gregory was the younger brother of Basil of Caesarea, and after education as an orator, he became a monk. He was consecrated bishop of the small town of Nyssa, in Cappadocia, *c.*371. Like Cyril of Jerusalem, he suffered at the hands of theological zealots, and at one stage was banished. Unlike the two other Cappadocians, Basil and Gregory of Nazianzus, Gregory of Nyssa was a speculative, mystical theologian, whose reputation suffered from being associated with the teaching of Origen. Geoffrey Lampe describes his five homilies on the Lord's Prayer as 'the most extensive and the most profound' of patristic expositions.[6] The homilies are not liturgical or baptismal in context. They are for the faithful in general, and they demonstrate Gregory's view that prayer is a means whereby the dimmed image of God can be restored in us, which means learning how to pray aright.

In the first homily, Gregory sets the scene by saying that 'the Divine Word teaches us the science of prayer' and 'all things depend indeed on the Divine Will, and life here below is ordered from above' – demonstrating his Platonism. Prayer is an ascent to heaven, because Christ has opened heaven to us; but we need instruction in how to understand prayer and thereby make it effective. There is also a strong hint of eschatology, for example in the second homily (which is on the first clause of the prayer), where he remarks that 'the words seem to me to indicate a deeper meaning, for they remind us of the fatherland from which we have fallen and of the noble birthright which we have lost'.

But the prayer is for the baptized alone: 'it is dangerous to dare' (a word we shall come across again) to use this prayer and call God one's Father before one's life has been purified. The third homily (on the name and the kingdom) places us at the mercy of God, without whose aid nothing good can be accomplished, for God is king of the universe. And we encounter for the first time in the preaching tradition the variant in Luke's version of the prayer which replaces the coming of the kingdom with 'may your Holy Spirit come upon us and purify us'. There are a number of witnesses to it, and, as we shall see, Maximus the Confessor alludes to this version also.[7] The Christian is initiated into the battlefield of the kingdom, with the help of the Holy Spirit. Trinitarian in his approach, Gregory explains that 'if therefore the Father forgives sins, the Son takes away the sins of the world, and the Holy Spirit cleanses from the stains of sin those in whom He dwells'.

In the next homily, Gregory regards the doing of the will like some of the other writers we have encountered; 'that the will of God may rule in us without hindrance, in the same way as it does in the life of heaven'. But we are in for a surprise with the bread: unlike the spiritualizing encountered in Origen and the *Mystagogic Catecheses*, and the ambiguity in Tertullian and Cyprian, but like Ephrem and Gregory, our preacher insists that *epiousios* is ordinary sustenance: 'ask for bread because life needs it, and you owe it to the body because of your nature'. And he relates it back to the kingdom: 'bread is for our use today; the Kingdom belongs to the beatitude for which we hope'. The fifth and final homily embraces the remainder of the prayer. Forgiveness is about the fact that we still commit sin; it therefore *must* be mutual, to the extent that when we forgive others, God imitates us when he forgives us our sins: 'I have shown great mercy to my neighbour – imitate your servant's charity, O Lord.' By contrast with this exaggerated view of forgiveness, his treatment of temptation is soft: it is about putting on luxuries instead of 'the divine garments' (a possible allusion to baptism). He sees the last two petitions as part of the same: 'if a man prays truly to be delivered from evil, he asks that he may be far from temptation'

– and he likens this to the baits of a fish-hook, in the same way that he likens the work of Christ in salvation to catching the devil. To pray against temptation is about keeping far away from it, because, as Gregory teaches elsewhere, evil is not the result of the divine will, but is the product of our free will; and the life of faith is about exercising it properly.[8]

Gregory shows a number of unusual traits. While his approach to temptation may not have the same grasp as other writers, his Platonism (the earthly ascent to the heavenly), his eschatology (the kingdom from which we were banished but to which we now have access), his this-worldly focus (bread and ordinary food, and his condemnation of luxury), and his insistence that we all sin (forgiveness is a continual gift of God and a responsibility between Christians) all show a depth that we have not so far seen. Gregory challenges his hearers with the need for a continued Christian lifestyle: they have in no sense 'arrived', just because they believe and have been baptized.

## John Chrysostom (c.347–407)

Like Gregory of Nyssa, John was educated as an orator, but was attracted to the monastic life, although having to care for his widowed mother prevented that vocation being fulfilled. He entered the monastic school of Diodore in Antioch in 369. He began his ministry at Antioch as a deacon in 381, becoming a presbyter in 386. In the following year, he preached a course of sermons 'On the Statues', in the aftermath of a riot following the overthrow of imperial statues in the city.[9] Preaching was the main part of his ministry (hence the nickname 'golden-mouth'). In 398, he was made Bishop of Constantinople against his wish; he preached against the moral laxity of the city, including the imperial family; a Synod in 403 condemned him, after which he was removed, recalled, and then exiled to Pontus, where he died.

John's one and only full treatment of the Lord's Prayer comes in the nineteenth of a series of eighty-eight homilies on Matthew's Gospel, delivered in Antioch in 390.[10] The homily in question is an exegesis of Matthew 6:1–14, so that the prayer is set in the wider context of Jesus' teaching. 'Our Father' is the way of speaking to God as a result of sharing the dignity of sonship, the 'Our' being a necessary indication of the *common* aspect of prayer. The hallowing of the name he sees as glorifying (cf. John 17:1), and the worship of God reflected in the *Sanctus* (Isaiah 6:3; Revelation 4:8), as we saw in Tertullian. The petition for the coming of the kingdom is 'the language of a right-minded child, not to be riveted to things that are seen' – and the spiritual warfare that the Christian life involves (cf. Gregory of Nyssa). The doing of the will reflects Jesus' teaching that 'he has bidden us to make the earth a heaven'; not just in 'me' and 'us', but everywhere.

Daily bread is the needful food for each day, as he echoes Gregory of Nyssa's teaching, with a similar 'earthy' emphasis that brings in Jesus' concern that we should not be anxious about tomorrow (Matthew 6:34); for John, such a way of living faithfully in the world is a way of seeing it in truly spiritual terms. He spends longer on forgiveness, which is consistent with the number of times this particular petition is referred to in the rest of his preaching.[11] For John, forgiveness – from God and of other people – is at the heart of the gospel. Forgiveness is 'surpassing mercy', and it is about living up to the baptismal life: 'the un-initiated could not call God Father. If then the prayer belongs to believers, and they pray, asking that sins may be forgiven them, it is clear that not even after the laver is the profit of repentance taken away.' The prayer and its challenges are part of the life of the baptized, and repentance is lifelong. (Augustine has a similar way of interpreting this petition, a tendency to refer to it repeatedly in his writings.) Echoing again Gregory of Nyssa, he lays responsibility on us: 'we ourselves have control over the judgement that is to be passed on us'. Again like Gregory, John treats the next two clauses as one prayer – unlike (as we shall see) Augustine. Temptation 'teaches us plainly about our own vileness, and quells our pride, instructing us to deprecate all conflicts, instead of rushing upon them'. Deliverance from the evil one, a personal reality, he suggests is about not holding grudges against those who have wronged us. John now gives us the earliest evidence we have of the full doxology,[12] which 'raises our spirits'; the reality of the kingdom of Christ, the power with which it is established, and the glory which is 'unspeakable'. He goes on to discuss the next verse (Matthew 6:14), which he has already brought into his observations about forgiveness.

John's handling of the prayer combines exegesis with challenge; there is an underlying balance between the goodness and mercy of God, and human response in a faithful and forgiving life. But for him as for Gregory of Nyssa, it is a prayer only for the initiated, to be said with boldness as he remarks in the third homily 'On the Statues' preached in Antioch – 'that prayer which those who initiated him into the sacred mystery taught him to offer up'.[13] He alludes to parts of the prayer in many other sermons, but for our purposes, the most significant are in two homilies preached at Constantinople. In the sixth on the Letter to the Colossians, delivered in 399, he turns his discussion on Christ's triumph on the cross (Colossians 2:13, 14 and 15) into an opportunity to describe the baptismal liturgy; after coming up from the font, the newly baptized recites the Lord's Prayer, and joins the Body of Christ, both the eucharistic community and sacramental sharing.[14] Then in the following year, he delivered two sermons on worldly vanity occasioned by Eutropios, an influential court official on whose friendship John depended, whose downfall was to have dire consequences for him. At the end of the second of these, he refers directly to the recitation of the Lord's Prayer before communion at the eucharist.[15] As with the Jerusalem *Mystagogic Catecheses*, we now have firm evidence of its use at Constantinople, both at baptism and at eucharist; but this time, it has the doxology as well. We shall return to John Chrysostom and the place of the Lord's Prayer in the liturgy later in this chapter.

## The 'Opus imperfectum in Matthaeum' (the 'imperfect work on Matthew')

Long associated with John Chrysostom, which ensured that it was read by many, this series of homilies on Matthew's Gospel, which has come down to us in Latin, is now regarded as the work of an early fifth-century Arian bishop or presbyter, in the Danube region, probably towards the coast. It is referred to as 'imperfect' to distinguish it from the authentic (and therefore 'perfect') work on Matthew by John Chrysostom, which we have just looked at. His treatment of the Lord's Prayer contains nothing explicitly Arian, and although a harsh note of judgement recurs, van Banning has shown that it is not Pelagian either. The author was probably a Latin speaker who knew Greek, and there are five features of his treatment of the Lord's Prayer which are Eastern. The prayer is divided into six petitions, not seven; daily bread is exclusively material, as with Gregory of Nyssa; he includes the doxology, and tries (not wholly successfully) to apply it to different parts of the prayer; and he maintains, like Origen, that 'on earth as in heaven' refers to the hallowing of the name and the coming of the kingdom as well as the doing of the will.[16]

## Theodore of Mopsuestia (c.350–428)

Theodore was a contemporary of John Chrysostom and trained with him in Antioch in the school of Diodore. He was ordained presbyter around the year 383, and in 392 he became Bishop of Mopsuestia, where he spent the rest of his life, unhassled by the kind of difficulties which John encountered at Constantinople and which led to his early death. Theodore, on the other hand, was condemned after his death at the Councils of Ephesus (431) and Constantinople (553), on the basis of what is now generally regarded as a false reading of his views on the Fall and the person and work of Christ. Most of his writings (including the baptismal homilies) have come down to us in Syriac only. His two sets of baptismal homilies were delivered either at Antioch between 383 and 392, or, more likely, at Mopsuestia. The original Greek version seems to have been used as a text-book for catechetical instruction until the time of his condemnation. Unlike John Chrysostom, whose baptismal homilies do not, unfortunately, contain any mystagogy on the Lord's Prayer,

Theodore's contain a full homily, which follows ten on the Creed and precedes three on baptism.[17]

Theodore is more verbose than the author of the *Mystagogic Catecheses* and John Chrysostom. The shape of the sermon resembles what we shall see in Augustine and Peter Chrysologus, with a general introduction and a conclusion, between which comes the treatment of the prayer itself. Theodore stresses from the outset the ethical character of the prayer – 'it contains the teaching for good works in a sufficient manner', and he almost implies that the Lord's Prayer is closely linked to the Creed in importance: 'for this reason, they joined to the words of the Creed a prayer which contains an adequate teaching on morals'. This could suggest that the prayer was a recent introduction for baptismal catechesis. He moves into the text of the prayer, which he gives in full and which (as for John Chrysostom) ends with the doxology. He weaves the Lucan context into his discussion, with Jesus teaching the disciples, and through them, the Church, how to pray. Divine sonship gives us 'conversation in Jerusalem, which is above' and 'that life of freedom' which is for those destined for the resurrection. This means, however, 'fellowship with one another, because you are brothers and under the hand of one Father'. Hallowing the name is about striving to do things which would glorify God, the opposite of which are blasphemous deeds. The kingdom is about the future for which we yearn – but it is also about us being ready to 'relinquish our fellowship' with the commerce of this world. Doing the will means inner conflict, as John Chrysostom also taught, so that we are not conformed to this world.

Daily bread for Theodore is 'our necessary bread', reflecting the *Peshitta* text, which we need both for the next world and for this world, thus resembling John's interpretation. 'It is not blameworthy to ask of God that which is necessary to us.' Forgiveness he links with bread; if we pray for what we need, then we should do what we need as well, which means receiving and giving forgiveness. 'How could a man who hates bad things and desires good things have stumbled voluntarily?' Forgiveness then leads into the 'afflictions' of this life over which we might have some control, such as resisting temptation; like Gregory of Nyssa, he means that we should pray against it coming near to us. But Theodore is more perceptive, singling out religious zeal among temptations. Deliverance from the evil one is an extension of dealing with temptation, less circumstantial and more direct. The prayer is, according to Theodore, an essential feature of the instruction 'for those who draw near the gift of baptism, so that along with an accurate doctrine concerning the creed of the faith, they might through prayer so order our life as to possess that perfection which is required of those who receive the gift of baptism'. For Theodore, prayer is about imitating the teaching of Christ. As Rowan Greer has written, 'if Theodore's teaching is rooted in Christ himself, it is also rooted in the tradition about Christ as found in the Church and in Scripture'.[18]

## *Titus of Bostra († before 378)*

Titus was Bishop of Bostra, in Syria, in the mid-to-late fourth century. He is known to have taken part in a synod at Antioch in 363 which in a letter to Emperor Jovian recognized the Nicene Creed. His writings are in Greek: he wrote a major work against the Manichees. He also wrote some homilies on Luke's Gospel, and it is from these that we have a short and engaging discussion of the Lord's Prayer, in the original Greek, where he includes, as many copyists did, the petitions for doing the will and against evil that are not in the authentic Lucan manuscripts.[19] The opening invocation, which he describes as an 'epiclesis', teaches us how we are God's children, and we hallow his name when we do deeds worthy of that holiness, as reborn from the dead. The kingdom is that of the risen Christ, not of a worldly kind. Doing the will is about being like the angels in heaven. Daily bread, which he interprets (with Luke's stress on 'daily') as the bread for the future, is for our souls as well as for our bodies; he embraces both, like Theodore. Forgiveness of sins is a mark of restoring communion with each other, and allowing the power of the Holy Spirit to work in us, a mark of Christian virtue. Not to be tempted by the devil, he says, is an impossibility! So not being led into it is to pray that the devil might not prevail in the conflict within the soul. Like John Chrysostom and Theodore, he links the last two petitions together. Titus gives us a variant of the kind of preaching we have seen in Chrysostom and Theodore: exegetical, practical, challenging.

## Cyril of Alexandria (†444)

Cyril became Patriarch of Alexandria in 412, succeeding his uncle, Theophilus. His episcopate was stormy, partly because of the time he lived through, partly because of the aggressive way he responded to theological controversy, especially in his sturdy support of the view gaining acceptance that the title *theotokos* ('God-bearer') should be applied to the Virgin Mary. He was a considerable thinker, who used his skills to express what was emerging as classical Greek theology. His discussion of the Lord's Prayer comes from a series of seven homilies on Luke's Gospel which have come down to us in Syriac, and which point back to a full-scale commentary which is lost.[20]

Cyril begins the first homily by defending Jesus' need to pray, on Christological terms, because he was praying 'in the flesh'. We are bold to call God our Father because of our divine sonship and rebirth (John 1:12; 3:5), which conveys to us, sinful as we are, divine richness dwelling in poor human nature. Holiness (second homily) is about God's nature, which is shown, for example, in our desire to pray, not for ourselves, but for others, indeed for the whole world; we do not add to it in any way. To pray for the coming of the kingdom (third homily) is to bring judgement on ourselves in the way we live (Matthew 24:46). Even though it does not appear in Luke, Cyril includes the petition for the doing of the will (fourth homily), like Titus of Bostra, and once more we come across the angelic comparison; for Cyril, to do that will is to live up to our calling as the first-born of the Church, as we try to imitate Christ, and live as if his image were in us, his light shining in us. Like Gregory, Cyril says it is right that we should pray for what we need; but the bread that we pray for (fifth homily) is both daily subsistence and also the bread that is about doing the will of Christ – he gently chides those who think it is wrong to pray for daily material needs. Forgiveness (sixth homily) is about imitating God in his abundant mercy (Romans 11:33) and in accepting that others have the capacity, too, to live forgiven and thankful lives. The petition against evil (not in Luke) is a personal force (seventh homily), according to Cyril, because it is the same as temptation; in this he takes a similar line to John Chrysostom and Titus of Bostra. Moreover, he recognizes that there are two sorts of temptation; religious, which is about departing from right faith (reflecting the theological controversies of the time) and worldly, which is about human passions. In either case, we pray to be victorious over both. Cyril's treatment is more self-consciously Christological (a strong sense of imitation) as well as churchly (doing the will as the first-born, as well as the religious temptation towards heresy).

## Isidore of Pelusium (†c.440)

Isidore was a monk and an ascetic who may have been a teacher in the Church in Pelusium, on the eastern estuary of the Nile, before retiring to a monastery nearby. He corresponded with Cyril of Alexandria and was a strong supporter of the Cappadocian Fathers and of John Chrysostom. He has left a vast correspondence, which includes a brief commentary on the Lord's Prayer in a letter to the deacon Eutonios.[21] He begins by drawing attention to its remarkable brevity, in which is to be found much wisdom that can be of great help in right Christian living. It is easy to say, but hard to understand. Hallowing the name contrasts with the tyranny of the devil; the coming of the kingdom is victory over that tyranny; we pray to do God's will when we have reached the point where we want to do nothing other than live virtuously; praying for daily bread, material as well as spiritual sustenance,[22] is about spurning luxury and relying on God's grace; we pray for forgiveness when we ourselves hold on to the memory of past faults; temptation leads us into the wrong paths, and can result from ridicule or anger; deliverance from the evil one results from wilfully following what is against human good; and the doxology proclaims the praise of God. In going on to summarize further, Isidore stresses that this prayer is for the baptized, and there is possibly a hint that he knew the practice of reciting it straight after baptism, as John Chrysostom preached in the homily on Colossians in 399.

## *Elishe the Armenian (mid-fifth century)*

Elishe is famous as the author of a history of an Armenian war which describes a revolt in 450 and the death of Vardan Mamikonean in the following year. He is variously described as Bishop of Amatunik' and a hermit. A number of homilies are attributed to him, including one on the Lord's Prayer which has recently been studied by Serop Jamourlian, who regards it as a baptismal homily preached at the Easter Vigil liturgy.[23] God is creator of all human beings, and we dare to call him Father as adopted children. Hallowing his name means entering the door, through which we are taught this prayer (an implicit reference to baptism). The kingdom comes through Christ, our brother, who transforms the material. The will of God is the sanctification of humanity, through the passion of Christ. The 'constant' bread is the eucharist: 'he gave himself as bread in the Upper Room, and continually gives himself now as bread in the Churches on the holy altar', through which we share in Christ, in spirit, soul and body. Forgiveness is what Jesus leads towards, through repentance. Temptation and deliverance are treated together, as we have seen already in John Chrysostom, Titus of Bostra and Cyril of Alexandria: it is not God's will to lead us there but to save us and deliver us. A truly paschal and sacramentally focused homily, it has some interesting textual variants: Armenia was evangelized from Syria, which explains the Old Syriac 'constant bread', but Elishe uses the first person – 'me' – at temptation, probably for dramatic effect. We can note two special features: God as creator of *all* humanity, and the style of eucharistic interpretation of the bread petition.

## Narsai (†c.503)

Narsai was a theologian of the Church of East Syria, who was born *c.*399, becoming head of the theological school at Edessa, perhaps in 437. Because of his identification with the views of Theodore and Nestorius, he fled to Nisibis *c.*471, where he was invited to found another school. He wrote a series of commentaries on the Old Testament which have not survived. Among his Liturgical Homilies, he provides important evidence for the Lord's Prayer both before and after communion.[24] In both cases, Narsai does not stick to the text but produces a farced version of the prayer, something which is not found in subsequent eucharistic rites but appears in the East Syrian daily offices, and is testimony to a Syriac tradition of enriching the text of the prayer. Here are some of its clauses in the translation by R. H. Connolly. It follows an introduction which, like the corresponding liturgy, stresses our privilege as adopted children to address God in the words taught us by Christ:

> Our Father, who dwellest above in heaven and in every place, hallowed be thy holy name in us by all peoples . . .
> Give us bread and every bodily need in this time of sojourning in this world . . .
> And make us not to enter into temptation nor trial, who are feeble and without thy power are nothing; but deliver us from the evil, of the crafty evil one . . .
> For thine is the power, also the kingdom, and to thee is due all glory for ever and ever.

A similar version appears after communion, where the rationale for a second recitation is thanksgiving after receiving 'the name (of Him) for whose name the world is not sufficient'.

Narsai takes us one step away from the homilies of the earlier writers and into the world of explaining the liturgy in all its detail, a process which we saw beginning with the *Mystagogic Catecheses* delivered in Jerusalem over a century and a half earlier. The Lord's Prayer has an established place in the eucharist, to which preachers bring their own insights. In Narsai's case, we can note the material interpretation of the petition for bread (with the *Peshitta* 'bread of our need' behind his words), the reliance on God's help in experiencing temptation and evil, and the presence of the doxology.

## Maximus the Confessor (c.580–662)

With Maximus the Confessor, we come to a figure who was both a theologian and an ascetical writer. An aristocrat by birth, he became a monk of Chrysopolis, later elected as abbot. He was involved in theological disputes against Monothelitism, which eventually ensured that he was exiled to the Caucasus. His title 'Confessor' indicates that, while he was not martyred, he suffered severely for his faith (according to tradition he had his tongue and right hand cut off), and was in consequence revered. Influenced by the earlier Greek Fathers, he also wrote a mystical commentary on the liturgy of the eucharist. His explanation of the Lord's Prayer written for a friend combines some of the features we have so far noted with a devotional approach that has much in common with Gregory of Nyssa, as well as some of the more challenging edges of Theodore. Reliant on Origen and Gregory of Nyssa (as Van Deun indicated), it is still the most carefully structured and theologically nuanced treatment we have so far encountered in the East.[25]

Maximus begins by placing the human worshipper in the position of being full of the fear of the Lord, and called to be deified (2 Peter 1:4), which is why the Lord's Prayer is so important. 'For the words of the prayer make request for whatever the Word of God himself wrought through the flesh in his self-abasement' (cf. Philippians 2:5–11). The prayer teaches us seven new mysteries: 'theology (the opening invocation, contemplating God), adoption in grace (the name), equality of honour with the angels (the kingdom), participation in eternal life (the will), the restoration of nature inclining toward itself to a tranquil state (bread), the abolition of the law of sin (forgiveness), and the overwhelming of the tyranny of evil which has dominated us by trickery (protection)'. Here we have for the first time an Eastern Father viewing the prayer in seven parts, which correspond to the opening invocation, and the remaining petitions, where (like other Eastern writers) he treats temptation and deliverance as one. His sevenfold approach on a basic shape which resembles that of Cyril of Alexandria, consisting of opening invocation followed by six petitions, differs from Augustine's, whose sevenfold scheme does not isolate the opening invocation but treats temptation and evil separately.

'Our Father' directs us 'to honour the consubstantial and superessential Trinity'. 'We sanctify his name on earth in taking after him as a Father.' To pray for the kingdom is to pray for the Holy Spirit; and here Maximus alludes to the Lucan variant which we saw in Gregory of Nyssa. Our salvation is seen in Trinitarian terms. 'No one should be astonished to hear corruption placed before generation' – we need to be faced with the weakness of human nature before we can be transformed; Maximus believes profoundly in human freedom, even though human will is wounded; as a strong opponent of Monothelitism (one will in Christ), this issue, along with his Trinitarian focus, is something of a touchstone to his theology. Prayer for the doing of the will inevitably leads us to 'be moved to seek God', so that the force of desire causes us to 'possess him'. Daily bread refers to today, and it is the Bread of Life, not earthly needs; here he follows Origen and not Gregory of Nyssa. 'Let us be scrupulous observers of the prayer in showing by our very acts that we hold on to the one and only life in the Spirit.' Forgiveness is the fruit of 'spiritual detachment', detachment from our own sins, through the God who involves himself in our life on earth. Temptation and deliverance from the evil one are treated together and concern how we use our freedom: temptation can start by being unforgiving. It can be 'the soul's voluntary inclination to the passions of the flesh'; so a forgiving soul will be more likely to resist temptation. Forgiveness is where the prayer against temptation and evil begins.

Maximus provides a basic definition: 'the aim of the prayer should direct us to the mystery of deification so that we might know from what things the condescension through the flesh of the Only Son kept us away and where he brought us by the strength of his gracious hand, those of us who had reached the lowest point of the universe where the weight of sin had confined us'. Although the exposition concludes with a Trinitarian ascription of glory, the prayer itself does not: Maximus does not include a doxology. The stress on adopted sonship finds expression in the definition of the prayer which he gives in his commentary on the eucharist, the *Mystagogia*, written *c.*628–630 for a monastic setting. In contrast to the Creed, which is described as the 'symbol of faith', the Lord's Prayer is the 'symbol of adoption' (*huiothēsias sumbolon*), a contrast which shows strong baptismal undercurrents, pointing to the uniqueness of the prayer. Even in the elaborate interpretation of the liturgy, the Lord's Prayer stands out on its own.[26] Although his exposition may lack some of the this-worldly admonitions of other writers, Maximus penetrates the internal coherence of the prayer in a way we have not so far seen, and among the Eastern writers he emerges as the spiritual giant.

## Main authors reviewed

- First of all, the *text*. As we have noted, the standard Greek version is a lightly edited version of Matthew 6:9–13, reflecting the early priority of Matthew over Luke. But what of the Syriac, as well as the Armenian, from which it is derived? Ephrem reflects the Old Syriac 'constant bread', as also Elishe the Armenian, but Narsai follows the *Peshitta*'s 'bread of our need'. What of the doxology? John Chrysostom includes it, as do Theodore, Isodore and Narsai, whereas there is no trace in other writers, notably the author of the *Mystagogic Catecheses*, with his liturgical focus; nor do we find it in Ephrem, Elishe, or Maximus. We can only conclude that the practice varied, with a gradual trend towards adding it as time went on, except in the case of Maximus, where he may have assumed its inclusion.

- Second, *variations in interpretation*. Despite differences of emphasis over hallowing the name and doing the will, there are other petitions which appear to cause real problems. Is daily bread the needful bread of the spiritual life, as Origen taught, which (in different ways) reappears in the *Mystagogic Catecheses*, Elishe the Armenian, and Maximus the Confessor? Or it is exclusively about material needs, as Ephrem, Gregory of Nyssa and Narsai taught so clearly, and John Chrysostom more circumspectly? Or it is both, as we saw in Titus of Bostra, Theodore, Cyril of Alexandria and Isidore of Pelusium? This question appears to have been openly disputed, as we know from contrasting views deliberately sought in correspondence from such notables as Basil of Caesarea (*c*.330–379) and John of Damascus (*c*.655–*c*.750): Basil (unsurprisingly) takes the same approach as Gregory and John Chrysostom, whereas John of Damascus interprets it in spiritual terms, along the lines of the *Mystagogic Catecheses*. When it comes to temptation, there are also differences; is it about being tested but not overwhelmed, as the *Mystagogic Catecheses*, or deliberately keeping away, as Gregory of Nyssa believed, or is it about being aware of different kinds, and not letting them prevail, as Titus of Bostra and Narsai thought? John Moschus (*c*.550–*c*.619/34) answered this specific issue, taking a more comprehensive approach; the petition against temptation is about not being overwhelmed.[27] These continuing debates apart, we can note the tendency among nearly all our writers to treat temptation and evil (always personal) as part of the same petition – which may well have been increasingly strengthened by the gradual addition of the doxology. This perhaps rescues them from the much more complex ways in which Western writers deal with the question of temptation.

- Third, *differences of context*. One adopts a different style and approach when addressing the newly baptized, as in the *Mystagogic Catecheses*, or preaching an expository sermon, like John Chrysostom, or writing a commentary, like Ephrem or Cyril of Alexandria, or writing ascetically about inner conflict, like Isidore, or explaining the liturgy for all the faithful, like Narsai. But because we are dealing with a prayer, the expositions have a common focus, which both lifts the commentaries out of Scripture, and lifts the prayer from the liturgical setting in which it is now being increasingly laid: Maximus' 'symbol of adoption' in that sense says it all. Some contexts – and writers – mean a penchant for allegory, like Gregory of Nyssa and Maximus the Confessor, whereas others, like John Chrysostom and Theodore, employ a more immediate use of Scripture, applying it directly to their hearers.

- Fourth, *liturgical setting*. Ephrem implies no more than that it is a prayer which is much used by Christians. The *Mystagogic Catecheses* and John Chrysostom give us evidence of the prayer's use before communion in the eucharist at Jerusalem and Constantinople. John Chrysostom likewise tells us of its use by the candidate immediately after baptism at Constantinople. But apart from that, we have no more. There also appears to be some ambiguity about exactly how the Lord's Prayer was covered by the so-called 'discipline of the secret'. John Chrysostom and Theodore imply it when they maintain that the prayer is restricted to the baptized. But we have to take into consideration the fact that John Chrysostom's sermons on Matthew's Gospel were public, not restricted; and the same goes for Gregory of Nyssa's. Juliette Day has shown how the 'discipline of the secret' was an ideal in certain places, more strictly applied in Alexandria than elsewhere (which may explain the paucity of our evidence from there); but it was not possible to exert it universally.[28] We would add our endorsement to such a view: the 'gaffe' had long been 'blown' on the Lord's Prayer, and much of that is to do with public teaching – and its place in worship.

## Liturgy

### Daily prayer

In his study of daily prayer in both the East and the West, Robert Taft has shown how the Lord's Prayer has been used in many different traditions. The earliest evidence comes from the monastic 'Regulations' attributed to Horsieios, who took charge of the Tabennesiot monastic communities in Egypt in 346, his two predecessors Petronius and Pachomius having died within a short time of each other in the plague.[29] It is not clear how often each day the following opening pattern was repeated, but this is how it began: prostration for prayer, silent confession, rising, signing with the cross (to recall baptism), followed by 'the prayer of the Gospel' (meaning the Lord's Prayer), followed by another signing, another prostration, silent penitential prayer, standing up, another signing, silent prayer, sitting down (for readings). From this we can see that the Lord's Prayer was referred to as 'the prayer of the Gospel', an indication of its uniqueness, and it is seen as a focus for preparation and penitence.

Our next evidence comes from Palestine, from what has been reconstructed at the time of John Cassian, who observes (*c*.382–386) the differences between the monastic traditions of Gaul and Bethlehem. The Vigil Office began with six psalms, followed by the Lord's Prayer, leading into three units of proper psalmody, each followed by the Lord's Prayer, followed by *Kyrie eleison* recited fifty times, and a Bible reading; these led into nine biblical canticles, with the Lord's Prayer and *Kyrie eleison*, after the third and sixth; then come the *Ainoi* Psalms 148–150, followed by the *Gloria in excelsis*, followed by the Creed and the Lord's Prayer, leading into the *Kyrie eleison* (fifty times) and the concluding prayer.[30] The Lord's Prayer had a central role, surrounding psalmody at the Vigil Office (the first part), and coming alongside the Creed (which it follows) at Mattins – the latter forming a kind of 'baptismal unit'. It is important to note the repetition of the Lord's Prayer – seven times in all. From the late fourth century, probably *c*.380, in Antioch, *Apostolic Constitutions* VII provides a text of the prayer, with the doxology, as in John Chrysostom; and it is to be recited three times a day (cf. *Didache* 8) after due preparation.[31]

The liturgical texts of the Eastern churches are hard to date, but the prayer tends to be placed either at the start or near the end. In the Armenian rite,[32] it comes at the beginning (after the opening doxology) at the Vigil Office and right at the beginning of Mattins; in the East Syrian rite, it comes at the start as well as near the end of Vespers, near the end of Mattins, and near the start of the Vigil Office. But the text comes in a farced version, in the manner noted in Narsai earlier, and with the *Peshitta* text 'bread of our need'.[33] In the Coptic rite, at Mattins the Lord's Prayer is placed in the middle, between the *Trisagion* and the 'Praise of Mary', which means that it concludes the intercession; and at Vespers, it is placed before the conclusion.[34] In the Ethiopic rite, the prayer comes at the end of Solemn Vespers and Mattins, but at the Vigil Office (an adaptation of the Coptic) it appears after the *Trisagion* and is followed by the Creed; this leads into a Gospel reading, Luke 11:5–13, which continues the narrative after Jesus gives the Lord's Prayer to the disciples.[35] As far as the Byzantine rite is concerned, in an account of a visit to Abbot Nilus of Sinai by Abbots John and Sophronius (late sixth or early seventh century) there is evidence of daily prayer in which the Lord's Prayer comes after Psalms 148–150, the *Gloria in excelsis* and the Creed,[36] but later practice placed it near the end. From this outline, we can see three tendencies, all of which seem to be motivated by a desire to draw out the uniqueness of the prayer – either at the start, or the end, or at a place in the body of the service where its function is clear. Monastic repetition of the prayer in Egypt and at Jerusalem is also to be noted.

## Baptism

Thomas Finn has suggested that the general practice in the late fourth century was for the newly baptized to recite the Lord's Prayer on coming up from the font.[37] In fact the evidence for such an assertion is paltry. We find the practice attested once only (as we have seen) in John Chrysostom at the end of the century at Constantinople, in a homily on Colossians.[38] The earliest evidence, however, comes from *Apostolic Constitutions* VII, where there is a description of baptismal practice, in which the newly baptized recites the Lord's Prayer, followed by a prayer for themselves.

> After this (the post-baptismal anointing) let him (the newly baptized) stand up, and pray the prayer which the Lord taught us. Of necessity he who is risen (again) ought to stand up and pray, because he that is raised stands upright. But let him pray (turning) towards the east . . . let him pray in these terms after the preceding prayer, saying: O God almighty, the Father of your Christ, your only begotten Son, give me a body undefiled, a pure heart, a watchful mind, a knowledge without error, and presence of your Holy Spirit, that I may be founded in the truth and have full assurance of the same, through your Christ, through whom glory be to you, in the Holy Spirit, for ever.

In *Apostolic Constitutions* III there is a full text of the Lord's Prayer as recited at this point with the doxology.[39]

It is important that we make neither too much nor too little of *Apostolic Constitutions*, which probably came from a heterodox community in a city which at the time had three rival bishops, and a single reference from John Chrysostom in Constantinople in 399. We do have a text, with the doxology; we have the outline of a rich but simple prayer by the newly baptized for a faithful life, immediately after the direction about saying the Lord's Prayer straight after baptism. There are no echoes of any of this in the *Mystagogic Catecheses*, which means we can probably discount it from late fourth/early fifth-century Jerusalem practice, and there is no sign of it in this position in Egypt either.[40] On the other hand, Gabriele Winkler has shown the persistence of this practice in Armenia, which was evangelized from Syria.[41] It is not hard to see why: once introduced for some time, it might be difficult to suppress a custom whereby the first words of the newly baptized is to recite the prayer which was the basis for much teaching and preparation. But as Brock has shown, the prayer was not originally part of the earlier Syriac liturgical texts: he suggests that it entered the rite when separate baptisms, apart from Epiphany and Easter eucharists, became the norm; he further suggests that it was moved to follow one or other of the anointings, where it is to be found in the current Syrian Orthodox rite. Armenian practice retained the simplicity of the earlier structure, reflected in John Chrysostom and *Apostolic Constitutions* VII but with the insertion of Matthew 3:13–17, the narrative of Jesus' baptism as a 'mimetic' (or an 'institution narrative'?) text for the candidate: the liturgical manuscripts used by Winkler all date from the ninth and tenth centuries, but she argues convincingly that they reflect earlier practice. Another variant is found in the Maronite practice of appending the Lord's Prayer to the blessing of the baptismal water, with an introductory prayer and an embolism, reflecting already existing usage at the eucharist.[42]

What, then, of John Chrysostom, and his witness to the practice at Constantinople? There appears to be no single usage overall. In the baptismal catecheses that have come down to us from his Antioch ministry, including one probably delivered in 387, there is no mention of the Lord's Prayer, but he exhorts the newly baptized to pray for the peace of the churches, and without diffidence, in a variant from the prayer by the newly baptized in *Apostolic Constitutions* VII.[43] Subsequent Byzantine rites of baptism make no mention of the Lord's Prayer immediately after the baptismal immersion.[44] What he is probably describing is a Syrian-inspired experiment that did not last at Constantinople – which would match the evidence of both *Apostolic Constitutions* VII and the Armenian rites. Be that as it may, we can assume from the abundance of other evidence that the Lord's Prayer, Maximus' 'symbol of adoption', would have been central to baptismal catechesis.

## Eucharist

We now come, finally, to the question of the place of the Lord's Prayer in the eucharist. We have already seen how the author of the *Mystagogic Catecheses* explains to the newly baptized the meaning of the prayer and its position is immediately after the eucharistic prayer, a position attested also by John Chrysostom, who includes the doxology as does Narsai. But we have no other fourth-century evidence in the East for this prayer at the eucharist. We might have expected it in the eucharist in *Apostolic Constitutions* VIII, but it is absent. Attempts to find it located in the eucharist of Sarapion of Thmuis, Egypt, have generally foundered; nor is it to be found anywhere in such fourth-century texts as the *Testamentum Domini* (Syria) or the *Canons of Hippolytus* (Egypt).[45] The strong indications so far are that it belongs to ordinary daily prayer, the monastic devotional and liturgical tradition, and baptismal preparation – which is compounded by the 'baptismal' way it is sometimes used in daily prayer, especially when juxtaposed to the Creed.

However, there is a wealth of evidence from the later Eastern Liturgies which all give a similar position to the Lord's Prayer that we found in Narsai – between the eucharistic prayer and the communion. The only difference is that the Byzantine rite places it *before* the breaking of the bread whereas all the other Eastern rites place it *after*, thus linking it more closely with the distribution of communion. As we shall see, this is also the position adopted by Gregory the Great for the Roman rite at the end of the sixth century. Robert Taft draws attention to this liturgical 'unit', consisting of introductory prayer, invariably on the theme of adopted sonship, the Lord's Prayer itself, and (usually) an interpolation (the embolism). It is interesting to note how (on the one hand) all rites opt for a pre-communion position, whereas (on the other hand) there are, inevitably, variations as to whether there should be a doxology, and if there should be an embolism between the prayer and the doxology. The old Byzantine way of chanting the Lord's Prayer in the Greek Church reflects a simple, congregational style, with the doxology at the end by the celebrant in a tone that matches his own prayer; a similar contrast is discernible in other musical settings of the Eastern Orthodox rite, Slavonic included.

There are variations. Greek James has both an embolism and the doxology, whereas Syriac James has only an embolism; in the same way Greek Mark has both an embolism and the doxology, whereas Coptic Mark only has an embolism. This suggests that the doxology is a Greek import. Uniquely for the East, the Coptic rite appears to have had for long a tradition of variable prayers of introduction (current practice includes an additional eighteen for seasonal use), which probably reflects an early custom of improvising the lead into the Lord's Prayer; we shall encounter a similar practice in the West, in the old Spanish, Gallican and Celtic rites. The liturgies of the Ethiopic Church and the East Syrian Church have the doxology only, whereas the Armenian rite has both an embolism and the doxology. The Byzantine rite, on the other hand, does not at first have an embolism, as the (early eighth-century) Barberini 336 manuscripts of the Liturgies of both Basil and St John Chrysostom show. It is only in the Ethiopic and the East Syrian rites that the *congregation* recites the doxology as a constituent part of the prayer; in all the others (where there is a doxology), it is recited by the priest. The East Syrian rite reflects Narsai's preaching in having a second recitation after communion, but using the standard *Peshitta* version, and not the farced texts noted in the Daily Office. Those rites which do have an embolism (Syriac and Greek James, Coptic and Greek Mark and the Armenian rite) begin on the theme of temptation, reflecting the Eastern consensus that the prayer consists of six petitions (not seven), because temptation and evil are treated together: this can be contrasted with Western practice, where, particularly after Augustine, the prayer is regarded as consisting of seven petitions (not six), because temptation and evil are taken as separate petitions, and where the embolism invariably begins on the theme of deliverance from evil, rather than temptation. If ever an example of textuality – the interplay of 'text in context' – were needed, it is in how the prayer is gradually filtered into the liturgy in this way.[46]

What motivated the prayer's introduction into the eucharist? It is clear from the *Didache* and from *Apostolic Constitutions*, to say nothing of the rest of the evidence, that the Lord's Prayer was a prayer frequently used by Christians in their daily lives. It is also clear that it had a baptismal focus, dramatically shown in *Apostolic Constitutions*, where it is recited immediately after baptism, but absent from the eucharist. It was, one supposes, only a matter of time before it entered the eucharist, and with astonishing unanimity – before communion.[47] Taft has signalled the sometimes piecemeal way in which the introductory words and embolism fit the prayer into the early parts of the Eastern rites; he has also suggested the 'terror-language' introduced into the liturgy from the late fourth century onwards, and the feeling of unworthiness to approach the table, as factors behind these texts. The prayer, however, shows a remarkable ability to stand on its own, and to resist any allegorical interpretations of the rest of the liturgy (unlike the medieval West, as we shall see).[48] My own view is that baptism and adopted sonship were fundamental motivating factors,[49] and that there may have been a two-stage introduction, first with the prayer itself, and then with surrounding material designed to make it 'fit in'. The 'symbol of adoption' in the end had to find an appropriate place at the table of the Lord.

# 4

# The Patristic West

How to connect the Lord's Prayer with baptism is an issue that has recurred through the centuries. And while it is possible to idealize the kind of catechesis that flourished in the fourth century, it is nonetheless true to say that there was a great deal of it, as this chapter will show. The foundations supplied by Tertullian and Cyprian are built upon by Ambrose. Jerome enters the scene with his revised text of the Gospels, posing questions, again, about how *epiousios* should be translated. Augustine towers over this era, partly because of his stature, partly because more has come down to us on the Lord's Prayer in terms of quantity than from anyone else at the time, and partly because of his determination that the prayer consists of seven petitions – which leaves its mark on the later West. We are fortunate, too, to have no fewer than six short homilies before baptism from Peter Chrysologus. Monastic tradition is represented by John Cassian and the *Rule of the Master*, as well as the directions in the *Rule of St Benedict*. As we move on into the sixth and seventh centuries, the tone begins to change. Augustine's readiness to adapt catechesis according to whether the candidates are adults or small children[1] has become something different: the catechesis of the growing child after infant baptism. And, as in the East, the liturgical commentary develops into a new genre of writing, in which the Lord's Prayer finds its proper place.

## Main authors

### *Ambrose of Milan (c.339–397)*

Born in Trier, Ambrose was the local governor in Milan when Bishop Auxentius died (in either 374 or 375). The local Catholic community (Auxentius was Arian) insisted that Ambrose should succeed him, even though he was not yet baptized. So began a distinguished and influential episcopate, in which figured the baptism of Augustine at Easter 387, as well as a number of confrontations with civil authority, Emperor Theodosius included. Ambrose brought his knowledge of Greek writings into his works. The *De Sacramentis* ('On the Sacraments') is one of his most famous works, consisting of six addresses (called 'books') to the newly baptized in Easter week; as with the *Mystagogic Catecheses*, the authorship has been contested, but they are now generally regarded as his. Probably written between 380 and 390, they were a popular resource in subsequent centuries.

Ambrose deals with the Lord's Prayer (which, like Cyprian, he calls 'oratio dominica'), in the fifth address, but recapitulates in the sixth. This may mean that the two are not as closely related as they might be, and provide evidence that the Lord's Prayer was only just being introduced into the eucharist at the time: the fifth address is specifically about the prayer; whereas the sixth is about the liturgy of the eucharist, and assumes a place for the prayer within it, some time before communion, and said by all, though exactly where (at the end of the anaphora? Before or after the fraction? Just before the distribution?) is not entirely clear.[2]

The heavenly Fatherhood gives us divine sonship, so that we ourselves might be hallowed. The kingdom and the will are about the triumph of God's purpose, and the casting down of the devil, with peace on earth; the kingdom is within us (Luke 17:21). In the petition for bread, which he spends more time on than any other, Ambrose, who was well read in Greek theology, uses the translation 'cottidianum' as in the Latin versions at the time, but he interprets it as 'substantialem' (or 'supersubstantialem', according to some later manuscripts), which echo Jerome's text of 384, of which he was probably unaware.[3] For

Ambrose, however, the bread has nothing to do with the body; *daily* waiting upon the Lord means offering the eucharist each day (cf. Cyrprian), as a medicine for our wounds. Forgiveness is about the generous mercy of God, which we should show to others; and here Ambrose contrasts Adam receiving the debt of sin from the devil with us receiving forgiveness from God. When it comes to temptation, Ambrose uses the North African paraphrase of Tertullian, the version of Cyprian: 'et ne patiaris induci nos in temptationem' – 'suffer us not to be led into temptation'. An athlete, he says, does not want temptation, but we want to be freed from evil, from sin. And he goes on to allude to deliverance from the devil by recourse to Paul's famous saying that if God is for us, who is against us (Romans 8:31). That conflict would apply particularly to the newly baptized, who have just renounced the powers of evil.

Ambrose gives us a series of short explanations, along the lines of the Jerusalem *Mystagogic Catecheses*, because his medium is that of post-baptismal teaching. What stands out is the mixture of traditions; he looks to the East over daily bread, but to North Africa over temptation. These ideas doubtless travelled, showing Ambrose as a cosmopolitan figure. Augustine might have heard something like this in connection with his own baptism.

## Jerome (c.345–420)

Jerome studied in Rome, but spent most of his life in the East, as a hermit for a few years in the Syrian desert, where he learnt Hebrew, a unique feat for someone of his background at the time. Ordained presbyter at Antioch, he went back to Rome, as secretary to Pope Damasus, after whose death in 384 he returned East, finally staying at Bethlehem from 386 for the rest of his life. His principal contribution for our purposes is his study of the Scriptures, and his work towards the production of a Latin text of most of the Bible, nicknamed the 'Vulgate', after its subsequent title 'editio vulgata', the 'common edition', which was produced in the sixth century. As Burton has shown, the need for such a text was apparent to those familiar with the various 'Old

Latin' versions, the quality of whose Latin was uneven, and whose instability was reflected, for example, in the theological glossing which lies behind the variants in the temptation petition which we saw in Cyprian (the third-century North African translation tradition is regarded as the oldest and most continuous). It was Damasus who asked Jerome to undertake this work, on the strength of his studies and life in the East; and he completed the Gospels in 384. His text matches what we find in his Commentary on Matthew's Gospel, which was finished (in some hurry) before Easter 398.[4]

The Fatherhood of God gives us sonship, and hallowing the name is about us, because God has no need to hallow himself; we ourselves do this, in contrast to the Gentiles, who blaspheme God's name, where he cites Romans 2:24 (= Isaiah 52:5). The kingdom is about conflict with the devil; to ask for its coming is to open oneself to the judgement of God. Doing the will of God is about being like the angels in heaven, a contrast between what they in heaven do by nature, and we on earth attempt, in our struggle against sin. Jerome then spends more time (like Ambrose) on daily bread, which he translates not as *quotidianum* but as *supersubstantialem*, following Origen's interpretation, whose influence on Jerome was strong. In his version of the Gospels, he keeps *quotidianum* in Luke, but replaces it with *supersubstantialem* in Matthew, as Burton suggests, clearly intended to reproduce the Greek term rather than to give a meaningful translation. This marks a radical departure for a Latin writer, and it is easy to see that he took this decision after careful study, reflected both in the Syriac version Ephrem knew, the Greek tradition of interpretation, as well as the second-century (lost) *Gospel of the Nazarenes*, thought to have been written in Aramaic or Syriac, and which (as we have seen), according to Jerome, uses the term *mahar*, meaning the (eschatological) bread of tomorrow. Jerome followed the tradition of Papias, that Matthew was originally written in Hebrew, hence the importance of Semitic tradition at this point. Like other writers, he cites Jesus' warning later on in the same chapter that we should not give any thought for the morrow (Matthew 6:34); he echoes these sentiments in his Commentary on Ezekiel, which was written in 412.[5] He omits any discussion of forgiveness or temptation, but provides (uniquely so far for the Scriptures) a concluding 'Amen' as the 'signaculum orationis Dominicae', the 'seal of the Lord's Prayer'; as we have seen, the Jerusalem *Mystagogic Catecheses* also provide an 'Amen', and refer to it as 'setting the seal' on the prayer. Perhaps this is Jerome's way of saying that there should be no doxology, a practice of which he will have known in the East.

Many of these ideas are contained, in briefer form, in his *Dialogue against the Pelagians*, which he wrote between 415 and 416. Here we have more baptismal allusions, as well as evidence for the use of the prayer said by all before communion at the eucharist. This he declares to be apostolic practice, which, while untrue, is evidence of a well-established practice. He also uses the word 'dare' of calling God Father, which we saw in Gregory of Nyssa, and which we shall come across in Augustine as well. But there is no 'Amen' at the end, and he paraphrases himself through the bread petition without quotation (whereas all the other petitions are given in full). This leaves us asking the question, which version of the Lord's Prayer did Jerome actually use, whether on his own or in his Bethlehem community – the Vulgate text, or one of the Old Latin versions? One suspects that his preferred version was the former.[6]

Jerome brings a certain sharpness to the Lord's Prayer, both in his stress on judgement and in his approach to the question of establishing a reliable text. The main variant is *supersubstantialem*, an unattractive word, but an accurate rendition of Eastern interpretation. This he succeeded in embedding in the official version of the Latin Bible, in contrast to the more limited (though still ambiguous) *quotidianum* ('each day' can stretch to include 'what we [really] need'). The other is the 'Amen', a hint that the prayer needs a conclusion; some writers, like Bede, follow Jerome here. What Jerome achieves is to supply two variants that are set to be at odds with liturgical practice for a long time to come.

## *Chromatius of Aquileia (†407)*

Chromatius was made Bishop of Aquileia, in the north of Italy, about the year 388. A learned man, he corresponded with Ambrose and Jerome, and supported John Chrysostom in the controversies surrounding his time at Constantinople. A number of his sermons have come down to us, including one entitled, 'Praefatio orationis dominicae', which was probably a short sermon on the Lord's Prayer for the benefit of the catechumens about to be baptized. We shall come across similar such short homilies in Augustine, Peter Chrysologus, and Caesarius of Arles. But we have the benefit, too, of a slightly longer 'Tractate' on Matthew 6: 9–13, which contains similar ideas.[7]

Chromatius uses Tertullian and Cyprian in both works. Both begin with a preliminary discussion of the meaning of the prayer, the 'Tractate' exhorting the faithful to 'guard the sacrament of our heavenly rebirth', the sermon stressing Jesus himself teaching the disciples about prayer (Matthew 6:6), with a delightful one-liner in the sermon, 'for our God listens to our faith, not our voice'; Fatherhood gives us sonship (John 1:12); hallowing the name means in our lives, as the baptized, not through our prayers; the kingdom has been established by Christ's blood and passion; the will is what we struggle to do on earth 'unblame-ably'; the bread is for sufficient daily needs, as well as spiritual food (John 6:51), and we ask for it daily on earth so that we may be worthy of heavenly nourishment; mutual forgiveness is essential – we are not forgiven unless we ourselves forgive; at temptation, he supplies the Tertullian paraphrase, used by Cyprian and Ambrose, as an explanation – we need to avoid it, for God does not tempt people with evil (James 1:13), since it is the devil who does so, as Jesus warned the disciples in Gethsemane (Matthew 26:41); but in the Tractate he refers to a version in the Gospels, 'et ne nos patiaris in temptationem, quam sufferre non possimus' ('and do not bring us into temptation which we cannot endure' – i.e. Cyprian with 1 Corinthians 10:13); deliverance from evil is brought about through prayer; he cites Romans 8:26, ('we do not know how to pray'), a text that

Peter Chrysologus also uses. The Tractate ends with a summary of the prayer as a progress into the life of God.

### Augustine (354–430)

Augustine's life is well chronicled, not least by himself.[8] Born in Thagaste, North Africa, he took himself to Rome, and then Milan, developing his skills as an orator, then a highly respected profession, especially for those keen to enter government service. At Milan, he encountered Ambrose's ministry, was finally converted in July 386 in a garden at Milan, and was baptized the following Easter by Ambrose himself. Returning to Africa in 388, he established a religious community in Thagaste, but was ordained presbyter in 391 at Hippo by the ageing Bishop Valerius, and succeeded him probably in 395. He became a powerful figure, both locally and beyond; and he died on 28 August 430, while all around him was falling apart, with the Vandal siege of his city.

Throughout his works, there are many references to the Lord's Prayer. Four in particular stand out. The first is contained in a lengthy exposition of what he was the first to call 'the Sermon on the Mount', which was written in 394; the most extensive, in it he sets out a coherent approach to the text of the prayer, which finds echoes in his subsequent works. They are contained in a correspondence with a family of aristocratic ladies, two widows called Proba and Juliana, and Demetrias, the granddaughter of Proba, who fled Rome after its fall in 410; four short *Sermons* for catechumens, in style similar to Chromatius, but longer, and probably preached from around 412; and finally his *De Fide, Spe, Caritate* ('On Faith, Hope and Charity'), often called the *Encheiridion*, a handbook to his theology, written 421–423; near the start, there is a chapter devoted to the Creed and the Lord's Prayer, directing their precepts towards the pursuit of faith, hope and charity, and towards the end, there are two short chapters on the prayer as it appears in Matthew and Luke. We have more from him than any other of our authors, as we shall also see in his use of the petition for forgiveness in his dealings with the Pelagians and the Donatists.[9]

The *Sermon on the Mount* is one of his earliest works of biblical exegesis and comes in two parts, the first dealing with Matthew 5, the second with Matthew 6 and 7. It is likely to have been based on preaching, and this is probably true as well of what he has to say on the Lord's Prayer. The preacher and the pastor walk side by side, as Augustine addresses not his own human frailty as in the *Confessions*, but the frailty of the human race, what Peter Brown describes eloquently as 'the lost future'.[10] He starts by giving us the full text of the prayer, with *quotidianum* ('daily') for the bread, following the Old Latin versions, but with *inferas* rather than *inducas* at the temptation petition, with its softer resonance ('do not bring us into temptation'). Then he describes the shape of the prayer: 'in all prayer we have to conciliate the goodwill of him to whom we pray, then to say what we pray for'. Following established tradition, Fatherhood means our adopted sonship, a status Jews never approached, as Tertullian had pointed out; it is God's love alone that confers this on us, with the moral implications involved, as Chrysostom also teaches. Heaven is where God dwells, and that means also 'in the hearts of the righteous'; which leads him on to a characteristically human-focused treatment of the hallowing of the name, 'that it may be held holy by men, that God may become known to them'.

The kingdom is 'a thing which belongs to the hallowing of God's name', and he goes on to point out that the petition 'is not used in such a way as if God were not now reigning'; the kingdom is eschatological, judging us now, as we wait in future hope. He deliberately gives four interpretations of doing the will, which we shall encounter again: by the holy and just; but also for the conversion of sinners; (in other words, we are praying for sinners to be converted, or for the righteous to be rewarded, but the wicked condemned at the judgement); the third interpretation is that heaven and earth signify spirit and flesh, so that doing the will is the triumph of spirit (God) in the frailty of humanity (flesh); and the fourth, inspired by Tertullian's view of 'Mother Church', interprets 'as in heaven, so on earth' to be 'as in Christ himself, so in the Church; as in the Husband, so in the Bride'. Augustine's sense of the unity of the prayer, moving from one petition to another, is heralded by his closing words on doing the will: 'earth is fruitful as a result of heaven fertilizing it'.

Augustine's readiness to see the will of God in different ways is also shown in his interpretation of daily bread, following in the steps of Tertullian and Cyprian. It is the bread of ordinary need, but it is also spiritual food, and, following Cyprian, it is also the eucharistic bread. Augustine is aware of Christians, 'most of them being in Eastern parts', who do not celebrate daily; and here he goes into a tactful parenthesis, not wanting to be confrontational, but at the same time firmly standing his ground! 'We must take all three meanings together.' Forgiveness is about attitude, but it is also about prayer; we have to pray for those we have pardoned; forgiveness is about asking for pardon, and granting it, by God, by us.

Then comes temptation; although aware of 'ne nos inducas' ('lead us not') in the Gospel texts, and Cyprian's (liturgical) version, 'ne patiaris' ('suffer us not'), he defends the translation 'bring' as being just as accurate a rendering of the Greek as 'lead', which is also what he uses elsewhere, the Sermons included.[11] For God does not do the 'leading' but suffers us to be led there. God's permissive will is his way round this difficult petition, which is at root about the human experience of suffering of any kind, and how to express our genuine fear and reluctance about it, the reality of the experience, and God's relationship with a fallen world. In this world, human beings have a choice, a responsibility, as Augustine points out; when faced with testing, we pray not to be brought into it, whether it is doing harm, or being deluded by prosperity. The final petition, separate, but clearly related to the previous one, is about 'being delivered from that into which we have already been led'. Here, Augustine breaks with Tertullian, Cyprian and Ambrose in translating *a malo* not as the devil, but as the force of evil, present in temptation, but in much more. In this, as in other things, he is set to influence the West in a significant way, at variance with much of the East, with its personal view of 'the evil one'. And he concludes by speaking of death being delivered from the bonds of this life, and the hope of blessedness to come, an appropriate note for a work that began with the beatitudes.

Augustine then goes on to do two things. First, he discusses the shape of the prayer. For him, unlike Tertullian and Cyprian, there are definitely seven petitions; but expanding on Tertullian, for him the first three are about eternal things, the remaining four about this life; this is a theme that recurs in the *Sermons* as well as the *Encheiridion*. Of course, he admits, there are earthly aspects to the first three, as well as eternal features of the other four, but this is the essential direction. Then he goes on to allegorize these petitions in a way which we do not encounter in his other writings. He is the first Western writer to apply allegory in full, in numerology, to the Lord's Prayer. He began his exposition of the Sermon on the Mount by applying the seven gifts of the Spirit (Isaiah 11:2–3) to the beatitudes (Matthew 5:3–10),[12] and these reappear together now. The fear of God and the poor in spirit are linked with hallowing of the name; the piety of the meek with the kingdom coming; knowledge and those who mourn with the doing of the will; fortitude and thirsting after righteousness with daily bread; prudence and the merciful with forgiveness; understanding and the pure in heart with temptation; and wisdom and peacemakers with deliverance from evil. He then reverts to the theme of forgiveness, so that he can lead into Jesus' injunctions in the ensuing verses (Matthew 6:14ff.) Where did he get this idea from? As the prayer of the baptized, the Lord's Prayer is what those who are Spirit-filled can say. But there is another, parallel source. At Milan, in Ambrose's time, the post-baptismal anointing (the 'spiritual seal') was accompanied by a prayer based on Isaiah 11:2–3 (the germ of what later came to be called the 'Confirmation Prayer'), which is bound to have had an influence on Augustine.[13]

Augustine builds an impressive edifice, in which he demonstrates his desire to throw the petitions of the prayer in many different corners, so that they can embrace every kind of important human experience. While his allegorical interpretation is not entirely convincing, it was in time to set later commentators on a similar track, working as they did on the common motto, 'si Augustinus adest, sufficit ipse tibi' – 'if Augustine is there, that is enough for you'. As we shall see, his sense of the internal shape of the prayer both in its constituent parts, and in the way one petition flows logically into another, was to leave a lasting legacy: Isidore of Seville took up the gifts of the Spirit, but the beatitudes were not to appear until Rabanus Maurus in the ninth century.

There is a consistency about Augustine's teaching on the prayer. The First Letter to Proba (412) is in some respects a compressed version, dealing with the main themes, but without the fullness or the subtlety; 'whoever says in prayer anything which cannot find its place in that gospel prayer is praying in a way which, if it is not unlawful, is at least not spiritual', having earlier warned her, in true anti-Pelagian style, that the prayer is not to be used for asking for personal gain.[14] Near the start of the *Encheiridion*, he explains briefly how the Lord's Prayer and the Creed contain everything that a Christian needs to learn by heart, clearly a baptismal context, with catechesis in view. Then in the two chapters much later on dealing with the two biblical versions of the prayer, Augustine returns to the 'three plus four' structure, compressing into a short space some of the themes we have encountered already, including the ambiguity of 'daily bread'; and in the next short chapter, he takes the opportunity of saying why Luke's version is not really substantially different, because of the internal unity of the prayer.[15]

The four *Sermons* take us into a different milieu. The same teaching comes through, but without the allegorization at the end of his treatment in *Sermon on the Mount*. In overall approach and style, they are similar to Chromatius of Aquileia and what we have yet to see in Peter Chrysologus and Caesarius of Arles. These are sermons preached for the *traditio orationis dominicae*, the 'handing over' of the Lord's Prayer to those about to be baptized. They could repeat the prayer, along with the Creed, probably on the Saturday morning; and the Gospel passage for the occasion is Matthew 6:9–13 – the Lord's Prayer itself.[16] The Creed teaches us what to believe, and the Lord's Prayer how to pray (56.1). Each sermon begins with an introduction on the need to know how to pray (using the text Romans 10:13), and moves into each petition in turn: sonship is granted in the womb of the Church (56.5), and as an inheritance (59.2); the hallowing of the name is by us (56.5), in us (57.4), and makes us holy (58.3, 59.3); the kingdom is to come (Matthew 25:34, the Great Assize again, 56.6, 57.5) and we can herald it by our behaviour; the doing of the will means not resisting God (56.8), echoing the subtlety of *Sermon on the Mount* with its four interpretations (57.6), and he mentions angels as well (58.4, 59.5); daily bread is ordinary, spiritual and eucharistic (56.9–10, 57.7, 58.5, 59.6); the prayer for forgiveness is both a 'bilge-pump' (a nautical image for a sea-faring community) (56.11) and a 'bargain with God' (56.13, 58.7), an image we came across in the Jerusalem *Mystagogic Catecheses*; Augustine also interprets the forgiveness petition as a daily renewal of baptism, meaning that grievous sins were recognized after baptism, and could be forgiven (56.11, 57.8, 59.7); temptation is about future sins, appropriate when thinking of baptism (56.19), it is about both bad (being subjugated) as well as good (being tested) (57.9), it is about giving in to the tempter (59.8); deliverance from evil is about admitting to being in evil (58.11) and a recognition of its reality (59.8). But Augustine's version of the third petition varies in these sermons. He uses Cyprian's *'in coelo et in terra'* ('in heaven and on earth') in 56.7, but he notes another possibility in 56.8, *'sicut in coelo et in terra'* ('as in heaven also on earth'), which is also Jerome's text, and the one used in the *Sermon on the Mount*, and it is what appears in 59.4; but a third text, *'sicut in coelo, ita in terra'* ('as in heaven, so also on earth'), is used in 57.6 and 58.4; as Edmund Hill suggests, the Sermons are probably chronological, and reflect a gradual move towards a standard liturgical text.

Baptismal allusions about rebirth and repentance, and 'entering the font' (56.29, 57.8), pervade these sermons: Augustine takes care, too, to get across to his hearers the internal shape of the prayer, with its three heavenly and four earthly petitions (56.19, 58.12, 59.8), although he does seem to waver on two occasions (perhaps a preacher's licence) over whether temptation and evil are part of the same petition (56.18, 57.10). There is only one reference to baptism eradicating original sin inherited from Adam (56.13), something we have not (perhaps surprisingly for Augustine) seen so far. More liturgical in context than the other writings, they refer, but only allusively, to the ideal of the 'discipline of the secret', whereby only those baptized knew the prayer (56.10). He makes clear that the candidates will have to recite the prayer before they are baptized, but he is less concerned about them getting this right than the Creed, because they will hear the priest recite it every day at the eucharist (58.12) – an important piece of evidence that, in Augustine's time, the prayer was part of the eucharist, but that it was not recited by everyone, as in the East. In another Letter, he tells us that the eucharistic prayer is the prayer 'that almost every church now concludes with the Lord's Prayer'.[17]

Augustine uses petitions of the Lord's Prayer frequently in his other writings, but two themes stand out as particularly important. One is the daily recitation of the prayer as a daily purification from sin, a renewal of baptism, which we have seen already.[18] The other is the extensive use he makes of the prayer for forgiveness. Against the Donatists and the Pelagians, who shun using this petition, Augustine insisted that even the apostles sinned, everyone sins, good people pray the Lord's Prayer right up to the end of their life, and through the grace given only by God, we are enabled to resist temptation. (At the Second Council of Milevis in 416 and the Sixteenth Council of Carthage in 418, in both of which Augustine took a prominent part, there were pronouncements against Pelagian omission of this petition.) For Augustine, the petition for forgiveness is central.[19] His extensive use of this particular petition shows a mind that is ready to apply the prayer of the Church to theological controversy; indeed, for him it becomes a criterion against which not only human behaviour but doctrinal orthodoxy can be measured.

A great deal emerges from Augustine's treatment of the prayer. Following on from Tertullian and Cyprian, it is the basis for all prayer, and in that sense summarizes the gospel. It is both God-directed and human-directed in its internal shape. It leaps out of the Sermon on the Mount, instructs Proba as to how to pray, and helps form new Christians preparing to enter the font. Augustine is probably the first exegete really to face up to the fact that the prayer not only *can* but *should* be interpreted in different ways and at different levels. It was, probably, his Platonism that inspired him to Tertullian's insight that the prayer is about heavenly and earthly petitions. And his profound sense of God's distance and grace enabled him to walk circumspectly around the thorny question of God's role in temptation, with the preferred translation 'bring', rather than 'lead'. Moreover, the challenging directness of the baptismal sermons shows the prayer to pervade human experience, and a sense that it belongs everywhere within it. There is, too, a 'Western' consciousness, which comes across in the way he implicitly chides the East for not having daily communion (and for not interpreting the bread-petition in a eucharistic way), in his ambiguous relationship with Jerome, whose Vulgate text he disliked, and which he shows no signs of using here, and in his deliberate (impersonal) translation of evil. But perhaps Augustine comes to the heart of Christian living when he refers to the 'two wings of prayer' – asking for God's forgiveness and giving alms to the poor (56.10), and he knew the custom of beating one's breast while reciting it.[20] For Augustine, the Lord's Prayer is something we 'dare' to say ('audemus quotidie dicere'). In an Easter season sermon, he goes as far as speaking of 'the sacrament of the Lord's Prayer', to which the congregation, though not joining in with the celebrant at the eucharist, assent with 'Amen'.[21] Above all, for Augustine, the Lord's Prayer is the prayer of the forgiven sinner, living a thankful life, and while his basic thought about the prayer remains unchanged, Michael Jackson rightly draws attention to his increasing distrust of the human will, in the face of the Pelagian heresy, and the need for that will to be purified by God's grace.[22]

## *John Cassian (c.360–after 430) and the* Regula Magistri *(c.500–525)*

We now turn from baptismal catechesis and public exposition to the monastic tradition, in which East and West mingled considerably. John Cassian's life reveals this; born in Scythia Minor, that area of the Roman Empire which corresponds with Dobrudja, the part of Bulgaria and Romania along the Black Sea Coast, after a time in Bethlehem and Egypt as a monk, he became a deacon at Constantinople, from where he was sent by John Chrysostom as an emissary to Pope Innocent I. He then moved to near Marseilles, where he founded two monasteries, and where he wrote his *Institutes* and his twenty-four *Conferences*, from material gathered during his time in the East. The former are about the way religious communities should function, whereas the latter, probably written about the year 426, are a series of conversations with great spiritual figures. In the ninth of these, which is the first of two conferences with Abbot Isaac, in the Egyptian desert of Scetis, addressed to Leontius, Bishop of Fréjus, and the monk Helladius, he gives an exposition of the Lord's Prayer.[23]

The style and tone, more Greek than Latin, take us back to Origen and Gregory of Nyssa. The heavenly Fatherhood is our soul's ascent to God, as adopted children, from our exile on earth. The hallowing of the name is God's glory, our feebleness, and God's desire to perfect us. The kingdom is God's reign, which the soul wants to reach, and by which it is judged (and here Cassian uses the by now familiar text from the Great Assize, Matthew 25:34). The doing of the will is salvation, where Cassian shows a little more optimism than Augustine when he prays in order that all should be saved. Cassian follows Jerome in translating *epiousion* as *supersubstantialem*, though he is aware of the Latin translation *quotidianum*; as a careful judge of the options, he asserts that we pray for bread which 'by its nobility and substance' makes it 'exceed all creatures', and realizes that *quotidianum* is a softer and more ambiguous description. This bread is necessary for the life to come; 'daily' does not mean daily communion, but the requirement to recite the prayer each day. Forgiveness stems from the mercy of God, and the need to forgive others from the heart; Cassian refers scornfully to the practice of some people omitting this petition when it is chanted in Church, a practice alluded to by Chrysostom and Augustine. Temptation is about not being overcome, in the knowledge that testing is part of the Christian life; and deliverance from evil, which Cassian places in the same chapter (therefore not treated separately), is a prayer that we should not be tempted by the devil more than we can bear. And he goes on to assert that the Lord's Prayer should be the principal guide in all prayer; everything that is necessary is contained within its bounds. Cassian's use of essentially Eastern material attributed to Abbot Isaac is mediated in a Latin text that takes cognizance of issues of translation and meaning. His theological approach is Eastern as is his discussion of temptation and evil (personal) as part of the same petition.

The *Rule of the Master*, an anonymous monastic rule, is now generally regarded as written in Italy, south-east of Rome, in the sixth century, but whether it is earlier than the *Rule of St Benedict*, with which it shares some common material, including the prologue and concerning the abbot, but not on the Lord's Prayer, is an open question. The main difference for our purposes is that, whereas the *Rule of the Master* discusses its meaning, the *Rule of St Benedict* confines itself to directions as to when it is to be used. It relies on previous Latin writers, reflecting its monastic milieu, and is beginning to bring us into a liturgical context as well.[24]

The Lord's Prayer is a prayer which we are instructed by Mother Church to 'dare' to say.[25] By the wood of the cross, we are reborn in another womb, at baptism, and become heirs of salvation. We hallow the name in good deeds, showing how the Spirit makes his dwelling in us; and here the author relies, not for the first time, on Cyprian.[26] The kingdom is about judgement; and the will, on which he spends more time than anything else, is a struggle against the power of evil, the exemplar of which is Jesus in Gethsemane; the angels in heaven do the Father's will, so should we try on earth. The discussion of daily bread is by contrast brief, and confined to a few words on living in daily fear of the Lord, a spiritual view, but unspecific. Forgiveness involves self-searching in respect of both our own sins and our capacity to match God's power to forgive in extending forgiveness to others. Temptation is testing, from which we pray that God may not leave us without help and protection, a passage which reappears in a prayer for use in a monastery in the 'Old' Gelasian Sacramentary (a book of prayers for the sacraments and other occasions written near Paris in the mid-eighth century, but containing material reflecting Roman practice going back to the sixth); we should make this petition by beating our hearts as well as our bodies.[27] Deliverance from the evil one is, ultimately, about being separated from God at the end.

## Peter Chrysologus (c.400–450) and Caesarius of Arles (c.470–542)

Peter was born at Imola, and made Bishop of Ravenna in 433; he knew Empress Galla Placida, who had close connections with Ravenna, where she built a number of churches, and with whom Peter shared a strong loyalty to the See of Rome. Of his sermons, 176 were collected together by one of his eighth-century successors, Felix (707–717), of which no fewer than six are pre-baptismal homilies on the Lord's Prayer: other sermons have more recently been identified, and they have been edited, together with the original 176, by Alexander Olivar.[28] They are marked by a literary style that is clear and simple; he was nicknamed 'Chrysologus' ('golden-word') to honour his reputation as a preacher as well as to distinguish him from John Chrysostom ('golden-mouth').

The six sermons (there are seven preceding ones on the Creed), like the four of Augustine, have the same shape, consisting of an introduction on prayer, followed by a clause-by-clause exposition, sometimes with a recapitulation at the end, which begin again with the opening words, 'Pater noster', as if to embed them further in the minds of those about to be baptized. (Only 69 fails to reach the end, because, as sometimes happens with preachers, he has taken so long about other matters, in this instance, speaking about prayer in general, that he has to stop after the petition for the coming of the kingdom.) The immediacy is conveyed in the opening sections (with repetitions of 'today', 67.1, 68.2, 70.1, 71.1). Baptismal allusions abound, in the pouring of divine grace at the font (72.8, cf. 68.2); repeated use of the image of becoming heirs of the kingdom (67.2, 68.3, 70.1, 71.2); and references to new birth, 'little children' (67.2), 'not yet born' (71.2), and 'in the womb' (72.2). The latter suggest that these homilies were delivered on Easter Eve, possibly in the morning, as the last instruction before the Easter liturgy. He implies that the congregation included (not uncontroversially) those who were not to be baptized ('Christians in the womb', 67.11; 68.3, 11; 69.6; 70.3), but who were still allowed to recite the prayer – a sure indication that the older baptismal discipline was breaking down.

The heavenly Fatherhood of God is about our rebirth at baptism, as heirs together of the kingdom (67.2), which requires of us heavenly behaviour (71.3). Hallowing the name is a witness to those who do not acknowledge Christ, who are blasphemers (67.4, 69.4, 70.4, 71.4). The kingdom, where he reads *veniat* (not *adveniat*, except at 68.5), means the reign of the Christian in the world to come, while evil and sin continue to reign in this life (67.5), with ourselves as faithful soldiers fighting for Christ (68.5); it is a kingdom to wait to receive (the Great Assize, Matthew 25:34 – 69.5, 70.5), a kingdom we await in hope (71.5, 72.5). Doing the will is turning our minds to the will of God (67.6), having one will, one mind (68.6, 72.6), and resisting evil (70.6). He spends no time on the niceties of translating daily bread, but follows Ambrose with a spiritual view, interpreting it on each occasion either explicitly or implicitly as the eucharist: it is the bread of heaven (67.7), which is the heavenly table (68.7, 70.7, 71.7), and he even uses the image of baking to illustrate the resurrection ('baked in the furnace of the sepulchre', 67.7). Forgiveness is a sharp challenge ('man', he addresses directly to each person about to be baptized, 67.8 and 71.8), for it is a 'bargain' with God (68.8), as we encountered both in the Jerusalem *Mystagogic Catecheses* and Augustine, from God the fount of all forgiveness. Temptation means, as we have seen before, not being left alone by God (67.9, 68.9, 70.9, 71.9), for it exposes our weaknesses, and makes us aware of the need for prayer (72.9). He is usually succinct on deliverance from evil, which he interprets personally, unlike Augustine; the devil cannot enjoy what is good (67.10), we live not in our own strength but in the strength of God (68.10), the devil as the source and action of all evil (70.10), the author of evil (71.10), for Christ brings us to everything that is good (72.9).

What Peter Chrysologus provides is a remarkable selection of baptismal homilies, which, while similar in structure, differ enough to enable us to see into the mind of an effective communicator. Like Augustine, he knows how to teach profound things in a simple way, keeps being taken with the brevity and depth of the prayer, preaches with a suitable array of biblical allusions and quotations, and is ready to spread the baptismal theme through the prayer, as well as stress the eucharistic meanings of daily bread. Unlike Augustine, whose writings he appears not to have known, he gives no hint of the three heavenly/four earthly interpretation, although he assumes an overall sevenfold shape; daily bread is exclusively spiritual; evil is personal; and the variant reading *veniat* is one more piece of evidence that the text of the prayer is not universally settled.

When we come to Caesarius, who, after twelve years as a monk at Lérins, was Archbishop of Arles from 502 until his death forty years later, we have the contrast of an influential figure who has left us only one baptismal homily on the Lord's Prayer.[29] He dominated church life in the area, securing, for example, the condemnation of Semipelagianism at the Council of Orange in 529.[30] Sermon 147 takes us back to the ambience of Augustine, by whom Caesarius was heavily influenced. The preceding sermon, on prayer, ends with a reference to this one, 'rather early tomorrow morning', which, along with the manner in which he begins ('you have recited what you believe, you have heard for what you should pray'), suggests another pre-baptism occasion. Heavenly Fatherhood gives us an inheritance; the name of God is always holy and is to be sanctified by us in baptism; the kingdom is to come, and we pray to be among the saints; doing the will is about 'the soul within us' being Heaven itself, and overcoming when there is conflict between the flesh and the spirit; daily bread, as in Augustine, is material survival, spiritual sustenance, as well as the eucharist; forgiveness of sins is what baptism is about, and – as in Augustine – we renew the sacrament daily when we recite this prayer. Unusually, he deals with temptation and deliverance (impersonal, following Augustine) together briefly; God helps us to come through these experiences; and he ends by asserting, with Augustine, that the prayer consists of three petitions that are about eternal life, and four that are about this life. The 'ideal' of the baptismal homily, if it ever existed in full measure, was already breaking down; Caesarius is the first preacher we know to encourage sponsors subsequently to teach the Creed and the Lord's Prayer to the baptized, a clear indication of a changing world.[31]

### *Venantius Fortunatus (c.530–600), Isidore of Seville (c.560–636), Hildefonsus of Toledo (c.607–667), and Bede (c.673–735)*

We now come to four different writers with distinct contributions: Venantius Fortunatus in Gaul with an exposition of the prayer, Isidore of Seville with a liturgical focus, Hildefonsus of Toledo providing part of a manual for the catechesis of the growing child, and, finally, Bede in England writing expositions of the Gospels.

Venantius Fortunatus who was born near Venice and educated at Ravenna, after various journeys in Gaul became Bishop of Poitiers towards the end of the sixth century. Best known for his two great hymns to the cross ('Pange lingua gloriosi' and 'Vexilla Regis prodeunt'), his *Exposition of the Lord's Prayer*[32] is a short Augustinian treatise, with a baptismal focus. He manages to weave baptism not only into the opening (baptism is the renewal of life, through which we learn to pray), addressing the heavenly Father (predictably, divine sonship), but also into the hallowing of the name (twice); the coming of the kingdom in the 'watering' of new Christians, whose life should be based on the beatitudes themselves; the doing of the will, based on the Ten Commandments (the first time mentioned in connection with baptism and the Lord's Prayer) with renewed manhood through baptism making us like the angels in our ability to obey; and forgiveness has started at the font, where we rise with Christ to receive communion. He runs out of time (or space, or energy) at temptation, but provides an explanation of daily bread that is as comprehensive as Augustine. In this treatment, we can see the ideal of baptismal preparation breaking down, for there is an almost self-conscious air about these baptismal allusions.

Isidore became Bishop of Seville *c*.600, succeeding his brother, Leander; the two of them had arrived at Seville after fleeing the conflicts between the Visigoths and the Byzantine imperial forces in the south of Spain. He was a committed scholar and is credited with establishing the liturgy at Seville; his works, which were influenced by Augustine, were popular in subsequent centuries. The *De Officiis Ecclesiasticis* ('On Ecclesiastical Offices')[33] contains an exposition of the meaning of the eucharist, going through each main part, including the Lord's Prayer, which he begins by identifying as an integral part of the mass, perhaps because in some places it was omitted. Relying on Augustine, he points to the 'three and four' shape of the prayer; the hallowing of the name, the kingdom and the will are about the Christian hope that is to come, whereas daily bread, both for material and spiritual needs, and forgiveness, protection and deliverance are for this life. He ends by suggesting that the 'sevenfold' shape corresponds with the fullness of the Church, or the gifts of the Spirit (Isaiah 11:2–3), the former of which is new, the latter taken straight from Augustine. Later on he discusses the meaning of daily bread in relation to the eucharist; it can (and should) be received daily, but it should be approached with due preparation.

Hildefonsus became Archbishop of Toledo in 657, after a time as Abbot of Agali, in which capacity he attended the Councils of

Toledo in 653 and 655. His *Annotationes de cognitione baptismi* ('Remarks on understanding baptism') relies on Augustine, as well as on Isidore of Seville. The Lord's Prayer no longer holds the central position that we saw in previous preachers and writers; instead, it comes after an explanation of such liturgical customs as the laying on of hands and chrismation, and before a discussion of the eucharistic presence.[34] We are in a different climate; the prayer is addressed to the whole of the Trinity, the name is hallowed by the redeemed humanity living faithful lives, the kingdom is what we pray to share in, the will is about obedience, daily bread is both material and spiritual, including the eucharist, forgiveness is needful both to receive and to extend; he uses the Augustine text at temptation (*ne inferas*, 'do not bring us'), which means not being deserted by God, and deliverance from evil results in being where we cannot suffer anything. Like John Cassian (and others), he goes on to say that everything that we can pray can be summed up in these brief words, the 'gospel prayer', as he describes it, in words taken from Augustine's First Letter to Proba.

We now come to Bede the Venerable, who began his long monastic career at Wearmouth, moving from there to Jarrow in 682. His many writings, including his *History of the English Church*, mark him out as the most distinguished scholar of his time. In his expositions of the Gospels of Matthew and Luke,[35] there are discussions of the Lord's Prayer. He does not follow Jerome's Vulgate text, with *supersubstantialem* – it is the Old Latin text, echoing liturgical practice, that he uses. In the Matthew exposition, the heavenly Father dwells among us; the name is hallowed in us at baptism; the kingdom is both promised and sought through the suffering of Christ; the will he interprets in the manner of Augustine (angels in heaven, the salvation of the just, judgement for the damned, heaven and earth correspond to soul and body); daily bread is, similarly, material, spiritual and eucharistic; forgiveness means praying for those who have wronged us, as well as for ourselves; temptation he regards as God allowing it to happen (*induci patitur*, 'to suffer to be led'), another Augustinian trait; and deliverance is about surviving into the life of blessedness. Interestingly, he adopts the Vulgate 'Amen', as a 'seal' of the Lord's Prayer, quoting Jerome, but without acknowledgement. Bede was influential not only in England but beyond. He refracts the teaching of Augustine, complete with three heavenly and four earthly petitions, for generations to come, and is in effect our main link between the Age of the Fathers and the long medieval period that follows.

## Main authors reviewed

- There is greater instability in the *text* than in the East. The significance of this factor, together with the need for translation from the Greek, cannot be overestimated in the long term. The instability can be traced back to Tertullian's inversion of the kingdom and will petitions, though the more significant stage is Cyprian's adoption of Tertullian's paraphrase into his text, *ne patiaris induci* – 'suffer us not to be led'. This Augustine knew well, hence his additional alternative, *ne inferas* – 'do not bring us', which we saw in Hildefonsus of Toledo, an influential source for the time, and his adjustments to the text of the petition of the doing of the will in Sermons are another case in point. Hilary of Poitiers' Gospel text at this point was 'non derelinquas nos in temptatione quam ferre non possimus' ('do not abandon us in temptation which we cannot bear'), which is similar to the variant referred to by Chromatius.[36] Peter Chrysologus' lone voice over *veniat* (instead of *adveniat*) is not without significance, even though it does not alter the meaning of the prayer at this point. The other main cause of debate concerns the translation of *epiousion*, where *quotidianum* (arguably a more attractive word) was clearly embedded in the Latin tradition but where Jerome went for a translation of the Greek tradition of interpretation, which was not taken seriously by commentators until the Carolingian era; apart from Jerome only Ambrose (who knew Greek well), and Cassian (who came from the East) discuss *epiousion* in any detail. The fact that Jerome adds 'Amen' to his

Vulgate text suggests that this was how he prayed the Lord's Prayer. Bede's 'Amen' is another suggestion of liturgical use of the prayer. These variants, particularly with *supersubstantialem*, periphrases over temptation, and 'Amen' reappear in the Irish Gospel Books of the seventh, eighth and ninth centuries. Unlike the standard Latin 'Evangeliaries', which contain only the liturgical Gospel-readings, these manuscripts, including the *Book of Dimma* and the *Book of Kells*, consist of the entire text of all four Gospels, although the Lord's Prayer was only read (if at all) as a liturgical Gospel in baptismal preparation. From a theological point of view, it is the instability of interpretation-text-gloss over temptation which is the most significant, and more extensive than anything we have seen in the East: it all began with Tertullian and Cyprian; it carries on in such late fifth-century North African Gospel text variants as 'et ne passus fueris induci nos in temptationem' ('and do not let yourself allow us to be led into temptation');[37] and it embraces not only interpretations of text, but a liturgical text that has to be more stable than the Gospel versions, which only gradually became standardized after Jerome. We shall encounter the question of liturgical versus biblical text at the Reformation, and after.

- When it comes to *interpretations*, the terrain is rich and plentiful. We are fortunate in having, unlike the East, more than just one view from every single author, thanks to Augustine's influence, and the reputation of Peter Chrysologus as a preacher. But unlike the East in this era, where a 'definitive' answer to the meaning of daily bread was sought (is it material, is it spiritual, is it the eucharist?), there is a more relaxed approach, with different authors opting for different views. This may, once more, be the result of Augustine's influence, for it is he who encourages a comprehensive view of the meaning of both this petition and the will of God as an internal struggle, as a conflict to be played out at the day of judgement, and as a delineation between heaven and earth, soul and body. His view of the overall shape of the prayer (three heavenly and four earthly petitions) does not appear in Peter Chrysologus, but it had a lasting influence, as we can see in Caesarius of Arles, Isidore of Seville, and Hildefonsus, who, moreover, is the only writer to bring the Trinity explicitly into his discussion (cf. Gregory of Nyssa in the East). Augustine is responsible for the innovation of translating evil in impersonal terms, and although this view does not appear in Cassian, the *Rule of the Master*, or Peter Chrysologus, subsequent writers follow in his steps. He therefore overshadows his Western successors, spreading an influence that, with modification, stretches into the Reformation, in such different figures as Martin Luther and Lancelot Andrewes.

- The *contexts* vary and yet we can see a discernible shift, which relates to the Lord's Prayer and baptism. Ambrose, like the Jerusalem *Mystagogic Catecheses*, preaches to the newly baptized, but he is the only author to do this. Augustine, Peter Chrysologus and Caesarius of Arles all preach before baptism. There are, moreover, other kinds of discourse, like Augustine writing to Proba, or his exposition of the Sermon on the Mount, to say nothing of the influence of a doctrinal handbook like the *Encheiridion*, and his repeated references to the petition for forgiveness, both in his other sermons, and in his polemical works. Then there is monastic spirituality, with John Cassian bringing the Egyptian desert tradition into southern Gaul, adapting his treatment of 'daily bread' so that his Latin-reading audience understands, but treating temptation and evil as the same petition; and the *Rule of the Master* builds on the North African tradition of Cyprian and Augustine in writing for a religious community. When we move further on, the climate changes. Venantius Fortunatus may emphasize the baptismal focus, but is this really where his audience are? A similar suspicion surfaces when looking at Hildefonsus of Toledo: the *Liber de cognitione baptismi* must have been written for the instruction of those already baptized and growing up in the faith. Paul Bradshaw has argued persuasively that the patristic 'ideal' was probably short-lived,[38] even if it did leave its mark on how the prayer was brought into the eucharist.

- That brings us to the fragments – and they are only fragments – of evidence we have for the *liturgical use* of the Lord's Prayer. Candidates for baptism were taught the prayer, but there is no evidence for it being part of the baptism service itself, as was the case in Antioch in the *Apostolic Constitutions* towards the end of the fourth century. But what of the eucharist? Taft has suggested that there was a rite of dismissal of penitents, with the laying on of hands, between the Lord's Prayer and the communion in North Africa, which may be echoed in Optatus, Bishop of Milevis, who, writing in 366, alludes to the use of the prayer at this point in Donatist liturgical practice.[39] It is also clear that Christians did use the prayer on their own in their daily prayer. But what of the eucharist? Ambrose and Augustine both give us evidence suggesting its position before communion, and said by the priest alone – unlike in the East, where it appears to have been said by all. Jerome is clear that it was not an innovation in his time, but he is probably referring to Eastern as well as Western practice. Isidore of Seville, later on, does not tell us how it is recited, but for him the prayer was essential for the eucharist, which is why it came straight after the eucharistic prayer, almost as if it were part of it. We now need, therefore, to look at the liturgical evidence in more detail.

## Liturgy

A similar process for the Lord's Prayer is discernible to what we observed in the East. At daily prayer it tends to find a position at the end, as a summary of all prayer; although no position is to be found of the newly baptized reciting the prayer on their own after coming out of the font, it remains central to catechesis, as the 'Old' Gelasian Sacramentary tells us; and at the eucharist, we find more and more evidence for its position before communion.

## Daily prayer

It is not until the sixth century that we know for certain when and where the prayer was recited, although we should not forget that many of the treatises we have been looking at refer to domestic prayer: Ambrose of Milan recommends saying the Lord's Prayer with hands raised up twice each day – when rising and when going to sleep. The Council of Gerona, 517, laid down that it should come at the end of morning and evening prayer. Jordi Pinell tried to reconstruct the old Spanish daily offices of Mattins and Vespers, suggesting that it came at the end of both services. And according to Pascher, it formed part of the conclusion to the form of Mattins used at Rome, presumably from around the fifth century, although the provision for a collect as an alternative may indicate that the Lord's Prayer was used when no priest was present.[40]

The *Rule of St Benedict* (mid-sixth century), however, is more forthcoming:

> Assuredly, the celebration of Lauds and Vespers must never pass by without the superior's reciting the Lord's Prayer at the end for all to hear, because the thorns of contention are likely to spring up. Thus warned by the pledge they make to one another in the very words of this prayer: 'Forgive us as we forgive' (Matthew 6:12), they may cleanse themselves of this kind of vice. At other celebrations, only the final part of the Lord's Prayer is said aloud, that all may reply: 'But deliver us from evil' (Matthew 6:13).[41]

This tells us a great deal. The prayer is not recited by everyone together, but by the superior at Mattins and Vespers, and silently by everyone at the other hours. Forgiveness is made the heart of the prayer, reflecting much of the teaching we have so far seen, and the way it ends at the other hours seems to cover the fact that there is no 'Amen'. The *Rule*, which probably reflects an older tradition of placing the prayer at the conclusion of the daily offices, left its influence all over Europe as time went on. Unlike in the East, where in the Armenian rite it comes at the start of the offices, the West opts unanimously for the later position – if, that is, it is used. The superior's solo recitation is echoed in the practice alluded to by Ambrose and Augustine of the celebrant at the eucharist; the practice of communal recitation of the final petition is taken up in parts of the West at the eucharist in later centuries.

## Baptism

As we have noted, Caesarius of Arles is the first to encourage sponsors to teach growing children about the Christian faith, which is also referred to by Boniface of Mainz (†c.754).[42] But what of the liturgy itself? Apart from what we have already seen from the authors themselves, the 'Old' Gelasian Sacramentary places baptism in the Easter Vigil, and some time beforehand, both the Creed and the Lord's Prayer are explained. The Gelasian book may reflect at this point Roman practice in the early sixth century, if not earlier; the *Ordo Romanus* XI (a description of services, in this case at Rome), while dating from the early ninth century, similarly indicates Roman practice as early as the late sixth century.[43]

The rite in question Bradshaw regards as archaic, the survival of something much earlier.[44] The deacon instructs those about to be baptized, reading out a brief explanation of the Lord's Prayer. In structure this is similar to what we came across in Augustine, Peter Chrysologus and Caesarius of Arles, consisting of an introduction on the importance of prayer, beginning with Jesus' teaching (Matthew 6:6), followed by a clause-by-clause treatment: adopted sonship (John 1:12); hallowing through baptism; God's own kingdom, brought by Christ's passion; doing the will unblameably, as Caesarius said; daily bread is spiritual (John 6:41) only; the prayer is seen to free the believer daily from sin (cf. Augustine); forgiveness must be mutual; temptation means 'suffer us not to be led'; deliverance from evil means being helped by God when human frailty is too weak. This text was studied by Pierre de Puniet long ago, from which it is clear that the compiler

98

knew the works of Tertullian and Cyprian (to which we would add Augustine), and they represent the liturgical and catechetical triumph of that succinct North African tradition.

## Eucharist

As far as the eucharist is concerned, the evidence becomes increasingly strong for the Lord's Prayer coming between the eucharistic prayer and the distribution of communion as the almost universal practice, as Augustine indicates, as well as Jerome; and Optatus of Milevis' evidence suggests it was used at this point in North Africa before the Donatist schism. Aurelian of Arles (fifth century) tells us that where there was no priest the monastic community would on Sundays after Terce say the Lord's Prayer and then receive communion (from the reserved sacrament).[45] The most public form of receiving communion this way in the West ('the mass of the presanctified', i.e. the already-consecrated elements) began to take place on Good Friday in Rome later in the seventh century when some of the congregation desired communion on a day when the eucharist was not celebrated: the consecrated bread would be brought to the altar, the Lord's Prayer would be recited, and the distribution followed.[46] It could well be that the prayer was used on such occasions in less formal contexts, for domestic communion from the consecrated bread, at an earlier period, but the evidence is lacking. The Lord's Prayer was, arguably, already embedded in the eucharist in most places by the early fifth century, but not everywhere; we need to take careful note of the implied criticism, as late as 633, of those who only used it on Sundays, and not on weekdays as well, in Canon 10 of the Fourth Council of Toledo, although Canon 32 of the Council of Arles in 538 forbade non-communicants to withdraw before the Lord's Prayer had been said.[47]

There is, however, important evidence for the exact place of the Lord's Prayer in the eucharist at Rome at the end of the sixth century in the form of the Letter of Gregory the Great (c.540–604) to John of Syracuse, written in October 598.[48] The context is not without irony. John has been berating Gregory for innovations in the liturgy, among which was the recitation of the Lord's Prayer at the eucharist straight after the eucharistic prayer, John regarding this as a lamentable Greek custom. Previous Roman practice was to recite it, not immediately after the eucharistic prayer, but between the breaking of the bread (which followed it) and the distribution. Gregory answers his correspondent with the patient firmness required for the occasion: for him, the Lord's Prayer has a sacred origin because Jesus himself wrote it; it should be part of the eucharistic prayer, and not be separated from it, since that is a prayer written by a scholar; moreover, the Lord's Prayer is said by the priest alone, whereas, Gregory writes, 'among the Greeks (it) is said by all the people'.

Why did Gregory change the position of the prayer? The way he replies to John of Syracuse suggests that bringing the Roman rite into line with Constantinople was not among his priorities, though Gregory knew the Byzantine liturgy. Willis suggests a more practical reason: at the papal mass, the pontiff's custom was to retire from the altar to the throne for the fraction, which was carried out by the deacons and often took a long time; saying the Lord's Prayer from the throne would be out of place, hence the need to recite it in the slightly earlier position. Plausible as the theory is on its own, it does not answer another question – why was the prayer recited by the celebrant alone, particularly when the universal practice in the East was for everyone to join in? Gregory appears to give the answer, and it is corroborated by Isidore of Seville: a prayer regarded as essentially part of the eucharistic prayer should properly be said only by the priest. But priestly recitation of the prayer was not universal practice in the West, as we have seen in Ambrose, and as we also gather from Gregory of Tours (538/9–594), who writes in his *Miracles of St Martin* that a deaf-mute woman was cured and able to recite the Lord's Prayer at mass.[49]

## The text

The earliest full text of the Lord's Prayer within the eucharist comes from the Gregorian Sacramentary, a book of prayers for baptism and eucharist with all the seasonal material whose main contents, in principle, go back to the time of Gregory the Great himself:

> Pater noster, qui es in caelis, sanctificetur nomen tuum; adveniat regnum tuum; fiat voluntas tua sicut in caelo et in terra. Panem nostrum quotidianum da nobis hodie; et dimitte nobis debita nostra sicut et nos dimittimus debitoribus nostris; et ne nos inducas in temptationem, sed libera nos a malo.[50]

Apart from the persistence of *quotidianum*, this is exactly what Jerome gives us in his version – with two further exceptions. The first is an interesting variant in the Sacramentary of Gellone, which was compiled in the north of France for the use of a monastery in the south at the end of the eighth century (part of the family of 'Gelasian' Sacramentaries); it is probably a scribal error, since the standard form appears in the baptismal rites, but it is nonetheless worth recording its (more poetic?) rendering of the opening line, 'qui in celis es'. Second, a group of manuscripts from the ninth century, most from what is now northern France and Germany, adds the 'Amen', which (as we saw) is what Bede gives us; we shall find this variant persisting through the Middle Ages.

In the mass, the prayer follows the eucharistic prayer. It is introduced with a special formula, echoing Cyprian, about following the teaching of Christ and daring to address God as Father (two common patristic themes), and it leads straight into a prayer beginning 'deliver us, Lord' (the embolism), inspired by the concluding petition, 'deliver us from evil'. Such a prayer occurs in most of the Eastern rites: the difference is that in the West, the embolism refers to 'every evil', reflecting the impersonal interpretation of Augustine, whereas in the East (as we have seen), the embolism (where it is used) begins on the theme of temptation. This is another symptom of the different ways in which the structure of the prayer is conceived. The presence in both East and West of this liturgical unit, consisting of short introduction, Lord's Prayer, followed by embolism, in the majority of these rites, suggests a common origin, based on the fixed Lord's Prayer text used in many contexts outside the eucharist, with a tradition of improvisation before and after it. This must reflect, in both East and West, a common desire to highlight its uniqueness. The austere Roman rite, with its simple, fixed introduction and concluding embolism, is something of a contrast to the varying, seasonal forms of both these texts that are to be found in northern Europe, in the Celtic and Gallican rites, and (with variable introductions only) in the 'Visigothic' Spanish rite; this rite, like the Roman, has the prayer sung by the priest alone to a simple chant, the congregation responding to each petition with 'Amen', except at 'daily bread', where they chant 'quia tu es Deus noster' – 'for you are our God'. One significant difference with the East is the recurring view that it forms a part of the eucharistic prayer, rather than looking forward to communion.[51] But as in the East, all this may point to a two-stage introduction into the eucharist; first with the prayer itself, with some kind of introduction, and then with the embolism, which in the West must be post-Augustine, because of its view of evil, and the absence of any reference to it in his writings. Above all, however, the Lord's Prayer reflects its function, as a mark of baptism, as a daily devotion, and as holding an essential place at the eucharist.

# 5

# The Later East

When we begin to take up the story from where we left off, it becomes clear that the East never ceased to be 'patristic' in the way that the West moved towards a more fragmented, differentiated theological and liturgical life, of which the Reformation was but one symptom. However, there are some noticeable shifts both in the kind of material and in interpretation. In the Greek and the Syriac, Armenian and Arabic sources, there are liturgical commentaries, which have replaced baptismal catechesis: people attend the liturgy and they need it explained in its entirety. There are still works of exposition of the Gospels, in which the Lord's Prayer takes its rightful place; these are in many ways similar to what we have seen, and influenced by John Chrysostom and Gregory of Nyssa, as the authors themselves point out. And then there are works of a more obviously devotional kind. As we move on in history, so there is a discernible trend to recognize the many different ways of interpreting the prayer, although the marks that distinguish East from West persist, particularly at the end of the prayer, where temptation and deliverance tend to be treated as one petition, evil as personal, and the doxology included at the conclusion. The liturgical commentaries are important, and we shall take the opportunity of showing how they fit into different eucharistic rites, since the authors (fortuitously) represent four of the main traditions of the Christian East, Byzantine, Syrian, Armenian, and Coptic.

## Byzantine

### *Germanus of Constantinople (c.640–c.733) and Nicholas of Andyda (1055–1063)*

Germanus was a priest at Hagia Sophia who, after a time as Metropolitan of Cyzicus, became Patriarch of Constantinople in 715. His tenure was by no means easy because – after 725 – he found himself in the position of having to resist the iconoclastic policy of Emperor Leo III. He had to resign five years later, spending the rest of his life at Platonium. He wrote several works, and his authorship of a liturgical commentary, the *Historia mystica ecclesiae catholicae*, 'The Mystical History of the Catholic Church', is generally accepted. In it, Germanus provides the text for the introduction to the prayer, stressing our confidence to address God as Father, which is the same as that found in the earliest manuscripts of the Byzantine liturgy, the eighth-century Barberini 336 manuscript.[1]

God is Father because he is creator, we are his children, and we have the responsibility to live lives worthy of his goodness. Hallowing the name is about living up to our name as Christians, followers of Christ: as Christ is blasphemed by me, so he is also glorified by me – a recognition of humanity's varying capabilities. The kingdom is the Second Coming. Doing the will means acting with the same readiness as the angels. The petition for bread feeds both the natures of humankind, the soul as well as the body, including through the eucharist. Sin after baptism is a reality; forgiveness therefore is about being ready to forget, and not keeping hold of the memory of hurts – by God of us as well as by us of other people. Temptation is about human weakness, by which we do not want to be overwhelmed. And we pray to be delivered not from evil men, but from 'the evil one', the personal force that contrasts with Augustine's impersonal interpretation. He ends by quoting in full Maximus' short passage in his *Mystagogy* on the prayer as the symbol of adoption.

Germanus' work was highly influential, and as 'Historia', its title is significant, indicating a shift away from allegorical interpretation of the liturgy, which is now moving towards contemplation of the events of salvation history, thereby drawing the worshipper into a fuller participation. His treatment of the Lord's Prayer, however, has a simple autonomy, making it stand out from the rest of the liturgy. It would be hard indeed to count the number of people who have benefited from its teaching. There is an element of challenge throughout, that these are not just words – the bread of the soul speaking to us now as we pray. In the liturgy itself, the prayer comes straight after the eucharistic prayer, with its introduction, which Germanus himself quotes. The earliest texts of the Liturgies of Basil and John Chrysostom date from the eighth century (MS Barberini 336); here the prayer appears in its opening words only, but the doxology is chanted by the priest alone.[2] For Western Christians, the doxology is unusual in liturgical prayer, but in the East, doxology is the normal way of concluding many prayers, and the Barberini 336 manuscript is no exception. In addition to the Lord's Prayer in the two liturgies, the doxology is also found (again by the priest after the rest of the prayer by the congregation) near the start of Vespers, as well as just before communion in the (Lenten) Liturgy of the Presanctified; there are many other doxologies of other kinds at the conclusion of other prayers. But why by the priest alone? Probably because that was standard practice with the doxology in the case of other prayers. Germanus' commentary dominated the Byzantine world for six hundred years, to the extent that it was embroidered; a twelfth-century version, for example, adds material on baptism and eucharist, the kingdom and the Spirit (cf. Gregory of Nyssa and Maximus the Confessor), as well as the doxology, keeping up to date with a changing liturgical climate.[3] Another but much briefer liturgical treatment is to be found in Nicholas Bishop of Andyda's *Protheōria*, dating from 1055–1063. In other respects it is a much more elaborate commentary, except for the Lord's Prayer, where he makes only general points, and the bread is what we need for the body.[4]

## Peter of Laodicea (seventh–eighth century)

Peter was a scholar of some note who wrote commentaries on the Gospels which, along with many others, have been lost. The only work that we can safely attribute to him is an exposition of the Lord's Prayer.[5] More elaborate than the brief catechetical discussion by Germanus, he is keen to bring the Trinity into the prayer, and to draw in different interpretations, once punctuated by *allōs*, 'in another way'. He does not disappoint us. We call God Father because through the coming of the Spirit we are adopted by Christ – a line of thought that goes back to the fourth-century writers such as John Chrysostom and Gregory of Nyssa, but which has not so far been expressed so explicitly. The hallowing of the name is not in the imperative, but the optative, he notes, but not drawing out its full nuances; we are called to show that holiness in our lives. The kingdom comes through the Spirit, another echo of Gregory of Nyssa and Maximus the Confessor. The doing of the will can be understood either as acting 'unblameably' like the angels, or in spiritual purity, or that the Church may have a peaceful existence on earth. He discusses the two possible derivations of *epiousios*, allowing either, but not as material, or earthly: it is the bread that will come, and it is the bread that we need, which leads him towards a spiritual interpretation, of Christ as that living bread. Forgiveness must mean forgetting wrongs (*amnēsikakein*), which applies both to God for us and to us for others. As in previous Eastern writers that we have noted earlier, including John Chrysostom, and Cyril of Alexandria, temptation and deliverance are treated together, because temptation is about succumbing to the devil. There is no mention of the doxology. In this treatment, we find a mixture of textual scholarship, patristic learning and practical application.

## Theophylactus the Bulgarian (c.1050/60–after 1125) and Euthymius Zigabenus (twelfth century)

We now come to two biblical exegetes. Theophylactus was born in Euboea, in Greece, and was taught by Michael Psellos, one of the great figures in the eleventh-century Byzantine world, who pioneered the revival of classical learning and a renewed interest in Platonism. Theophylactus was made Archbishop of Ohrid, in Bulgaria (hence his nickname 'the Bulgarian'), an environment he found uncongenial for his studies which included commentaries on every book in the New Testament (except Revelation, not used in the Byzantine liturgy because it was regarded as suspect). He was much influenced by fourth-century writers, particularly John Chrysostom.

He discusses the Lord's Prayer in his commentaries on Matthew and Luke.[6] At the start of the former, he follows Origen by distinguishing between a vow (*euchē*) and a prayer (*proseuchē*), which is the essence of the Lord's Prayer, said by us, who are his children. Hallowing the name is about us being holy; the kingdom is about judgement; the bread is both material and the body of Christ, which we ask to share in the eucharist without condemnation. Forgiveness is about living the baptismal life, and being an example of God himself (he does not reach Gregory of Nyssa's heights in suggesting that God imitates us as forgiving people). The temptation petition, as John Moschus, is about not being absorbed and taken over by it; he ends with the doxology. The commentary on Luke, as with Cyril of Alexandria, uses the same version as Matthew, which he quotes in full (i.e. not clause by clause).[7] He repeats some of the same themes, including kingdom and judgement, but is more explicit on daily bread; we are asking for what is necessary, not what is superfluous, for if we have more than enough, that can lead us into temptation. These, moreover, come in two kinds, voluntary (what we deliberately do) and involuntary (what circumstances provide); voluntary refers to temptation, whereas involuntary refers to the evil one, from which we rightly pray to be delivered. All in all, his Lucan treatment, though directed at the Matthean text, is more unitive in style.

Euthymius Zigabenus was a scholar who wrote against heresies at the command of Emperor Alexis Commenus, with a great deal of patristic knowledge, including John Chrysostom; he sought the literal sense of Scripture rather than its allegorical or mystical meanings, which made him an unusual figure at the time. His commentary on Matthew's Gospel is longer than that of Theophylactus.[8] The heavenly fatherhood is, once again, the sign of our adoption, and we are called to ascend the ladder of virtues to heaven: this is the first time we have encountered this particular image in the East in relation to the Lord's Prayer, and we shall see it in the West, in the same century, with Honorius of Autun. But unlike John Chrysostom, Euthymius is clear that the prayer can be addressed to each person of the Trinity, and not just to the Father. Hallowing the name means glorifying it in good works (Matthew 5:16 again). The kingdom is about being ready for judgement. At both the kingdom and the will he notes an imperative mood in the Greek, even though they are optative (cf. Peter of Laodicea). The bread he interprets in both senses, again like Peter of Laodicea; he gives the 'bread of substance' first place; we ask for what we need. Forgiveness starts at baptism, which leads him to see this prayer's function as a renewal of baptism (cf. Augustine). Over temptation, he nearly reaches the North African 'suffer us not to be led' when he suggests it means 'do not allow us to be led'. He is aware that testing can bring out virtues in how we live; also we need divine help in the fight against the devil. No mention is made of the doxology, but he goes straight on to offer another interpretation, which he describes as anagogical, in which he draws in the Trinity more explicitly; we call God Father as the son of the Father; the kingdom is the Holy Spirit (cf. Gregory of Nyssa and Maximus the Confessor); the will of God is the exercise of heavenly virtues; the bread is both for the soul and for the body; temptation is voluntary as evil is involuntary (following Theophylactus); and the doxology (mentioned now) completes the prayer on a note of praise.

Theophylactus and Euthymius represent the late flowering of the earlier school of patristic exegesis but on new terrain. The more explicit drawing in of the Trinity, the open recognition of different layers of meaning (e.g. the bread-petition), and the exercise of virtues, are three significant examples.

## Nicholas Cabasilas (c.1350) and Symeon of Thessalonica (†1429)

The last two principal Greek commentators of the later East are Nicholas Cabasilas and Symeon of Thessalonica, both of whom write from a specifically liturgical context. Cabasilas, a layman, wrote an influential commentary, but he passes over the Lord's Prayer in a matter of words, stressing only its importance as the prayer Jesus has given to us, as adopted children.[9] The same can be said of Symeon; the prayer is offered by those who have been made adopted children by being cleansed from original sin (mentioned here, unusually in the East), and are brought together in union with the Father and the Holy Spirit. For Symeon, this is a prayer of redemption, and it is profoundly Trinitarian.[10]

## Syriac, Armenian and Arabic

When we look at Christian writers outside the Byzantine world, we come across a different culture. In terms of genre, there is a similar mixture, which includes works of a directly devotional kind (Martyrius' *On Perfection* and Yuhanna ibn Saba's *Precious Pearl*); commentaries on Matthew's Gospel (by Isho'dad of Merv and Dionysius bar Salibi); and liturgical commentaries (by Moses bar Kepha, George of the Arabs and Khosrov). And as far as church allegiance is concerned, we have a spread between East Syrian (Martyrius and Isho'dad), Syrian Orthodox (Moses bar Kepha, George of the Arabs, and Dionysius bar Salibi), Khosrov the Great (Armenian) and Coptic (Yuhanna ibn Saba). All wrote in Syriac, with the exception of Khosrov (Armenian) and Yuhanna ibn Saba (Arabic).

## Martyrius and Isho'dad

Martyrius (or Sahdona, as he is known in Syriac) was a spiritual writer in the seventh century, from the Persian Empire. He was educated at Nisibis, and became Bishop of Mehoze c.635–640, from which position he was expelled for apparently false teaching on the Person of Christ. He fled to Edessa, where he probably wrote *On Perfection*, which is regarded as a work of considerable depth.[11] The Lord's Prayer is set in the spiritual search for the heavenly city, by pilgrims on earth. The Fatherhood of God is the only fatherhood we need, for there is nothing like it on earth (cf. Gregory of Nyssa), where we possess neither a fatherland nor a family; this is our inheritance. The kingdom we are led to by the Holy Spirit (cf. Gregory of Nyssa again); the doing of the will is an angelic ministry, akin to hallowing the name, but by exiles on earth. Following the Syriac tradition which we saw in Theodore, daily bread is 'the bread of necessity', which he interprets broadly in terms of human need, but the direction is spiritual – place us in rich pastures (Psalm 23:2); forgiveness is a gift from the nourishing God; temptation can be circumvented by the grace of God, who can provide a table for us against the enemy (the devil) (Psalm 23:5); and he ends with the doxology, which in the East Syrian liturgy follows straight on from the rest of the prayer, and, unlike the Byzantine rite, is supposed to be recited by all. It is also (uniquely) repeated after communion, and has an established place in the daily offices, as we have already seen. For Martyrius, the Lord's Prayer is about following Christ in his perfection; we must not be encumbered by earthly distractions in our search for grace, mercy, forgiveness – and, above all, spiritual nourishment.

Isho'dad of Merv (ninth century), in Central Asia, was Bishop of Hedatta, also of the East Syrian Church, who wrote commentaries on books of the Old and New Testaments, in which he relies on earlier writers such as Theodore of Mopsuestia. He writes in a compressed style, aware of the many levels of meaning to which his text can direct us. He deals with the Lord's Prayer in his commentary on Matthew.[12] Prayer is about both words and deeds, but it is also about the mind, the spiritual, which is the context for the Lord's Prayer. God is our Father because we are brothers and sisters together, but he is heavenly, to distinguish him from our earthly fathers, to show what glory he is given, and to show us our inheritance. Hallowing the name is not about us adding something to it, but living lives that others can see

(Matthew 6:16). The kingdom is for the future, and yet it is near, and it is granted through repentance; and it is also given through the Holy Spirit, in baptism. Doing the will 'in heaven' is where there is no opposition to rational beings, which is why we pray that God's will may be perfected in us. 'The bread that we need' is about the body only (cf. Gregory of Nyssa). Of forgiveness he writes: 'He binds pardon wisely with pardon.' Temptation is about worldly distractions, from which we pray to be liberated. He passes over deliverance from evil, although he refers to 'Satanic temptations'. He divides the prayer rather like Augustine, into ten sentences, the first five of which are about the soul, the second five about the body. He does not include the doxology.

### George of the Arabs and Moses bar Kepha

George and Moses were two Syrian Orthodox bishops who wrote liturgical commentaries; this provides a different kind of context. As we saw in Chapter 3, the Liturgy of St James places the Lord's Prayer after the breaking of the bread, not before it; as in the other Eastern churches, it has an introductory prayer, asking for worthiness to call God Father, and an embolism immediately follows, but with a doxology (said by the priest) only in the Greek version. George was born near Antioch and in 686 was made bishop for the Arab nomads in Mesopotamia, based at Akula; he wrote many works, which included translations of Aristotle. His *Exposition of the Mysteries of the Church* is a short work on baptism, the eucharist and the consecration of the chrism. He stresses the importance of the candidate learning the Lord's Prayer, which 'makes known that they are now become sons of God'; the Lord's Prayer comes before communion, and he writes briefly about it, in baptismal terms, as 'a prayer of confidence, which shows us to be sons of God by grace; and there is in it a confession of the Creator, and love of things good, and rejection of things evil, and hope, and forgiveness of sins, and a request for what is needful'.[13]

Moses bar Kepha was born *c.*815, in Balad, and was made Bishop of Mosul and the vicinity (Iraq) *c.*863, where he stayed for around forty years; he wrote commentaries on most of the books of the Bible. His liturgical commentary is more extensive than that of George of the Arabs, and in style has something of the compressed yet comprehensive approach of Isho'dad.[14] After dealing with the fraction, he leads into the Lord's Prayer by alluding to its introductory prayer in terms of baptismal sonship. His opening comments are a virtual repeat of what we read in the commentary of George of the Arabs.[15] There are no fewer than six reasons for addressing the heavenly Father, though they are an amalgam of much of what we have already encountered: a father different from ours, Christ's teaching, heaven above and earth beneath; but he goes on in yet more detail, alluding to baptism, including the sponsor, and the image of the womb, strong in the Syrian tradition.[16] Through the prayer, Jesus teaches us 'to display in ourselves the likeness of God'. This is proportionately the most extensive treatment of the theme, and it demonstrates an abiding sensitivity towards the baptismal aspect of the prayer.

Hallowing the name, again, is about holy and exemplary living (Matthew 6:16), as well as the mission of the Church in converting those who do not hallow it. The kingdom brings us into conflict with our own lives, as we await its final revelation (Matthew 25:34); and doing the will tells us of our 'two abodes', heaven and earth, where he echoes the Jerusalem *Mystagogic Catecheses*. Praying for 'the bread we need' places us where we can look at this world and judge what it is, in material terms, that is really necessary for us.[17] Moses combines Matthew and Luke by referring to 'debts and sins'. Forgiveness means remembering our own, but not other peoples' sins (he says), and provides a further opportunity for repentance, even after baptism, in spite of what some may say to the contrary. We can triumph over temptation, but it can also be what the devil draws us towards, 'a sin which cannot be blotted out'. Deliverance from the devil is about a personal struggle with the evil one. The doxology points us to the kingdom. Immediately afterwards, he alludes to the embolism, 'bring us not to that temptation which we are not able to bear', even though it would have come straight after the petition for deliverance. This may reflect how embedded the doxology was in popular usage, as well as the importance of the liturgy.

## Khosrov Andzevatsi

Khosrov was probably born around the turn of the tenth century and died in *c.*960. He was well versed in theology, and knew Greek. He was made Bishop of Andzevatsik'. It appears to have been a not uncontroversial episcopate, because of his pro-Byzantine views, which included a positive attitude to the Council of Chalcedon (451). His liturgical work was influential in the Armenian Church. His exposition of the Armenian Liturgy,[18] where the Lord's Prayer follows the eucharistic prayer, deals with each petition briefly. We address God as Father not just as the baptized but also through the body and blood of Christ; when the kingdom comes, Satan will be crushed; doing the will on earth as in heaven means always wanting to do the will of God and becoming like angels; the bread is for 'essential needs of the body'; forgiveness is mutual; temptation is either sins or dangers, and evil the assaults of Satan. A doxology of a more extended kind, which mentions 'kingdom, power and glory', follows the embolism.

## Dionysius bar Salibi

Dionysius bar Salibi was Bishop of Amid, and died in 1171. Among his many learned writings is his commentary on Matthew's Gospel.[19] Like Moses bar Kepha, he sets out to be as comprehensive as possible, and begins with a discussion of the prayer in terms of Christ's baptism, and ourselves made up of one body. Hallowing the name is about purity of living. The kingdom is the reign of God in our souls, and therefore is the gospel, the contemplation of the Trinity. The bread is sufficient material provision, and no more. He distinguishes between voluntary (what we take on) and involuntary (circumstantial) temptation, and sees deliverance from the evil one as an extension of temptation; he includes the doxology in the text of the prayer.

## Yuhanna ibn Saba

Nothing is known about Yuhanna ibn Saba except that he wrote *The Precious Pearl* in Egypt in Arabic in the fourteenth century. It is a lengthy work about the Christian life, the thirty-third chapter of which is devoted to the Lord's Prayer, following a chapter on the Creed.[20] In style expansive, it draws the reader into Christ's own life of prayer, a tone which Yuhanna sets right at the start when he quotes the prayer in full, adding 'through Jesus Christ our Lord', before the concluding doxology. Like Moses bar Kepha, he gives careful attention to the prayer's opening: the 'spiritual and metaphysical' sense that the Father has sent the son into the world, and its 'material and sensible' meaning that we are saved from the consequences of Adam's parentage. For Yuhanna, the prayer is about our sanctification, the work of the Holy Spirit in us. Hallowing the name is a consequence of the Spirit of Truth (John 15:26); the coming of the kingdom is the conflict of the soul with Satan, in which we can triumph; doing the will can result from the power of the Spirit in us, as in heaven, the dwelling-place of the Trinity.

We ask for bread but it is not material, for it is 'substantial' bread, the living bread (John 6:51), and it is also the bread of the eucharist; and here John refers directly to the Last Supper (Matthew 26:28; 1 Corinthians 11:24). Forgiveness he applies to the human condition, listing three ages, childhood innocence, the rough and tumble of youth and early adulthood, followed by maturity. He indicates that maturity is a time when we can be more aware of ourselves, other people, and the world in general than before, and conscious of the divine light that can guide us. Temptation is what Jesus experienced; we can triumph over it, just as he was able to triumph over the devil himself. (He treats temptation and evil as essentially the same petition.) All prayer should be made through Christ, which is why he adds these words before the doxology. Yuhanna even regards them as spoken by Jesus himself to the Father, an indication that this is *his* prayer and not the prayer of a teacher or Father of the Church, which would have required the conclusion, 'Through

Jesus Christ our Lord.' Yuhanna ends this unusual treatment of the prayer by referring to two contrasting scenes: Jesus at prayer in Gethsemane (Matthew 26:18) and the risen Jesus who has triumphed over death being the same Jesus who sent out his disciples with neither purse, bag or sandals, and yet they lacked nothing (Luke 22:35–36).

Yuhanna spreads the prayer over Scripture and human experience in a way that we have not seen since Augustine. It is not a liturgical treatment and he gives us no clues as to liturgical setting, although one may note that, as with the introductory prayer (uniquely in the East variable), the Coptic rite places the prayer after the fraction, and follows it with an embolism; and, in the Greek version, with a doxology. Yuhanna represents the tradition of Egyptian monasticism, in which the prayer holds such a central place, both for liturgical prayer and for personal devotion.

## Conclusion

- The kind of evidence has changed. There has been a move away from the earlier tradition of strictly baptismal catechesis, represented by such figures as John Chrysostom and Theodore of Mopsuestia, to a *catechesis based on the eucharistic liturgy*; and the persistence of biblical commentaries, as well as the development of works of a devotional kind, are also apparent.

- As far as the text is concerned, we note the expansion on forgiveness in Moses bar Kepha, a symptom of the East Syrian liturgical practice that we saw in the teaching of Narsai. The main variant is the doxology, which does not appear in Germanus (a liturgical commentary), or Peter of Laodicea (a biblical commentary), or Isho'dad (a biblical commentary), or George of the Arabs (a liturgical commentary). But it *is* present in every other writer, regardless of genre. Its absence in Isho'dad could be explained by the fact that he does not comment on every verse of Matthew; and in George of the Arabs by his reticence over the full text of the prayer. But what of Germanus and Peter of Laodicea? Peter was a scholar who may well have known the doxology was not original to the text. Germanus, on the other hand, is bound to have been aware of its existence in the praying life of the Church. The existence of the doxology, but recited by the celebrant alone, in MS Barberini 336 (contemporary with Germanus) may give us an explanation: the doxology was recited by the celebrant, not by the congregation. Whether or not it had always been congregational is not known: it was certainly part of the prayer, as witness the preaching of John Chrysostom.

- When it comes to *interpretation*, many of these writers are building upon an already existing tradition, as witness Euthymius citing Chrysostom, and Moses bar Kepha referring to the Jerusalem *Mystagogic Catecheses*. There are, too, different approaches to levels of meaning, with Peter of Laodicea, Isho'dad, Moses bar Kepha and Yuhanna ibn Saba ready to provide them lavishly, as they enjoy themselves with the prayer, the Scriptures, the tradition and their observations about life. On the other hand, there is a more restrictive approach in Theophylactus, Khosrov and Dionysius bar Salibi, who limit themselves to simple explanation. The petition for bread, although univocally 'the bread of necessity' in Greek, Syriac, Armenian and Arabic traditions, nevertheless continues to be interpreted differently, the material perhaps prevailing, thanks to Ephrem and Gregory of Nyssa, but moving beyond the broadly Christ-centred to the eucharist in Yuhanna ibn Saba. Deliverance from evil retains its personal force, in contrast to Augustine in the West.

- But what we see, particularly in the liturgical commentaries, is the persistence of an older, simpler layer of teaching on the Lord's Prayer epitomized by Germanus' use of Maximus' description of the 'symbol of adoption', which does not absorb the elaborate interpretations of the rest of the liturgy. In that respect, for all that the Christian East likewise used the Lord's Prayer as part of the rosary, the medieval West has a rather different story to tell.[21]

# 6

# The Medieval West

## Introduction

What happened to the Lord's Prayer in the medieval West is, on one level, complex and, on another level, relatively simple. It is complex because of the range and amount of material at our disposal. But it is relatively simple because the prayer has a fixed role in the eucharist, before communion; in baptism (along with the Creed), to be taught to growing Christians; and at the daily offices, near the end. It has, too, a powerful place in private devotion, for as early as 800, the lay brother monks of St Gall and Reichenau, in Switzerland, said fifty Paternosters for the deceased. In the *Rule of St Benedict*, the monks who have to work away from the monastery or who are on long journeys are not expected to recite all the offices, but only a minimum, which we may safely assume would include the Lord's Prayer.[1] The medieval period saw the flowering of repetition, whether by lay brothers at work in the fields as a substitute for the choir offices they were unable to attend, or by the faithful, along with the 'Hail Mary', as a penance. The Lord's Prayer then found extra places in public liturgy, but as a private devotion, as witness the late medieval priest's preparation for celebrating mass.[2] It is this non-liturgical repetition that the Reformers resisted so strongly. In terms of the Latin text, there are only two variations, whether to end with 'Amen' at mass, and whether to use Jerome's *super-substantialem* of the bread, as was the custom (uniquely) of Peter Abelard's community at Lauds and Vespers. Vernacular versions become an increasing need as time goes on.

Does the literature reflect these shifts? There is a distinct move away from the liturgical catecheses of the fourth century, signs of which were apparent, for example, in the preaching of Caesarius of Arles, towards the sermon, increasingly seen as an entity on its own rather than an integral part of the liturgy. Augustine's influence (which Bede the Venerable did so much to propagate) continues, among not only those who cite his writings, but those who develop the sevenfold structure of the prayer, such as Amalar of Metz in the ninth century, or Hugh of Amiens in the twelfth: and his impersonal interpretation of evil is a legacy that pervades the medieval West. The influence of the Fathers is palpable, whether from those who quote them directly, like Rabanus Maurus, Ralph of Laon in the *Glossa Ordinaria*, or Bonaventura, or those who simply allude to them, like Bruno of Segni. Augustine's numerological scheme was adapted, so that from the twelfth century onwards, the petition for daily bread is seen as both heavenly and earthly or else as only heavenly.

From the beginning of our story we have noted different ways of *teaching* about the Lord's Prayer, whether in the discourses of Tertullian or Cyprian; the pre-baptismal preaching of Augustine or Peter Chrysologus; or the post-baptismal preaching of Ambrose of Milan or the Jerusalem *Mystagogic Catecheses*. But there have also been *theological* shifts, manifested in two ways. One is the desire to load the prayer with more and more about Christian teaching, Frowin of Engelberg being an example. Another concerns free will; while Augustine's ready grasp of the need to accept different kinds of interpretation influences many of these writers, the twelfth century places an increasing emphasis on the importance of free will in the life of grace, and the role of virtues within it; the theological legacy of Peter Lombard left its mark – in the same century in which public consent emerged at marriage as a necessary prelude to the nuptial mass.[3] There is, however, one lamentable gap – a commentary from Visigothic Spain, where some time after Isidore of Seville, the practice grew up of inserting a congregational 'Amen' after each petition, with the celebrant reciting the prayer. Gregory VII's policy to give the Roman rite pre-eminence during the time of the reconquest of Spain from the Arabs resulted in the demise of this liturgy.[4]

In what follows, we shall approach the material in five over-lapping ways. First, *expositions*, whether based directly on the Gospels (like Rabanus Maurus), or, as time goes on, increasingly focused on the prayer on its own (like Albert the Great). Second, *sermons*, which include those which stand in the tradition of Augustine, like Yvo of Chartres, or the kind of systematic exposition of the search for the Ultimate Good that we see in Thomas Aquinas. Third, *liturgical commentaries*, which at first sight seem recondite, but which turn the mass into an allegory of Christ's life, and draw the Lord's Prayer into much of the teaching (e.g. on virtues and vices) that we see in the expositions. Fourth, *Latin paraphrases*, including one by Francis of Assisi, which expand on the prayer in a devotional style that, in effect, flows from the kind of theological works that are in circulation. Fifth, *vernacular texts*, which are partly taken from sermons, or from translations of the Scriptures, or are versions of the prayer which were not allowed to be used liturgically but which helped people who did not understand Latin to grasp its meaning. Here, the focus moves from the big names of European theology to England, where, as elsewhere in Europe in later centuries, vernacular texts became the seed-bed of theological and liturgical reconstruction at the Reformation, which pushed the Lord's Prayer into a central position, as a guide to prayer, and (in the case of Luther and Calvin) tried to develop the paraphrase so that it had a place in the liturgy itself.

## Expositions

Three biblical commentators of the Carolingian period are Rabanus Maurus (*c.*780–853), Paschasius Radbertus (*c.*790–*c.*860) and Christian of Stavelot (†*c.*880). Rabanus Maurus is probably the biggest name of this group; a child-monk at the abbey of Fulda, he went to Tours *c.*800, to study under Alcuin, returning to Fulda in 818, as master of the choir school and from 824–842 as abbot; he was Archbishop of Mainz from 847 until his death. He wrote commentaries on nearly every book of the Bible. There is a full treatment of the Lord's Prayer in his commentary on Matthew, in which there are several direct quotations from Cyprian and Augustine.[5] He stresses the teaching of Jesus; divine sonship is the gift of grace (Galatians 4:6; Romans 8:14); hallowing the name is about our daily sanctification; the kingdom is about its rule in our hearts (he refers to Augustine); doing the will means doing it in the Church (as we shall see in Remigius); daily bread is about material needs as well as spiritual; he observes, as Augustine did, that a daily eucharist is not practised in the East; and he also notes the reading *supersubstantialem* (from Jerome's Vulgate), which he takes to mean what we spiritually (not physically) need; forgiveness provides an opportunity for a one-liner, 'if we lie over this bargain, the fruit of the whole prayer comes to nothing'; temptation he interprets (like Augustine) that God might not 'suffer us to be led', for we do not pray not to be tempted, but not to be overcome by it; deliverance is about protection, the last thing we ask for in this life; which leads Rabanus to summarize the prayer in terms of three heavenly and four earthly petitions, and he finally applies the seven gifts of the Spirit to the beatitudes in the same way as Augustine. Around the same time, Walafrid Strabo ('Walafrid the Squinter'), who was born near Reichenau and educated at Fulda under Rabanus Maurus (827–829), wrote his *Libellus de Exordiis et Incrementis Quarundam in Observationibus Ecclesiasticis Rerum* ('Little Book about the Beginnings and Growth of certain Ecclesiastical Matters'), in which he rejects the tendency to interpret 'daily' as *supersubstantialem*, on the grounds that it is used by those who do not believe in daily communion (i.e. Greeks), and he calls in Cyprian and Augustine for support; the Lord's Prayer, according to him, has been used since the very earliest times at the eucharist.[6]

Paschasius Radbertus became a monk at Corbie, Saxony, in 822. He was made abbot in 843/4, a position which he resigned in 849 in order to study; apart from writing controversially on the eucharist, championing a view of the presence considered too spiritual by Rabanus Maurus, he wrote a commentary on Matthew's Gospel.[7] The heavenly Fatherhood of God unites the community together as one body in prayer, through the washing of baptism; hallowing the name is where the Spirit dwells, which prompts Paschasius to refer to the Trinity, for the work of sanctification is a constant rebirth; the kingdom is in the future (the Great Assize, Matthew 25:34 again), which should lead us to pray for its coming, 'with the eye of faith and love'; the doing of the will is our work on earth, but so that heaven will come, not earth remain; the will of God is that of the whole Trinity, and the three first precepts of the Ten Commandments (cf. Venantius Fortunatus) will help us discover and do that will. When it comes to daily bread, Paschasius follows Jerome's Vulgate text, by now increasingly authoritative. Going one step further than Rabanus Maurus, he uses the reading *supersubstantialem*, which he interprets (at some length) as what we need for this life so that we may reach the next (he uses John 6:53ff.); he notes, as did Rabanus (and Augustine before him), that the Eastern churches do not practise a daily eucharist everywhere, but recommends daily communion, even though (as he observes) not everyone is ready or prepared to do so. Forgiveness leads him to discuss different sins, our need for forgiveness, our need to forgive, without any excuse; temptations come in many different forms, including infidelity of heart; and to pray for deliverance from 'every kind of evil' (an allusion to the embolism, 'deliver us, Lord') is the best way to conclude the prayer. Paschasius is the first commentator to follow Jerome's text at *supersubstantialem*; he does not include his 'Amen', unlike Bede (whose context is a biblical commentary). He also reflects the growing emphasis on the Church, the Ten Commandments, and the place of forgiveness.

Christian of Stavelot is a lesser figure who wrote a commentary on Matthew's Gospel *c.*865; it was his most original work, which demonstrated an attachment to the more traditional kind of exegesis that was free from allegorical interpretation.[8] God is our Father through condition, as creator, and through adoption, in our baptism; hallowing is through good works; the kingdom is when the whole world recognizes God as true; the will means humans acting on earth as angels in heaven; although he uses *quotidianum* of the bread, he is aware of *supersubstantialem* and the reasoning for the Greek tradition of interpretation, but he regards it as spiritual, and eucharistic; forgiveness is the needful consequence of our weakness and the assaults of the devil; deliverance concerns both the present age, the future and the eternal. The petitions concern both the present age and the future (he does not differentiate between them like Augustine); but he adds, following Jerome, the 'Amen', which really means (for him) that there are eight petitions. The tenor of these commentaries is not towards originality, but to maintain an older tradition, applying it gradually to new needs, like the Latin over against the Greek Church, the place of the Church as an institution, as well as the challenges of the Christian life.

Rupert of Deutz (*c.*1075–1129/30) was a monk at St Laurent, Liège, who was expelled with his abbot because of the investiture controversy; he was ordained priest in 1106 and made Abbot of Deutz in 1120. Like Yvo of Chartres, whose preaching we shall see later, he represents a mixture of the older 'patristic' and newer 'scholastic' approaches. In his commentary on Matthew's Gospel,[9] he distinguishes between the two versions, pointing out the 'omissions' in Luke, but fixing on seven petitions as the basis of the prayer. There are references to baptism and eucharist; he uses Jerome's Vulgate text at *supersubstantialem*, but he applies it (Augustine-style) to daily material need, spiritual need and the eucharist; and when discussing temptation, distinguishes between 'concupiscence' (greed) and tribulations, and the crown of martyrdom.

Bruno of Segni (*c.*1045/9–1123) was a monk who after a time as Canon of Siena became Bishop of Segni in 1079; a friend of Gregory VII, he retired to Monte Cassino, where he became abbot, but he was encouraged to return to his diocese. Among his writings is a commentary on Matthew's Gospel, which is full of references to Tertullian, Augustine and the *Opus Imperfectum* attributed to John Chrysostom.[10] While the discussion is short, there are some notable features which reflect the times he lived in, especially as he took up a position on the eucharist which opposed Berengar, who like Paschasius Radbertus advocated a more 'spiritual' understanding of the presence of Christ. So when it comes to the petition for the coming of the kingdom, Bruno brings in the Church, a tendency we shall note elsewhere from this time onwards, and the need to fight heretics. But he also does something else unusual; God's rule over the heavens includes the planets – and he names Jove, Mercury, Mars and Saturn; this is taken much further by Gunther the Cistercian. He uses Jerome's text at *supersubstantialem*, but applies it specifically to the eucharist, celebrated every day by the Church, though he allows a wider interpretation as well.

A different approach is to be found in the *Allegories on the New Testament* attributed to Hugh of St Victor (†1142), but now more generally agreed to be the work of his colleague Richard of St Victor (†1173).[11] Richard is supposed to have been born in Scotland, and came to Paris, where he joined the Victorine community, and became prior in 1162. We now move away from the monastic environment of some of the previous writers to the more public context of teaching which is more akin to a university, where influence is more immediate. He wrote a number of works, including on the Trinity, which showed a deep knowledge of patristic literature. In the *Allegories*, his lengthy treatment of the prayer (with the 'Amen') concentrates on different kinds of virtues throughout; the heavenly hierarchies are also given full treatment; there is a stress on the 'elect' (as opposed to those who are not to be saved), that we have not seen before with such strength; he expounds a 'hierarchy of charity', in which the Jews have 'faith', ordinary Christians have 'consummated faith', whereas the Christian whose faith is informed by charity has *dilectio*, love; he discusses different kinds of temptation, leading to different kinds of sin; he also points out that the congregation joins in with 'but deliver us from evil', which was a custom found in the *Rule of St Benedict*, in some places at the eucharist. He draws three virtues into the opening of the prayer: 'Father' brings benevolence, 'our' excludes pride, 'who is in heaven' shows reverence. There are rhetorical asides, such as 'feed, shepherd, you yourself feed your sheep' in his discussion of daily bread. The second exposition applies the prayer to the seven sins, of which there were a few signs in the earlier part of the work. These appear in the order established by Gregory VII: pride, envy, anger, sloth, covetousness, gluttony and lechery. He applies them to hallowing the name, the coming of the kingdom, the doing of the will, daily bread, forgiveness, temptation and deliverance from evil. While the scheme may not convince the astringent biblical exegete, it certainly brings the prayer into the orbit of the human condition, and reflects a growing consciousness of different kinds of sin.

Anselm of Laon (†1117), was one of the leading theological figures of his time, and contributed to the *Glossa Ordinaria*, a collection of extracts from the Fathers on the Scriptures which became a standard commentary for many years to come. He taught at the Cathedral School at Laon, where he was Chancellor, Dean and Archdeacon from 1115 until his death two years later. His lectures on the Bible were known for their traditional approach to exegesis, based on the style of the Fathers, and they had considerable influence after his death.[12] He offers a prayer-like exposition which starts with the end of the prayer, and concludes at the beginning with the vision of God. He divides the prayer in a different way from Augustine, though he takes care not to controvert him, in the deferential style of the time. There are three heavenly and three earthly petitions, but the central petition – for daily bread – is both heavenly and earthly. This is a bold step, considering the influence which Augustine's interpretation so manifestly wielded, but it shows the interest taken by these expositors over the meaning of this particular petition. Anselm starts with deliverance from evil, and with original sin, and following the inversion of Augustine's scheme over the gifts of the Spirit which (we shall see) began with Amalar, he applies this petition to the fear of the Lord; he also inverts Augustine's order over the beatitudes, identifying the poor in spirit with deliverance from evil. With this point of departure, the soul journeys through each petition to the hallowing of the name, and the heavenly Father himself. He notes the reading, *supersubstantialem*, and follows Augustine in seeing daily bread in material, spiritual and sacramental terms. When it comes to doing the will, he asks the rhetorical question, Who can resist the will of God? By turning the prayer round, he makes it clear that his purpose is for reading and meditation; it is not a liturgical exercise. Anselm grasps the nettle concerning the shape of the prayer, gently setting aside Augustine's 'three-and-four' pattern in favour of an approach that does better justice to an increasing focus on daily bread as the eucharist, and at a time when eucharistic presence was being debated, and moving towards transubstantiation.[13] In the treatment of the prayer in the *Glossa Ordinaria*, however, thought to be by his brother Ralph of Laon, there is a series of brief quotations from Augustine and Bede, which illuminate an arrangement of the seven petitions in the Augustine framework (three heavenly and four earthly), together with the gifts of the Spirit; this resembles another biblical work a little later in the century, the *In Unum ex Quattuor* ('Into One from Four'), a harmony of the Gospels, with similar quotations from the same Latin Fathers, by Zacharias of Besançon (†*c*.1155) a Canon of St Martin's Abbey, also in Laon.[14]

Hugh of Amiens (*c*.1085–1164) provides one of the most comprehensive interpretations of the prayer so far.[15] After studying at Laon, probably under Anselm, he became a Benedictine monk at Cluny, then a flourishing monastery, from where he moved in 1112 to Limoges, as prior at St Martial; he then went to England at the request of Henry I, as prior of the abbey of St Pancras, Lewes, and in 1125 he became the first abbot of Reading Abbey. In 1130, he was made Archbishop of Rouen. He wrote two main works devoted entirely to the Lord's Prayer, the *De Ecclesia et Eius Ministris* ('On the Church and its Ministers'), between 1145 and 1148, and the *De Fide Catholica, et Oratione Dominica* ('On the Catholic faith, and the Lord's Prayer') later in his life, between 1155 and 1157. The *De Fide* is a more straightforward work, in which, for example, much is made of the kingdom of God and the Church; and he notes the reading *supersubstantialem*, like other expositors more with the intention of drawing out its rich meaning than of suggesting it as a viable liturgical alternative. It is in the *De Ecclesia* that Hugh excels himself in complexity, drawing together the seven orders, the seven gifts of the Spirit, the seven petitions of the Lord's Prayer, and the seven beatitudes:

| Presbyters | Wisdom | Hallowing of name | Peacemakers |
| Deacons | Understanding | Kingdom | Pure in heart |
| Subdeacons | Counsel | Will | Merciful |
| Acolytes | Fortitude | Daily bread | Hunger for right |
| Exorcists | Knowledge | Forgiveness | Mourn |
| Readers | Piety | Temptation | Meek |
| Doorkeepers | Fear of Lord | Deliverance | Poor in Spirit |

The seven gifts of the Spirit invert the order adopted by Augustine, which we shall see from Amalar onwards; the beatitudes are similarly inverted. His primary task is to root the whole life and ministry of the Church in the words and teaching of Christ; the Lord's Prayer is no longer baptismal: it is ecclesiological. Such an approach is a far cry from Augustine – and also Anselm.

Frowin of Engelberg wrote probably one of the longest ever works on the Lord's Prayer, but its influence was not nearly as great as, for example, Anselm or, in the coming century, Aquinas. The abbey of Engelberg in the mountains of the Obwalden, south of Lucerne, was founded in 1120, and gained prominence with the election of Frowin, then a monk of the abbey of St Blasien in the Black Forest. He built up the library, and secured ecclesiastical independence for the abbey, so that it was directly under the Emperor. His *Explanatio Dominicae Orationis* ('Explanation of the Lord's Prayer') demonstrates the author's extensive learning, with many quotations from writers including Paschasius Radbertus and Anselm of Laon, as well as Augustine and Cyprian.[16] In an earlier work, *De laude liberi arbitrii* ('On the praise of free will'), Frowin had written about the place of free will in the life of the Christian in general, and in prayer in particular. It is therefore no surprise to find that Frowin hangs much of his discussion on free will, which the heavenly Father has given us; hallowing the name and doing the will result from that gracious freedom, in the same way that we ask to be delivered from evil, and are enabled to say 'Amen' at the prayer's end. As befits a discourse of this kind, the length given to each of the seven petitions is uneven. The longest is his treatment of daily bread, which is spiritual in scope, but refers primarily to the eucharist, in which connection he quotes from the Roman eucharistic prayer. He links his discussion of forgiveness to the growing practice of private confession. His starting-point is the fact that we are made in the image of God but live under his judgement, and we are left with the choice to seek either what is good or what is evil. For Frowin, the will is central to the human condition, and to the life of faith. It therefore needs guidance, correction, constant attention – and forgiveness. And true to the twelfth-century trajectory which we saw beginning with Anselm of Laon, and which we shall see in Honorius of Autun, he sees the prayer divided between four heavenly, and three earthly, a consequence of a sacramentally focused understanding of daily bread.

Gunther the Cistercian (†c.1220) was a Rhenish scholar who became a monk of the abbey at Pariis, in the Diocese of Basel, and therefore like Frowin writes from a monastic (and not a Cathedral) base. His *De Oratione, Jejunio et Eleemosyna* ('On Prayer, Fasting and Almsgiving') opens with a lengthy exposition of the Lord's Prayer.[17] The seven petitions are to be matched with the seven gifts of the Spirit, the seven virtues and the seven beatitudes, although he does not specify exactly how this is to be worked out. There is a mass of detail, with no fewer than six different overlapping ways of understanding God as Father; like Bruno of Segni, he elaborates on the planets when it comes to heavenly bodies; hallowing the name starts for the Christian with baptism; the kingdom means the reign of God in the Church; an effective will is the cause of everything that is good; daily bread is both material and spiritual, including the eucharist; forgiveness meets many different forms of sin (nature, justice, piety, honesty, need, grace, blame); temptation is what happens when we are ignorant, and resist the grace of God; and evil comes in many kinds. Just when we think he has had enough, Gunther turns the prayer the other way round, like Anselm of Laon, and for the same reason; we can start with our awareness of evil, and travel through temptation, forgiveness and daily bread, and move through doing the will and praying for the coming of the kingdom, until we reach the hallowing of the name. He makes no use in this section of any of the sevenfold schemes.

Bonaventura (*c.*1217–1274) studied in Paris, where he entered the Franciscan Order, being elected Minister General in 1257, and wrote a biography of St Francis. In 1273, he was made Bishop of Albano in his native Italy. Among his many works, which had considerable authority, given the position he held in a preaching order, are his Expositions of the Gospels.[18] Full of quotations from Augustine, Jerome, Bede and the *Opus Imperfectum* attributed to John Chrysostom, they abound in discussion of the virtues; and Bonaventura uses Jerome's Vulgate text reading of *supersubstantialem* of bread, as well as including the 'Amen'. The seven virtues of the beatitudes match the seven deadly sins: poverty of spirit against pride; meekness against anger; mourning against envy; hunger for righteousness against sloth; mercy against covetousness; purity of heart against gluttony; and peacemaking against lust. Bonaventura applies the gifts of the Spirit in the opposite order to Augustine, as we shall see beginning with Amalar; he preaches fervently about them, in order to answer extreme Aristotelians, who (some at the time, he thought) relied insufficiently on divine grace in the pursuit of virtuous living. His discussion of each petition is comprehensive (the kingdom includes the Church Militant). His treatment of Luke's narrative includes discussion of the variations from Matthew, but there are no substantial differences in meaning. In another work for the specific use of lay brothers, Bonaventura divides the prayer into three heavenly and four earthly petitions (retaining Augustine's division), and recommends that it be said twenty-four times a day, corresponding to the hours, and the twelve patriarchs and apostles. Franciscan practice commonly allowed the prayer as a substitute for the reciting of the Office.

Albert the Great (†1280) was born near Ulm, and became a Dominican at Cologne *c.*1229, where he was soon brought into the teaching ministry of the Order both at Hildesheim, Ratisbon (where he was a reluctant bishop for two years from 1260–1262), and Strasbourg; among his pupils was Thomas Aquinas. He can, therefore, claim to have had very considerable influence.

He produced commentaries on the Gospels, which are more detailed than those of Bonaventura.[19] The prayer's shape is about four requests for good things, followed by three that are about averting evil things; this is a clear break from the long tradition of Augustine, even as adjusted in the previous century, and it reflects a more Aristotelian approach. His attention to different categories of good things is exemplified in his handling of hallowing the name, which is achieved by the destruction of sin, destruction of earthly love, the confirmation of good, and God dwelling in us; the kingdom is about God's power; the will means his determination to carry it out; daily bread is material, spiritual and eucharistic; his discussion of temptation provokes him into listing the virtues that will combat against the vices; and he uses *supersubstantialem* and has the concluding 'Amen'.

Meister Eckhart (*c.*1260–*c.*1328) was born in Hochheim, Thuringia, and became a Dominican at Erfurt, after which he studied in Paris and then back at Erfurt. He was famous as a vernacular preacher, where he showed his ability to bring out different shades of meaning in Scripture, a tendency which helped to bring his works into disrepute. His Treatise on the Lord's Prayer[20] is full of quotations from the Fathers, including the *Opus Imperfectum* attributed to John Chrysostom, as well as more recent writers, Aquinas included. Unlike previous authors, Eckhart insists that nothing temporal is to be asked for – the Lord's Prayer is exclusively about the *eternal*. Following the *Opus Imperfectum*, he maintains that 'on earth as in heaven' refers to all three opening petitions, the name and the kingdom as well as the will – a position we have not so far seen in the West, and therefore worth noting. Over daily bread he notes that not everyone receives at mass, but they can still participate by being present – a concession to late medieval eucharistic piety. He notes Jerome's Vulgate reading, *supersubstantialem*. Elaborate in style, Eckhart takes the reader through a great deal of detail, but keeps steering towards his goal, which is the goodness of God, and the distractions of this life; in that sense, he builds on the teaching of his predecessors.

## Sermons

Haimo of Auxerre was a monk at St Germain-des-Prés, Paris, where he taught in the school, from 845 until his death in 896. In a sermon on the Lord's Prayer,[21] he carefully differentiates between the Lucan and Matthean settings, and follows Augustine in directing the first three petitions towards the future life, and the other four towards the present. For example, the petition for bread is about this age, and is addressed to God not as creator but as giver of grace, an important piece of exegesis which rescues a potentially superficial following of Augustine over the shape of the prayer into making the second part of the prayer too earthly in its focus. Like Augustine, he is comprehensive about what the petitions mean, from what we need in material terms, through spiritual nourishment, to the eucharist itself. Reflecting Carolingian concerns over making the 'Tariff' penance of the Irish missionaries too easy, Haimo lists seven ways of forgiveness: baptism, penitence, mercy, forgiveness of others, laying hold of true charity, receiving the body and blood of Christ, and by the blood of martyrdom.

Yvo of Chartres (*c*.1040–1115) also provides a classic Augustine-inspired homily.[22] Educated at Paris, and later at Bec under Lanfranc, he was Prior of the Canons Regular in St Quentin, Beauvais, in 1079, and made Bishop of Chartres in 1090. The sermon begins by contrasting 'the dignity of our condition and the excellence of our restoration', and goes on to make his hearers aware of their need of that restoration, because of our fall into sin. He then goes through Jesus' teaching on prayer in the lead-up to the Lord's Prayer itself (Matthew 6:5–8); there are seven petitions, divided into three heavenly and four earthly (Augustine again), which he expands into the life of the Church; we call God Father as a sign of our redemption, and pray standing, facing east, looking to the rising sun, from where the kingdom will come. He applies the seven petitions to the seven gifts of the Spirit in the way of Amalar rather than Augustine: the fear of the Lord with hallowing the name, the kingdom with piety, doing the will with knowledge, daily bread

with fortitude, forgiveness with counsel, temptation with understanding, and deliverance with wisdom. And he concludes the
sermon by providing three remedies against sin (almsgiving,
fasting and prayer), applying them as medicines against illness
to the human condition. Yvo thus stands between the earlier
patristic tradition represented by Augustine and the newer
approach to preaching, which was less exegetical and more
systematic. In an earlier sermon, he describes the purpose of the
prayer at mass as completing the consecration and purifying the
communicants. This teaching reflects the view we have already
seen in the West, of the Lord's Prayer as an integral part of the
mass.

Maurice of Sully was made Bishop of Paris in 1160, successor
to Peter Lombard. A sermon he preached on the prayer represents a distillation of much of the teaching that he encountered in
Paris from his student days, which began in 1140: Robson has
shown the influence of Richard of St Victor on Maurice.[23] He
begins with a recitation of the Latin text, with a contemporary
French translation, a text that includes 'Amen'. He appeals to the
fragility of his hearers, and the need for them to understand the
prayer; he alludes to Richard's 'hierarchy of charity'; like other
writers at this time he stresses the role of the Church in the kingdom of God; the hierarchy of heaven has pride of place in the
doing of the will; daily bread is the Word of God, and therefore
not material in any sense; at temptation, he supplies the North
African paraphrase referred to by Augustine, 'suffer us not to be
led'; and the prayer ends with 'Amen', leading straight into the
embolism, 'deliver us, Lord', thus showing the liturgical context
of the sermon.

Alan of Lille, a major twelfth-century figure (†1203), studied
in Paris and became involved in fighting the Catharist heresy in
the South of France, ending his days at Cîteaux. His major work
was the *Ars Praedicandi* ('The Art of Preaching'), which was one
of the first works of its kind, and which was highly influential. It
contains twenty-seven model sermons, but the substance is the
main part, which deals with virtues; one of these, patience, provides him with the opportunity of suggesting what should be said

about the Lord's Prayer.[24] Working backwards, as did Anselm of Laon, he applies the beatitudes in yet another way; deliverance from evil is linked with the poor in spirit, temptation with the meek, forgiveness with the merciful, daily bread with hungering after righteousness, the coming of the kingdom with those who mourn, the doing of the will with the pure in heart, and the hallowing of the name with peacemakers. (Only three of these, the kingdom, daily bread and forgiveness, reproduce Augustine's pattern.) There is a simplicity of approach which would have appealed to many a preacher; the material probably reflected Alan's own experience.

Jocelyn of Soissons († before 1152),[25] although influenced by Augustine, follows Anselm of Laon's pioneering division of the prayer into three heavenly, three earthly, and daily bread as both; also, like Anselm, he asks whether anyone can resist the will of God. He provides a comprehensive interpretation of each petition, drawing baptism into the hallowing of the name; at daily bread, he notes the reading *supersubstantialem*, and brings in the eucharistic community by referring to the sharing of the kiss of peace; when dealing with forgiveness, he enumerates different kinds of sin and also praises the practice of offering the mass for the departed. He ends with 'Amen', which he describes as the *sigullum confirmationis* ('the sign of confirmation') of the prayer, adapting Jerome's word here. And he takes the opportunity, in conclusion, of alluding to the briefer version of the prayer in Luke's Gospel, and the tradition of associating the seven petitions with the seven gifts of the Spirit and the seven beatitudes, without specifying which scheme he would follow.

Thomas Aquinas (*c.*1225–1274) was born in Roccasecca, near Aquino, not far from Naples, and at an early age was given to the Benedictine monks at Monte Cassino, who sent him to study in Paris where he joined the Dominican Order; he went to Cologne in 1248, where he met Albert the Great, and after a teaching career which saw him in Paris, Rome and back in Paris, he finally went to Naples in 1272, where he died two years later. In the spring of 1273, he preached a course of sermons on the Lord's Prayer which have come down to us in note form. Full of the teaching which permeates his *Summa Theologiae*, they relate to the shape of the prayer, and the way it leads human beings towards finding what is good.[26] The sermons end with a summary of his overall message:

> *Our Father*. Let it be understood that everything which should be desired is contained in the Lord's Prayer, and everything which should be avoided. Amongst everything which is desirable is that which should be most desired and loved, and this is God: therefore you seek first the glory of God when you say *Hallowed be your name*. Three things, however, are desired by God in your respect. Firstly, that you should attain everlasting life, and you ask for this when you say: *Your kingdom come*. Secondly, that you should do the will of God and act justly, and you ask this when you say: *Your will be done on earth as in heaven*. Thirdly, that you should have those things necessary for everyday life, and you ask this when you say: *Give us today our daily bread*. The Lord talks about these three things in Matthew 6:33, with respect to the first when he says, *strive first for the kingdom of God*, to the second, *and his righteousness*, and to the third, *and all these other things will be given to you*. Those things which are to be avoided, and from which you should be free, are contrary to the good. Moreover, good, which is first to be desired, is fourfold. First is the glory of God, and to this no evil is injurious. Job 35:6, 7: *if you have sinned, what do you accomplish against him? If you are righteous, what do you give to him?* For the glory of God resounds as much when he punishes evil as when he rewards good. The second is eternal life, to which sin is deleterious since through sin it is lost. Therefore we ask for this to be removed when we say, *Forgive us our sins as we forgive* . . . The third good is justice, and good works, and against these is set temptation, for temptations hold us back from doing good. We ask for these to be taken away when we pray, *Lead us not into temptation*. The fourth good is the good things of life, to which are opposed adversities and tribulations: we seek to be spared these when we ask, *but deliver us from evil*.

Aquinas was first and foremost a preacher, and these sermons reflect his Aristotelianism: the desire for the good, as a remedy against evil, as an effective means towards realizing our desires, and a way of making us familiar with God, the ultimate Good, who is ready to listen to our prayers and to grant them. His name is admirable, lovable, venerable, and inexpressible, and holy because it is firm, it is not earthly, it is tinged with love (Revelation 7:14). The kingdom requires perfect submission and leads to the glory of paradise and the destruction of sin. The will stems from God's desire for us to have eternal life, to observe his commandments, our desire for which can involve struggle. Daily bread is the strength to persevere, avoiding greed and excessive care about worldly things; it therefore means material, spiritual and sacramental realities. Temptation derives from our need to live in fear, humility and hope, so that we are able to see our faults and our need of grace, including the sacrament of penance. Temptation means fleshly delights, and the devil's trickery; we pray not for the grace not to be tempted, but to avoid being put into the kind of passive position in which we could be easily tempted. Finally, God does deliver us from affliction, but rarely; however, he grants us consolations and gives us benefits, turning temptation into good. Like many preachers of his time, he uses the beatitudes and the gifts of the Spirit, but not always precisely; they are not the mainspring of his exposition.

Although he cites Augustine, this treatment is far away from Augustine's approach, where the narrative quality of the preaching draws the hearer into the movement of the prayer in terms of the famous 'three heavenly' and 'four earthly' petitions. We have moved, too, from the adaptation of that shape which we first saw beginning in Anselm of Laon, resulting in 'four heavenly' and 'three earthly'. Instead, following Albert the Great, Aquinas regards the prayer as drawing us towards God by addressing our basic needs, the desire for good, and desire to avoid evil. Throughout the prayer, there is a conflict between good and evil but there is always the possibility that good will prevail, hence the need for virtues in the face of temptation.

## Liturgical commentaries

The established place of the Lord's Prayer in the liturgy comes through in three Carolingian liturgical commentaries, by Amalar of Metz (*c.*780–850), Florus of Lyon (†*c.*860) and Remigius of Auxerre (*c.*840–*c.*908), of whom the most influential figure was Amalar. A pupil of Alcuin, he became Bishop of Trier from *c.*809–813, and after being sent on a mission to Constantinople, he devoted himself to writing. But he was appointed administrator of the Primatial See of Lyon in 835 after the deposition of Agobard. His *De Ecclesiasticis Officiis* ('On Ecclesiastical Offices') is a series of works on the liturgy, some of whose elaborate views were condemned, causing him to be removed in 838. The Lord's Prayer figures in three of them, the *Canonis Missae Interpretatio* ('Interpretation of the Canon of the Mass'), the *Liber Officialis* ('Official Book'), and the *Ordinis Missae Expositio* ('Exposition of the Order of the Mass').[27] He regards the Lord's Prayer as part of the Canon (i.e. the eucharistic prayer), and it represents the three days' burial of Christ in the tomb, along with the introduction and the embolism. As far as the text is concerned, he begins by stressing the divine institution of the prayer, from the Christ who is both God and Man; the prayer is our way of showing what we believe, coming from the same mouth which gave us the institution of the eucharist, the heavenly prayer alongside the heavenly food. Hallowing the name is the angelic ministry in heaven, and it is ours on earth, in the kingdom which judges the works of the devil, and the will which it is our task to fulfil. Amalar is aware of the Greek tradition of interpreting the bread, which he regards as both spiritual and material in its focus; forgiveness is mutual (Matthew 18:35 is quoted, with good patristic precedent); temptation is about not entering into what the devil would like us to do. He goes straight into the embolism, 'deliver us, Lord', although there is a version of this text that indicates that the congregation respond with the petition for deliverance from evil, as in the *Rule of St Benedict*.

The *Liber Officialis* reads more like an exposition, another variant in the interpreting tradition, although he once again roots the prayer in the teaching of Christ in the form of the introductory words at mass. There are quotations from Cyprian, which Amalar uses to forge an even closer link between the prayer and the eucharist.[28] The *Exposition of the Order of the Mass* devotes a short section to the seven petitions of the prayer. He applies them to the seven gifts of the Spirit (Isaiah 11:2–3): the hallowing of the name with wisdom; the kingdom with understanding; the will with counsel; daily bread with fortitude; forgiveness with knowledge; temptation with piety; and deliverance with the fear of God. This is, arguably, a better scheme than Augustine's. Amalar then suggests another interpretation, based on the seven deacons and seven subdeacons assisting at the altar at High Mass.

Florus, on the other hand, who was a deacon at Lyon, wrote extensively on the liturgy for the hierarchy. His *Expositio Missae* ('Exposition of the Mass') appeared around the year 835, when Amalar took temporary charge of the See of Lyon, and it was aimed at his innovative teaching. His treatment of the Lord's Prayer[29] is a more conservative, patristic exercise, and less related to its liturgical context than other treatises on the mass. The heavenly Fatherhood is a direct consequence of regeneration; for although God may be everywhere, he is not present everywhere in his divine grace; the hallowing of the name is by baptism; the kingdom is in the future, but one we pray that we may recognize; doing the will he interprets in a way similar to Augustine, realizing the distinction between spirit and flesh, the need to pray for unbelievers, and the hope of salvation; daily bread is not just about material need, according to the Greeks (he maintains), but it is spiritual (John 6:41), and includes the eucharist; forgiveness is binding on us as well (Matthew 6:14); we pray not to be deserted by God, whether it relates to what we ourselves do or what we suffer; deliverance from evil is the last thing to be asked in life, punishment in the future; and like Bede, he follows Jerome in adding 'Amen', as a 'seal' ('signaculum') of the prayer.

Remigius was a monk at the abbey of St Germanus, Auxerre, until 893, when Archbishop Fulc had him come to rebuild his Cathedral school at Reims. Remigius takes us into the world of the scholar, manifested in his *Liber de Divinis Officiis*, in which there is a short discussion of the Lord's Prayer in the course of the mass.[30] Divine institution constitutes both the prayer's uniqueness and its importance, hence the introductory words. Hallowing the name is the privilege of those who have been reborn by water and the Spirit, an expression he has just used in relation to divine Fatherhood, but it also means good deeds; the kingdom is in the future (the Great Assize, Matthew 25:34), for God is able to reign in faith, hope and charity, while the devil reigns in luxury, drunkenness, and hatred; doing the will on earth is performed in the Church, Christ's body, and in the repentance of sinners; daily bread is what we need in material terms, our spiritual needs, including the eucharist, and the teaching of the Scriptures (a comprehensive list, like Augustine); forgiveness places us in the position of owing two debts to God, our own sins, and our inability to forgive others; temptation is about being tested by life, being tempted by the devil; like Florus, he adds 'Amen'; and along the lines of Augustine, he stresses that of the seven petitions, the first three are about the future, the remaining four about the present. There is no hint of applying the sevenfold structure to the gifts of the Spirit.

The tradition of liturgical commentary lived on, as we see in a group of twelfth-century writers. Hildebert of Lavardin (†1134) was Archbishop of Tours, and wrote a *Liber de Expositione Missae* ('Exposition of the Mass') which, as one would expect, encounters the Lord's Prayer in a eucharistic context.[31] The introductory words about following the teaching of Christ relate not only to the prayer but to the institution of the eucharist. The opening invocation to the heavenly Father indicates our inheritance as adopted children; doing the will refers to the life and work of the Church; the bread, citing Augustine, is material, spiritual and eucharistic; temptation is by testing as well as seduction; and after dealing with the embolism, he praises the allegorical interpretation of the introduction, the prayer and the embolism symbolizing the three days Christ laid in the tomb that was first propounded by Amalar. Stephen II of Autun (†1189) applied the prayer to the seven gifts of the Spirit, the seven virtues of the beatitudes, and their seven fulfilments.[32] Sicard (c.1155–1250) was Bishop of Cremona from 1185 and wrote his *Mitrale* ('Book of the Mitre'), probably before 1198.[33] He follows Amalar's allegorical interpretation of the three days' burial. The eucharistic context of the prayer is central; the kingdom is the coming of the Church to Christ; free will is steered and corrected by grace; at daily bread he notes *supersubstantialem* as the Latin reading.

Lothar of Segni (1160–1216), was a cardinal in papal service while not even yet a priest; he was elected Pope (as Innocent III) in 1198. Responsible for establishing further the position of the Papacy in secular affairs, he called the Fourth Lateran Council in 1215. His *De Sacro Altaris Mysterio* ('On the Sacred Mystery of the Altar') was completed between 1195 and 1197.[34] Following the lead taken by Anselm of Laon he divides the prayer into three heavenly and three earthly petitions, the first three directed towards our native land (*patria*), the second three to the way there (*via*); daily bread concerns both. The seven gifts, virtues and vices are woven together with the beatitudes (so dividing the beatitudes into their virtues and their fulfilment like Stephen II); he begins with the address to the Father, and then goes to the final petition, working backwards (like Anselm) to the beginning. He enumerates three kinds of evil, what is innate, what is circumstantial, what is inflicted; and five kinds of daily bread, bodily, spiritual, doctrinal, sacramental, and eternal. What these writers do is draw together the increasingly sevenfold focus on the Lord's Prayer in liturgical allegorization. In an allegorical commentary on the liturgy attributed to Hugh of St Victor (†1142), there is a strong emphasis on the representative role of the priest; as Christ enters the holy of holies, and returns to his people, like the High Priest of old, washing his clothes, so the priest at mass 'returns to the people', with the Lord's Prayer, whose seven petitions correspond to the gifts of the Spirit, which combat the seven deadly sins.[35] Such a view of priesthood was common at the time, but is not often encountered so explicitly in relation to the Lord's Prayer at mass.

Finally, William Durandus (c.1230–1296) was born near

Narbonne, and after spending most of his career in papal and curial service, he was consecrated Bishop of Mende, also in the south of France, when he began writing his lengthy *Rationale Divinorum Officiorum* ('Rationale of Divine Offices'),[36] which covers an array of ecclesiastical and liturgical matters, with allegorical interpretation a constant feature. It shows a mind that is not original, but easily gathers together material from established sources, and the Lord's Prayer in the mass is no exception. Following contemporary teaching, he sees the spiritual and temporal aspects as mixed throughout; in addition to the seven spiritual gifts, virtues, beatitudes and vices, he adds the seven words from the cross (Luke 23:34; John 19:26, 27; Luke 23:43; Matthew 15:34; Luke 23:46; John 19:30), which were first treated by Arnold of Marmoutier, Abbot of Bonneval, in 1138; and the seven words of the Virgin Mary (Luke 1:34, 38, 44, 46; John 2:3, 5; Luke 2:48). Following Lothar of Segni's rationalization of Anselm of Laon, the petitions are divided into three for our native land, three for the journey, the middle petition for daily bread being for both. Like Lothar and following Anselm of Laon (and others), he works backwards from the end of the prayer to the beginning. What we have not seen before are the seven words from the cross and the seven words of the Virgin Mary, the former are the only set of 'seven' that fit into allegorical interpretation.

These liturgical commentaries show a way of absorbing the same kinds of insights (the shape of the prayer, the sevenfold schemes) that were the common coin in the works of exposition and preaching at the time. They also point forward to popular works like Langforde's *Meditations*, in the fifteenth century, which we shall see in the next chapter. Daily bread is the turning-point of the prayer in every sense, and these writers have to cope with its heavenly and earthly dimensions, or else forswear the latter in favour of the former.

## Latin paraphrases

The paraphrase in some respects resembles the farced versions of the prayer which we saw in Narsai in the late fifth to early sixth-century East, but takes the process much further. Anselm was a reluctant Bishop of Lucca (*c.*1035–1086) who resigned to become a monk but who was pressed back into episcopal service by Gregory VII. There are three 'meditations' on the Lord's Prayer to his name, one lengthy, two much shorter, all in the form of an extended prayer, which may therefore be regarded as paraphrases.[37] The atmosphere is rhetorical and devotional, with rich invocations of God's goodness and mercy, but there is a systematic mind underneath, as each petition is related to a particular need; the opening invocation to devotion; hallowing the name to wisdom; the kingdom to sublimeness; the will to love (offering as alternatives understanding to the name, and desire to the kingdom); daily bread to the sacrament of the eucharist; goodness to forgiveness; baptism to temptation; mercy to deliverance.

A different approach is to be found in the *Speculum Ecclesiae* ('Mirror of the Church') by Honorius of Autun, an early twelfth-century monk, who came from Germany, and who had connections with Canterbury at the time of Archbishop Anselm. Liturgical in context, the *Speculum* contains directions for certain occasions, including how to teach about the Lord's Prayer on festivals.[38] Honorius was a popular theological writer whose purpose was to help preachers enable ordinary people to see in the Lord's Prayer seven steps on a ladder to heaven (the ladder is also used, in the East, by the twelfth-century exegete Euthymius Zigabenus), of which we ourselves are heirs. Taking Anselm of Laon's approach further, he adapts Augustine's division of the prayer into four heavenly and three earthly, offering a full treatment of daily bread that is at once material, spiritual and sacramental, but he then applies this shape to the contemplative (four heavenly) and the active (three earthly). If someone like Honorius is propounding such a change, we can conclude that it was already common coin at the time. In another section he looks at the gifts of the Spirit, but he does not identify them specifically with parts of the prayer, instead beginning (like Anselm of Laon) with the last, the fear of the Lord, and ending with the first, the gift of wisdom; this is another ladder into heaven. He refers to the practice of infrequent communion in his discussion of daily bread, and ends by inviting the congregation to recite the prayer with him, for without this prayer, they are like fish without water. Such a participation in the prayer at mass would have been mental rather than aloud.

Francis of Assisi (1181–1230) was the son of a nobleman who, on hearing at mass one day the mission of the twelve (Matthew 10:7–19), decided to found a new religious order to work among the poor, permission for which was granted by the Pope in 1209. Franciscan spirituality was marked by simplicity, with a special devotion to the cross. It would not, therefore, be unexpected to find a paraphrase of the Lord's Prayer among Francis' writings, particularly as he is bound to have preached repeatedly on it – but no sermons have come down to us. Although its authorship has been contested, the paraphrase that has his name is generally regarded as authentic, and Fumagalli has shown linguistic parallels with Francis' 'Canticle'.[39] In style, it is made up of blank-verse invocations, with a frequent use of abstract nouns: 'O most holy Father, our creator, redeemer, consoler and saviour' is how it begins. Throughout, one is struck by the contrast between the goodness of God, the depth of his mercies, and the weakness and sinfulness of humankind. The paraphrase follows each petition; daily bread is the memory of everything Jesus has done for us (implying the eucharist); and forgiveness is achieved by the cross and passion, and aided by the prayers of the Virgin Mary; and the embolism, 'deliver us Lord', is echoed in what he has to say about evil, 'past, present and future'.

### Vernacular material

What, then, of the text of the prayer in the vernacular? The material is potentially vast, but selection has to move in favour of England.

The *Lindisfarne Gospels* (667–698) contain a vernacular translation by Aldred, a monk of Cheste-le-Street, from the mid-tenth century.[40] It is intended to reflect the rhythms and meaning of the original (the difficult word *oferwistlic* appears to be an attempt to render *supersubstantialem*). We offer here a modern translation, because of the nature of the Anglo-Saxon original.

> Our Father who is in the heavens,
> hallowed be your name;
> your kingdom come;
> let your will be done as in heaven so on earth;
> give us today our bread of sustenance (*oferwistlic*);
> And forgive our debts, as we forgive our debtors;
> And lead us not into temptation;
> But free us from evil.

At the end of the tenth century, we come across a vernacular paraphrase of the Lord's Prayer in Anglo-Saxon, emanating from Worcester. It comes in ten short paragraphs, consisting of the Latin text of the prayer followed by the paraphrase, and gives something of a background to the later Latin texts which we saw earlier. The opening invocation is separated from the hallowing of the name, the petition for forgiveness is split into two sections (one about God, the other about other people) and 'Amen' appears as the conclusion. Translated into modern English, and with the Latin omitted, this is what results:

> Father of mankind, I pray for your healing, holy Lord in the heavens.
> May this your name be hallowed now, fast fixed in our minds, redeeming Christ.
> May your kingdom now come to us mortals, wielder of mighty powers, righteous Judge, and may your glorious faith remain in our hearts for the span of our lives.
> And may your will be fulfilled among us in the habitation of the kingdom of earth, as clear as it is in the glory of heaven, made both dear and lovely for ever and to eternity.

Give us now today, Lord of men, high King of the heavens, our bread, which you sent into the world as salvation to the souls of mankind: that is the pure Christ, the Lord God.

Forgive, guardian of men, our guilt and sins, and pardon our crimes, the body's wounds, and our wicked deeds, although we often offend against you, the almighty God, in your mercies,

Just as we pardon on earth the crimes of those who often do wrong against us, and do not think to accuse them of their evil deeds, in order to have eternal life.

Do not lead us to punishment, to the grief of affliction, nor to the testing, redeeming Christ, lest we, devoid of grace, become out of enmity estranged from all your mercies.

And also free us now from the evil of every fiend; we in our hearts shall eagerly speak of thanks and glory, Prince of the angels, true Lord of victories, because you have mercifully set us free from the bondage of hell's torments by your mighty power.

Let this be.[41]

The paraphrase is an expansion of the original, addressed throughout to Christ; and while each paragraph is different in length, there is still a sense of shape. Much of the teaching in the prayer we have come across already: we hallow the name by dedication; the kingdom coming in us; the will manifested; daily bread as Christ himself (and not material); forgiveness as mutual (hence the division of this petition); temptation and deliverance merge from one into the other; and the presence of the 'Amen' reflects popular use, rather than what the priest says (on his own) at mass. Phrases such as 'High King' reflect, too, the social order of the times. The advantages of such a paraphrase lie in its memorability and devotional fervour; the disadvantages accrue from its specific application, limiting the rich ambiguity of the prayer itself.

As if to answer such a text, there is a homily on the Lord's Prayer by Wulfstan, who was Bishop of London from 996–1002, and Bishop of Worcester as well as Archbishop of York from

1002–1016.[42] A short, instructive homily, reflecting some of the Augustinian teaching we have encountered already, it uses an Anglo-Saxon version of the prayer which is brief, and tries to reflect the quick, rhyming character of the Latin text on which it is based; and it ends with 'Amen'. Dorothy Bethurum regards this version as Wulfstan's own, because it bears traces of his style, which would give it some authority.

> Oh! Our Father who is in heaven,
> Be your name eternally blessed.
> And your kingdom over us reign always.
> And your will be done just as in heaven also as on earth.
> Grant us for this day daily food.
> And show mercy just as we show mercy
> to those who offend against us.
> And do not let us be tested all too greatly.
> But release us from evil. Amen.

An English homily from around this time[43] appears in blank verse, and adopts a popular style, carefully including Christian teaching throughout. Near the start come words which set the tone:

> We must to these words look,
> That are good for both body and soul,
> That we may be as his begotten sons,
> That he may be our father and we his chosen,
> That we may do all his behests
> And act according to his will.

Hallowing the name means good deeds that show that 'in the font we were born again'; the kingdom means 'looking upwards'; the will means being like 'thy archangels, and thy beloved holy angels'; daily bread is 'our livelihood' but also 'doctrine to us indeed', to feed the soul; a forgiving heart is essential for the Christian life, otherwise 'the Pater Noster availeth me nought'; he begins the following petition with the definition,

'Lead us not into temptation. That is a kind of trial', and he goes on to enumerate them, taking over the whole human person, whether it be lust or ill-will, which can be corrected by fasting, prayer and almsgiving; deliverance from evil can be achieved by thanking God for the help he brings.

Piecing together the opening lines of each section, we can provide a version of the prayer as follows:

> Our Father that art in heaven,
> Thy name be blessed,
> Thy kingdom come,
> Thine own will be in earth and heaven;
> Give us today our daily bread;
> Our sins, Lord, be forgiven us,
> As we do unto all men that live;
> Lead us not into temptation;
> But do thou deliver us from all evil. Amen.

The *Lay Folks Mass Book* is thought to be a thirteenth-century English translation of a twelfth-century guide to the mass, by a Canon of Rouen for Anglo-Norman use.[44] Written in rhyming verse, and in four different manuscripts, it is an extended devotional paraphrase on the eucharist. The verse-style has an influence on the text of the prayer (there were similar verse-translations in France at the time); and the worshipper is intended to say the prayer either with the priest aloud or else silently:

> Father our, that is in heaven,
> Blessed be thy name to name.
> Come to us thy kingdom.
> In heaven and earth thy will be done.
> Our each day bread grant us today,
> And our misdeeds forgive us aye,
> As we do them that trespass us,
> Right so have mercy upon us;
> And lead us into no testing,
> But shield us from all wicked thing. Amen.

The resemblance between this text and the metrical version in the English homily quoted earlier is striking, as also to a thirteenth-century English version:

> Father our that art in heaven,
> Hallowed be thy name;
> Come thy kingdom,
> Be done thy will also as in heaven,
> So on earth;
> Our each day's bread give us today,
> And forgive us our guilts,
> Also we forgive our guilters;
> And do not lead us into testing,
> But deliver us from harm.

And another, from later in the thirteenth century, with additions:

> Our Father that art in hevene,
> Hallowed be thy name with gifts seven:
> May thy kingdom come;
> Thy will in earth as in heaven be done;
> Our bread that lasts for aye,
> Give it to us each day;
> And our misdeeds do forgive us,
> As we forgive them that have misdone us;
> And lead us not into testing;
> But free us from all evil things. Amen.[45]

The second version is more creative, with the addition of the 'gifts seven', an echo of the long tradition of drawing the gifts of the Spirit into the prayer's heart. A tradition of vernacular translation (if not of 'rendering') according to a common form has emerged. There is an interplay between the Latin text of the mass and the vernacular tradition, as witness the recurrence of 'every evil', from the beginning of the embolism prayer both in the vernacular poems and texts as well as in commentaries. The nearest parallel, also from England, is to be found in the blank-verse contrasting phrases of the vernacular marriage-vow, which began its life in the fourteenth century, but with the essential difference that, while the vow was of necessity in liturgical use, the Lord's Prayer in the vernacular was not.[46]

## Conclusion

For all these vernacular versions, the standard liturgical Latin text remained that found in the Gregorian Sacramentary. The only variant is the sporadic persistence of the concluding 'Amen', which reflects Jerome's Vulgate text, endorsed by Bede (and others), and also as it appears in some ninth-century northern manuscripts of the Sacramentary.[47] But what of Jerome's other variant, *supersubstantialem* instead of *quotidianum*? Nearly all expositors of the New Testament text draw attention to it, from Rabanus Maurus onwards, and Paschasius Radbertus, among others, adopts it. But it was actually used liturgically, at Lauds and Vespers, in the convent of Héloise, close friend of Peter Abelard (1079–1143/4). After a visit there, Bernard of Clairvaux confided to Héloise that he was somewhat taken aback by the experience, which provoked a detailed missive from Peter Abelard, outlining the authorities for the use of this particular text; interestingly, he did not appeal to the authority of the Vulgate on its own but to the authorities who endorsed it.[48]

The period that begins with the Carolingians in the eighth century and ends with Dante in the fourteenth – a stretch of five hundred years – experienced major changes in the way the Lord's Prayer was thought about. It is a rich scene, but the following appeared to be the main features:

- Augustine's structure, like his sevenfold shape, mediated through Bede, was adapted in the twelfth century by such figures as Anselm of Laon and Honorius of Autun, and then began to lose its appeal with Albert the Great and Aquinas, as theologians and expositors became more confident about breaking with tradition, and bringing some clarity to an increasingly complex terrain.

- There is an abundance of different genres of works, including the 'Commentary' of Rabanus Maurus, the 'Allegories' of Hugh of St Victor, the 'Meditations' of Anselm of Lucca, and the 'Explanation' of Frowin of Engelberg. This is a very different scene from the twofold discourse–homily pattern of the Fathers.

- Virtues emerge to combat vices, as preaching becomes no longer a narrative of a prayer into which the hearer is caught up but a series of steps on a journey through a sinful world, in the search for the ultimate good, which is God alone.

- The will emerges as essential in the Christian life, but in need of direction, as with Frowin and Bonaventura, hence the abiding interest in the gifts of the Spirit.

- Daily bread is persistently regarded as material, spiritual and eucharistic, whether in the Platonist interpretation of Augustine, or its subsequently modified forms in the interpretations noted from Albert the Great onwards, and Jerome's reading, *supersubstantialem*, not noted by his immediate successors, is constantly referred to by writers from Rabanus Maurus onwards.

- Daily bread may be eucharistic, as a 'heavenly' petition, but it is infrequently sacramentally 'received', as writers such as Paschasius Radberthus, Honorius of Autun and Eckhart recognize.

- The practice grows of preaching specifically on the Lord's Prayer as a separate exercise, as we saw with Alan of Lille, not for the catechesis of the newly baptized,[49] but for the edification of the whole People of God.

- The elaborate sevenfold schemes are more popular with some writers than others, if we compare Richard of St Victor and Durandus of Mende with the more muted treatment in Jocelyn and Aquinas.

- Vernacular translations become a necessity as language develops, but for the instruction of the faithful, not for liturgical use.

- The Church looms larger as part of the prayer's meaning, as witness Gunther the Cistercian, and particularly Hugh of Amiens' elaborate hierarchical scheme, all of which helped to lay the ground for the Reformation.

- The considerable contrasts of the life of the Prayer, which the Reformation was to try to narrow, are aptly summed up by Jordan of Saxony (*c*.1300–1370/80), another Saxon Dominican, who, when asked the difference between the Lord's Prayer recited by a layman ignorant of its value and clerics who know about what they are saying replied that the prayer was like a precious stone, which is just as valuable in the hands of someone who does *not* know its virtue as it is in the hands of someone who does.[50]

We cannot conclude, however, without looking at Dante Alighieri (1264–1321). The middle volume of his epic, *The Divine Comedy*, entitled *Purgatory*, deals (among other things) with those who have fallen victim to the seven deadly sins; each category is given a penance, a focus of meditation, a guardian-angel, a Beatitude – and a prayer. The first are the Proud, whose penance is heavy stones, whose meditations are examples of humility contrasting with pride, whose guardian angel is the angel of humility, whose beatitude is the poor in spirit. Significantly, their prayer is the Lord's Prayer:

Our Father Who in Heaven dost abide,
not there constrained but dwelling there because
Thou lovest more Thy lofty first effects.

The first stanza sets the style, each interpreting a particular petition. Two in particular are worth attention, the doing of the will and daily bread:

And as Thine angels offer up their wills
to Thee in sacrifice, singing Hosannah,
let all men offer up to Thee their own.

Give us this day our daily manna, Lord;
Without it, those most eager to advance
Go backwards through this wild wasteland of ours.[51]

The union of angels with men has not so far been so strongly stated, as the will is 'offered' in sacrifice. Nor have we come across a stronger, yet more ambiguous, petition for bread – which is manna, needful for each day's spiritual and material sustenance. The purpose of this whole Canto is for the Proud to pray for the souls of those left behind on earth in order to cleanse themselves of their own pride, because they are weighed down by their sins – 'unequally tormented by their loads'. There is a hint here of the ending of the Lord's Prayer, deliverance from evil, and its embolism, setting the whole context of the remainder of this Canto, as the poet asks the reader to pray for them, who now only ask good things for us. For Dante, even purgatory, so central to medieval piety, can be an environment for prayer, where the Lord's own – in yet one more sevenfold scheme – finds its primal place.

# 7

# Renaissance and Reformation

As long ago as 1945, Gregory Dix highlighted how the Reformers relied to a great extent on the piety of the late medieval, and more recently, Eamon Duffy has drawn attention to the enduring quality of popular religion before and during the Reformation.[1] In few areas is this borne out more strongly than in the way the Lord's Prayer figured in late medieval piety as a central tool for Christian teaching, and in the way the Reformers made it a central plank in the spiritual ark they were trying to construct for a renewed Church. The Lord's Prayer had always carried considerable weight in Christian discourse and prayer, along with the Creed, and as the Middle Ages moved onwards, the Decalogue as well. The question lay in how the prayer was to be understood and used, and in that sense, revisionist views of the Reformation need to be treated with some care. It must also be remembered that, in the words of David Daniell, 'the English Bible was made in blood' – a boy discovered in Norwich in 1526 with a piece of paper on which was written the Lord's Prayer in English was burnt alive.[2]

What we shall see in these vivacious centuries is, first of all, the persistence and development of many of the features of the medieval period; Theodoric of Paderborn's commentary on the prayer, still in the traditions of its predecessors, but more credal and contemplative; lay piety given a voice, with Langforde's *Meditations* drawing the worshipper into the seven words from the cross; the York Mystery Plays, whose texts have been long lost, but whose basic message can be guessed at; the traditions of medieval preaching; and the vernacular versions of the prayer. Then we shall look at Luther and Calvin, both of whom isolated the Lord's Prayer in different ways, Luther making it central to virtually every liturgy, and Calvin seeing it as a quotation from Scripture, which should function primarily as a guide (rather than a text) on how we should pray; both of them were sufficiently imbued by the paraphrase tradition of medieval devotion to try (with differing degrees of success) to use a *liturgical* paraphrase as a substitute in public worship. Luther and Calvin also represent an era in which the Fathers were read in full, rather than in the snatched selections of the medieval schools, exemplified by the *Glossa Ordinaria*. The Counter-Reformation produces first of all a Catechism in 1566 which concludes with the Lord's Prayer as the basis for all teaching about prayer; and continues in two contrasting figures, Teresa of Avila's *Way of Perfection*, in the same year as the Trent Catechism, and Francis de Sales's lengthy paraphrase from early in the following century. Then we go to England, and to the work of Thomas Cranmer in the first two Prayer Books, which in turn provoke controversy among those who took Calvin's view of its function; which leads to the radical rejection of the prayer among the first Baptists. The Lord's Prayer becomes a touchstone of how 'reformed' one really is, and what would be the 'correct' way of using it (or not) in public. Apart from bringing it into public vernacular usage, the Reformers in the end ensure that the doxology becomes part of the prayer as well (as in the Restoration Prayer Book of 1662), and develop their own rich tradition of interpretation. In previous chapters, details of liturgy have been dealt with separately, but because the Reformers applied their views on the nature of the prayer to its liturgical function, we shall be looking at these aspects together.

## The fifteenth and sixteenth centuries

Theodoric of Paderborn was a Canon Regular, who died in 1417.[3] For him, the prayer comes in seven parts, but (like Maximus the Confessor) he splits the first (invocation of the Father, and hallowing the name) into two, and he combines the last two (temptation and deliverance from evil) into one. The sevenfold structure expounded by the Fathers carried considerable weight, but we saw in the previous chapter how this was loosened by Anselm of Laon in the twelfth century, and moved on further by Aquinas in the thirteenth. Theodoric's exposition is thus a break with tradition, and is clearly intended for private prayer, probably for a clerical audience; by combining the last two petitions, he is only doing what previous Western writers have been approaching by stealth, what Eastern writers long recognized, and what Calvin is soon to work out more systematically.

The invocation by the Christian of the heavenly Father who both creates and redeems, Theodoric regards as primarily 'the confession of the faith of his own existence'; and he carries on with similar words about contemplation, linking each petition with the next. The kingdom is the Church, in which Christ reigns, as other medieval writers had maintained. Doing the will leads Theodoric into the Christian life; some are called to share in 'beatitude', the vision of the Eternal King, and the Immaculate Virgin (her first appearance in this way in any exposition of the prayer); our calling is to the 'consummation of sanctity'. With such an internalized view of the prayer, it is no surprise that daily bread is what we need for the sustenance of our faith in this age, as we prepare for the next: the various gifts of the Spirit, the Word of God, spiritual growth; we who are baptized have died with Christ (Romans 6:3–11), and shall rise with him, in heavenly virtues; there is nothing about the eucharist here. Forgiveness, however, is a need in this life, including the sacrament of penance, as we examine ourselves for the different kinds of sin we have committed. He rounds off the exposition with a brief treatment of temptation and evil together; we pray that God will not 'permit' us to be tempted (as a Canon Regular, Theodoric follows the Rule of St Augustine, and will have known his writings); and the prayer concludes with 'Amen'.

Langforde's *Meditations in the Time of Mass* is a small collection of devotions for use during the eucharist, which dates from the fifteenth century.[4] Practically nothing is known of Langforde, except that his initial was 'B' and he was probably a priest. Following in the tradition of allegorical interpretation, he regards the mass as representing 'the very process of the passion of Christ', and his meditations are to 'move souls to the devotion of the mass and to the loving remembrance of the passion of Christ'. The Lord's Prayer has a central role in this scheme, because it represents Christ on the cross; the 'seven petitions contained' are for the faithful to 'remember the seven words of great mystery which our Lord did speak hanging quick upon the cross in His great agony, distress and pain of death; and specially follow the example of that holy word in the which He prayed for His enemies'. And in a phrase that echoes, unconsciously, the commemoration of the departed in the 1637 Scottish Prayer Book eucharist, Langforde writes that those who truly forgive are real disciples: 'then shall you be the chosen vessels apt to receive His grace, and both meet and able to receive the fruit of this most blessed sacrament'.[5]

The Seven Words from the Cross, pioneered by Arnold of Marmoutier in 1138, and subsequently polished in the form which we saw in Durandus of Mende at the end of the thirteenth century (Luke 23:34, 43; John 19:26f.; Matthew 27:46; John 19:28; 17:30; and Luke 23:46), had become an important part of devotion. They were to bear fruit in the seventeenth century under the influence of Alonso Messia, in Peru, with a popular Good Friday service, which involved an address on each of the 'Words', which was followed by the recitation of ten Paternosters and Aves.[6] But this is yet to come: to base the Seven Words of Christ around the Lord's Prayer is a further flight of numerology and allegory; not that Langforde is trying to relate each to a corresponding petition, but he is locating the narrative of the Lord's Prayer within two others – that of Christ's Seven Words, which is already within the narrative of the mass.

It is important to try to gauge the different effects of some of this disparate literature. Theodoric's commentary may only have been read by clerics, although it could well have influenced local preaching. Langforde, on the other hand, is trying to reach ordinary worshippers, and the lasting influence of works like this was probably considerable. More dramatic still are the York Mystery Plays, the importance of which was identified by John Wycliffe (*c*.1330–1384) when arguing for an English Bible. These apparently survived the Reformation until 1572, after which, in 1575, Archbishop Edmund Grindal commandeered the script – and it has not been seen since. The Pater Noster Guild, as it was called, used to produce a series of seven plays, each dealing with a single petition, and probably relating them to one or other of the seven deadly sins, or virtues, or gifts of the Spirit.[7] The emotional effect of such plays could have been great, as people watched the drama of their lives (negative in the case of vices, positive in the case of virtues) worked out before their eyes. It is also interesting to note the mutual relationship between the probable content of these plays and popular preaching, which, as we saw in the previous chapter, tended to concentrate on the sevenfold character of the prayer, and its application to godly living.

As far as preaching is concerned, Alan of Lille pioneered the notion of the *Ars Praedicandi*, which became something of a feature from the fourteenth century onwards. The production of these works effectively meant a sermon that had a life of its own, apart from the liturgy, even if it was preached at mass. The Lord's Prayer figured as the topic of the sermon itself, with careful attention paid to structure, illustration, and message, in which the sevenfold possibilities would form an important consideration; or it would figure as a subsidiary *exemplum* ('example'), or else by proper use of the 'ante-theme', a section of the sermon immediately following on from the introduction of the theme, which was a short way of capturing the attention of the hearers.[8]

When it comes to daily prayer, we may assume that the use of the Lord's Prayer among the religious orders as a substitute for the canonical hours, whether by lay brothers toiling in the fields, or by travelling friars without books, would persist throughout this period. But what of the mass? The Sarum Missal was the mass-book of the Salisbury diocese, a liturgical tradition which was highly influential throughout England from the fourteenth century onwards. And while no substantial alterations were made to the mass, there are some noticeable variations. For example, in England it was common for the Lord's Prayer to be recited along with other devotions, the *Veni Creator Spiritus* included, as part of the preparation before mass, but this custom is not found in the first printed edition of the Roman Missal in 1474. Another variant concerns how the prayer is to end; the 'Amen' noted in some earlier eucharistic books gives way either to the custom of the final petition as congregational response, 'sed libera nos a malo' (also noted earlier), and perhaps arising from Benedictine practice; or else there was no response at all, the priest continuing straight away with the embolism, 'deliver us, Lord'. Sarum practice used the final petition as a response, both before mass and during, whereas the Roman Missal of 1474 has 'Amen'.[9] What lies behind these variations is different ways of using the prayer by clergy and ministers at public liturgies. The incursion of the prayer into the preparation before mass is an example of popular piety making its place known in the liturgy. Two other late medieval practices are noted in some missals; to delay the elevation of chalice and paten together from the end of the canon until during the Lord's Prayer, especially at the petition for bread, and for everyone to prostrate themselves, except at festivals.[10]

When it comes to vernacular versions, there is ample material; and, as in the thirteenth and fourteenth centuries, a remarkable convergence is taking place, especially when one considers the potential margins of creativity of such an exercise. Here is a fourteenth-century version:

> Father our that art in heaven,
> Hallowed be thy name;
> Come thy kingdom;
> Fulfilled be thy will in heaven as in earth;
> Our each day bread give us today;
> And forgive us our debts,
> As we forgive to our debtors;
> And do not lead us in temptation;
> But deliver us of evil. So be it.

A fifteenth-century version is similar, but it is interesting to note 'heavens', more accurately translating *caelis*, and 'come to thee' of the kingdom:

> Father our that art in heavens,
> Hallowed be thy name;
> Thy kingdom come to thee;
> Thy will be done in earth as in heaven;
> Our each day's bread give us today;
> And forgive us our debts
> As we forgive to our debtors;
> And lead us not into temptation;
> But deliver us from evil. Amen.

A 1505 woodcut, to which Eamon Duffy has drawn attention as a means of popular education, has this version, which, unlike the previous, reads 'come to be' of the kingdom instead of 'come to thee':

> Our Father that art in heaven
> Sanctified be thy name;
> Thy kingdom come to be,
> Thy will be done
> In earth as in heaven.
> Our daily bread give us today,
> And forgive us our debts
> As we forgive our debtors;
> And lead us not unto temptation,
> But deliver us from evil. Amen.[11]

We shall return to the evolution of a definitive English version in due course, where the Reformers were also to take up the search for proper instruction – as well as, for them, enlightened use – of the Lord's Prayer, using much of this inheritance. The text, which is not even entirely stable in its liturgical form because of different ways of ending it, is already widely used in different vernacular versions alongside the liturgies, as these struggle for both accuracy and rhythm, and against attempts at paraphrase, e.g 'come to be' and 'come to thee'. Even though interpretations of 'daily bread' vary, there is no hint of a translation that would express Jerome's *supersubstantialem*. The 'Wycliffe' (1388) rendering 'our bread over other substance' was a one-off. The Latin *debita* produces 'debts' as a translation, in contrast to the thirteenth-century writers we saw in the previous chapter, with 'trespasses' (Lay Folks Mass Book), and 'guilts' and 'misdeeds' in the other two.[12] The Lord's Prayer remains an essential item in the Christian repertoire that godparents had to recite, along with the Creed (and, now, the Ave Maria), before baptism, with the rest of the congregation. It was their duty to teach it to the growing child for repetition in piety and in penance. It figured so prominently in the lives of the devout that it was deemed an adequate substitute for the canonical hours for lay brothers in the religious orders.[13]

## Martin Luther and John Calvin

Luther and Calvin dominate the sixteenth-century Reformation. Although Calvin's work on the Lord's Prayer is small in comparison with the rest of his theological output, what they both have to say is significant. It highlights their different but complementary doctrinal emphases and demonstrates how they viewed the prayer, its function and meaning. What they strip away is considerable: although Luther retained the sevenfold structure of the prayer, he rejected any symbolism attached to that number. Calvin followed suit, taking the view that the prayer consisted of six petitions. This effectively eliminates discussion of gifts of the Spirit, virtues and vices; any identification of the kingdom with the Church; of daily bread with the eucharist; or of the petition for forgiveness with penance; and there is an emphasis throughout on the sincere use of the prayer, rather than on its repetition. But there are differences between them in how the prayer should function in the life of the Church. Luther remained in part an Augustinian, convinced of its effects as a prayer, even though these are the consequences of God's grace in initiating a new relationship with the believer rather than the believer's initiative in reaching up to God. And, while Luther's works on the prayer are considerable, and full of theological content, they are catechetical and devotional in focus. Calvin's more radical work is represented by what he has to say in the *Institutes of the Christian Religion*. Both mistrust the Church they inherit, emphasizing the place of the laity, in whom the work of divine grace is able to move freely. For their texts, Luther uses his own translation of the Bible into German, while Calvin relies on Erasmus's version. Both results are simple and direct, and end with 'Amen'; and while Calvin rejects Erasmus's *supersubstantialem* at 'daily bread', he follows Erasmus in including the doxology.[14]

Martin Luther (1483–1546) is rightly regarded as the inaugurator of the German Reformation. After studying at Magdeburg and Eisenach, where he was attracted to Nominalism, he became an Augustinian hermit at Erfurt in 1505, and was ordained two years later; in 1508 he became professor of moral philosophy at the new University of Wittenberg. In the ensuing years, he moved away from the assured position of his theological inheritance and became increasingly concerned about humanity's inability to justify himself. The '95 Theses' which he is supposed to have nailed against the Castle Church at Wittenberg on 31 October 1517 are taken to be the symbolic start of the Reformation. From then on, a growing conflict with the Catholic Church authorities was inevitable, particularly after the public disputation with Johannes Eck at Leipzig two years later, with Luther denying the primacy of the Pope and the infallibility of the Church.

Luther's ecclesiastical and liturgical reforms find an echo in his works on the Lord's Prayer, which are many and varied. Carmignac lists no fewer than twenty-one, starting with a sermon preached on 12 October 1516, and ending with 'A Simple Way to Pray' (1535).[15] Each publication is either a sermon or a practical-doctrinal discourse. This echoes in many ways his medieval predecessors, perhaps the best-known of his works being the so-called Large and Small Catechisms, both published in 1529, using the version of the prayer found in Luther's translation of the New Testament of 1522. In an important article which compares Luther and Calvin on the Lord's Prayer, Marc Lienhard draws attention to two distinctive features in Luther, the soteriological and the existential, which reflects accurately the atmosphere and the substance of his writing. There is not a great deal of movement, except that, as Carmignac points out, in two sermons preached in 1523, we begin to see a change of emphasis over how to interpret 'daily bread'; no longer exclusively spiritual, he is taking material needs more seriously, and such a view becomes central from 1528 onwards.[16]

For Luther, the Lord's Prayer's structure is sevenfold, but with a difference; the first three petitions are about spiritual blessing, the fourth about material, and the last three about deliverance from evil. This is a shift of perspective, and it owes something to the late medieval sense of sinfulness colouring the second part of the prayer. It has much in common with Albert the Great's view that the first four petitions are about good things whereas the last three are about averting bad things. The opening invocation is an invitation by God to us to believe that he is our true Father; the hallowing of the name has to start by acknowledging (along the lines of Augustine) that we cannot add anything to it, for the name of God is eternally holy, but it must lead into holy lives resulting from right teaching; the kingdom will come anyway but we must pray that we can share in it, when the Holy Spirit is given, so that we can believe and live righteously; similarly, the will of God will be effective anyway, but we must pray that it may be done among us, which involves conflict with the devil; daily bread is the sustenance God gives regardless of our prayers, and to the wicked as well, but we must pray that we may appreciate it, and receive it with thanksgiving, as food, clothing, money, goods, pious and faithful rulers, good weather, honour, faithful friends; forgiveness is our claim for something from God for which we are unworthy but only deserve punishment, which means that we too must heartily forgive; temptation comes from the devil, the world and the flesh, and we must pray not to be seduced into misbelief, despair, or any other vice, so that through temptation we may be purified and strengthened; we pray for deliverance from every evil, of body, soul, property and honour, so that we may have a blessed end: Luther is aware of the power of the devil, but following in the steps of Augustine, this petition is about evil in general.

Luther's view of the Lord's Prayer has something patristic,

something medieval, and something Reformation about it. It is patristic, in that the prayer has a narrative in which the believer (particularly in the latter part) is caught up; it is medieval, in that the believer is aware of inadequacy and sinfulness; and it is Reformation, in that God is seen to act regardless of human beings and institutions, and the believer is put passively in the position of receiving divine grace. But his most original emphasis is on the fact that it is Christ's own words of prayer *now*, a testament of his work for us. Much of this is borne out in his liturgical reforms, whose most unusual contribution was the composition in 1539 of the metrical paraphrase, 'Vater Unser', which was probably written for use with the Catechism. We have already seen verse forms of the prayer but Luther's can claim to have pride of place. While English translations are inadequate, here is the first stanza, in which (as in the remaining eight) Luther's teaching can be clearly seen:

> Our Father in the heaven who art,
> Who callest all of us, in heart
> Brothers to be, and on thee call,
> And wilt have prayer from us all,
> Grant that the mouth not only pray,
> From deepest heart, O help its way.[17]

With the liturgy, Luther was both radical and innovative. In 1523 and 1526, he produced versions of both baptism and the eucharist; the 1523 rites are more conservative than those of 1526.[18] For Luther, sacraments on their own justify nobody, but they are efficacious in that when faith is present (meaning the faith of the Church), they assuredly impart grace.[19] In the 1523 baptism rite, which, as Fisher shows, relies on the 1497 Magdeburg service (his local pre-Reformation rite) for its basic structure, the Lord's Prayer is recited before the renunciations, and by the priest, together with the godparents. Luther also adapts a local custom in the 1497 rite, where the priest lays his hand with his stole on the head of the child while reciting the prayer, but the godparents are not involved: Luther instead directs that the pastor lay his hand on the child's head while reciting the prayer, along with the godparents. The more simplified rite of 1526 has the same practice; and the custom of the laying on of hands survived into Lutheran practice elsewhere. The gesture seems to indicate imparting, blessing, and responsibility.

In the eucharist, Luther is equally bold; in the *Formula Missae* ('Form of Mass') 1523, the communion rite is reduced to short preface (still sung to the old music), followed by the Institution Narrative; the Sanctus and Benedictus come next, followed by the Lord's Prayer, which is chanted by the pastor, and introduced with the traditional words and is also sung, but the embolism, 'deliver us Lord' is omitted; and the communion (in both kinds) is introduced by the Peace. In 1526, the *Deutsche Messe* ('German Mass') which also encourages services of a less formal kind for teaching on the Ten Commandments, the Creed, and the Lord's Prayer, reduces the service further, so that the Lord's Prayer is turned into a devotional paraphrase in preparation for communion. This is to be said either at the end of the sermon from the pulpit (which Luther seems to favour), or else at the altar, before the Institution Narrative. In practice, subsequent Lutheran rites tended to opt for a common mean between the 1523 and 1526 forms, with the Lord's Prayer as liturgical text between the preface (or its equivalent) and the Institution Narrrative, forming a liturgical unit of thanksgiving, prayer in the name of the Lord and recitation of the words of Christ at the Supper: the paraphrase-version appears to have survived on solemn occasions such as Lent, as was the custom at Leipzig during J. S. Bach's time.[20] Although local rites began to add the doxology from the late sixteenth century onwards, Luther's reforms resemble (in this respect) those of the Swiss Reformer Ulrich Zwingli, who places the prayer (without doxology) at communion immediately before the Institution Narrative in the Zurich 1523 and 1525 rites. But perhaps the most 'Lutheran' – and baptismal – use of the prayer comes not from Luther himself, but from his close colleague, Johannes Bugenhagen (1485–1558), in the 1537 Schleswig-Holstein and 1539 Danish (and Norwegian) ordination rites, where for both pastors and superintendents (bishops), the Lord's Prayer is recited before the ordination prayer, both with the laying on of hands. This is unique, and inspired by Luther's practice at baptism, and it is still in use in Denmark.

For Luther, the Lord's Prayer belongs both to the catechesis of the Church, to baptism and to the celebration of the eucharist, because of its central place in the life of the believer, with meanings great enough to bear the load of liturgical recitation. Unlike his medieval predecessors, he was in a position to reform the liturgy, rather than to work around it. In actual celebration, it is possible to see the stark isolation of the prayer at both these sacraments, as well as at ordination, reflecting what Lienhard calls the 'soteriological' and the 'existential' emphases that lie at the heart of Luther's teaching.

John Calvin (1509–1564) was born at Noyon, France. Although intended for an ecclesiastical career, he instead studied civil law at Orléans and Bourges, after a brief foray with theology in Paris. Becoming increasingly influenced by Humanism, and also (possibly) Martin Luther, he fled Paris in 1533 after an incident in which the Rector of the University gave a lecture criticizing the Church, which was widely believed to have been composed by Calvin himself. Leaving France because of possible persecution, he went to Basel in 1535 and then Geneva in 1536, where his reforming zeal was not to the liking of the citizenry. This resulted in a ministry at Strasbourg from 1538 to 1541, after which he was able to return once more to Geneva. Calvin's influence on what came to be described as the 'Reformed' churches was considerable, thanks both to his preaching and to the *Institutes of the Christian Religion* (successive editions, 1536, 1539, 1543, 1550 and 1559), as well as an array of biblical commentaries that displayed, like the *Institutes*, a wide reading of the Fathers. But the fact that he began with the *Institutes* shows a systematic approach to theology and the life of faith that his legal training had honed.

There is a section on prayer in general followed by an exposition of the Lord's Prayer as a quotation from Matthew 6:9–13 at the end of the third volume of the *Institutes*, which can be compared with the corresponding section in the 1542 Geneva

Catechism.[21] Calvin's ideas were already formed in 1536, though there are small revisions in 1539 and 1559. To read Calvin is different from Luther. The style is less homiletic and directly edificatory, and more systematic and reflective. In words that date from 1536, he begins his discussion in the *Institutes* by describing the prayer as 'a table' which contains 'all that (Jesus) allows us to seek of him, all that is of benefit to us, all that we need ask'. He then discusses the structure; for him there are six petitions, and he openly disagrees with those who contend for seven (by which he means, principally, Augustine and Luther). The first three petitions are about God's glory, and the second three about 'the care of ourselves, and are especially assigned to those things which we should ask for our own benefit'; but he quickly adds that if we are tempted, we must not think of ourselves, but consider his glory alone, 'to gaze with eyes intent on this one thing'.

Of the opening invocation he writes that 'by the sweetness of this name he frees us from all distrust, since no greater feeling of love can be found elsewhere than in the Father'. It is an address that can encourage us, in fellowship with others, for there is an ecclesial dimension – 'all prayers ought to be such as to look to that community which our Lord has established in his Kingdom and his household', the elect Church; a section added in 1559 expands on the heavenly dwelling of God. Hallowing the name is more than hallowing in us, as Luther taught; it is done not only in 'highest reverence', but by God's action among us, in teaching and in works, with a corporate dimension. The kingdom is about the Spirit correcting fleshly desires, and our obedience to his rule; it is already set up (cf. Luther's view that it will come anyway), and challenges us into 'daily desire that God gather churches unto himself'; for God 'protects his own'. There are two wills of God, first, the secret, 'by which he controls all things and directs them to their end' and, second, that 'to which voluntary obedience corresponds'; this may be compared to Luther's view that the will of God will be done anyway, but we nevertheless have the responsibility to exercise ours; 'by this prayer we are formed to self-denial so God may rule us according to his decision'.

Daily bread brings us to our own affairs, without bidding 'farewell to God's glory'! But in a 1559 addition, he stresses that we should not seek anything for ourselves that will prevent us from living and dying in him (Romans 14:7–9); in a short aside inserted in 1539, he rejects Jerome's *supersubstantialem*, which 'seems to agree very little with Christ's meaning'; and in 1559, he added that this petition comes before forgiveness, which he regards as more important, so that in praying for both forgiveness and protection we can focus on 'the heavenly life'. Forgiveness comes from the 'free mercy' of God; he chides those who rely on their merits; forgiveness is an essential part of the new covenant, and mutual forgiveness is a way for Jesus 'to comfort the weakness of our faith'. The last petition (temptation and deliverance together) concerns 'the continual warfare and hard and trying struggles' of this life, for which we pray for the Spirit's grace to 'soften our hearts and to bend and direct them to obey God'; and in an insertion made in 1539, aware of the unresolved issue between East and West, he says that it 'makes very little difference whether we understand by the word "evil" the devil or sin'. Calvin then gives his approval to the doxology, where he follows Erasmus's 1516 version but is aware that it is not in the earliest texts of the New Testament, because it concludes the prayer in the 'firm and tranquil repose of our faith'.

Although he lacks Luther's pastoral zeal, and his sense of the prayer's immediacy and contemporaneity, Calvin on the Lord's Prayer has a profundity that places him on a par with Augustine and Aquinas. It is both theocentric and anthropocentric; and even if the ecclesial points of reference are more exclusive than others would wish, the context of his writing (active persecution threatened from outside, and internal dissension because of the uncertainty of the new 'reformed' church) indicates the clarity and originality of his mind. What were the main influences on his work? He rejects Augustine's structure, putting paid to any sevenfold associations in consequence; but there is an Augustinian sense of dependence on God throughout. The sixfold structure and daily bread as exclusively material read more like the Eastern patristic tradition. For the first five petitions, he is influenced by his Strasbourg colleague Martin Bucer (1491–1551), who wrote on the prayer in a Commentary on the Gospels in 1520; but not on temptation or deliverance, because he does not see these as separate, nor is he prepared to say whether evil is personal or impersonal; but he includes the doxology for reasons similar to Bucer, as an appropriate act of praise.[22] Calvin ends his discussion in the *Institutes* with a warning, dating from 1539, that 'we are not so bound by this form of prayer that we are not allowed to change it in either word or syllable'; all our prayers should, nonetheless, be tested by what is included 'by way of summary' in this prayer. This is the ambiguity that Reformed churches struggled with as a result: for Calvin, the Lord's Prayer is a scriptural warrant about prayer, not a liturgical text, and yet this was not the solution that was to stand the test of time.

In the Geneva *Form of Prayers* of 1542, 1547 and 1559, the Lord's Prayer and the Creed both appear just before the baptism. The prayer is introduced in 1542 in a periphrastic manner: 'Grant us, Father of mercy, that the baptism which we minister to him according to thine ordinance may bring forth its fruit and virtue. Such as has been declared by thy gospel'; however, the 1556 Genevan service-book of John Knox (*c*.1513–1572), compiled for the use of exiles from Scotland and England, follows the 1545 Strasbourg rite, praying for the infant about to be baptized and concluding with the words, 'in whose name we pray as he hath taught us', which also appears in the 1564 Scottish *Book of Common Order*. The 1542 wording is less confident than 1545 and Knox. There is also a form of 'evangelical confirmation', at which the duly catechized candidate must publicly recite the Lord's Prayer (as well as the Apostles' Creed). But with the eucharist (usually only quarterly, and celebrated as the second part of the morning service), there is some hesitation. In the 1542 Strasbourg rite, a public catechesis of the Lord's Prayer follows the Creed (during which the elements are prepared), whereas in the 1542 Geneva rite, it does not appear at all. Calvin thus avoids a pre-communion use of the Lord's Prayer at the eucharist, preferring instead an intercession, which leads into a paraphrase of the Lord's Prayer (as Maxwell has shown, adapted from Bucer's

German Psalter of 1539), whether the eucharist is celebrated or not. The Lord's Prayer as a liturgical text is therefore not to be recited at all at most Sunday morning services. Knox similarly avoids the prayer before communion, and provides a lengthy intercession, but this ends with the full text of the Lord's Prayer. In both the 1556 Genevan and 1564 Scottish books, the text reflects the (1560) Geneva Bible in English translation, with 'debts' and 'debtors', reflecting the late medieval vernacular English versions rather than the more recent 'trespasses' and 'those who trespass against us' which were to appear in the English Prayer Books; and 'for thine is the kingdom and the power and the glory for ever', as the translation of the doxology, a more accurate rendition of the Greek than what was to appear in the 1662 Prayer Book, 'for thine is the kingdom, the power and the glory, for ever and ever'. The difference between Calvin and Knox over liturgy is to be discerned through various stages of Reformed church practice: Calvin's exposition is accepted but his liturgical strictures are not entirley taken on board. This tension, as we shall see, is to break out in another way in England later on in the sixteenth century.

When we compare Luther and Calvin, we are not dealing with the same kind of mind or context. Luther wrote far more on the Lord's Prayer than most others, using similar themes as he communicated with different audiences, whereas Calvin stuck to the medium of his *Institutes*, sharpening his focus as the years progressed, as the successive editions show. Both wrestled with the need to express the ecclesiological aspects of the prayer in a manner less self-confident than the Catholic inheritance, and while successive editions of the Geneva Psalter contained metrical versions of the Ten Commandments, the Creed, and the Lord's Prayer, Luther's 'Vater Unser' had, arguably, a more lasting influence altogether, encouraged by composers such as Dietrich Buxtehude (*c.*1637–1707), J. S. Bach (1685–1750), and J. L. Krebs (1713–1780). Calvin's legacy, however, is the *Institutes*, and an ambiguous relationship with the text of the prayer. Luther, on the other hand, was less averse to its popular, liturgical purpose, and could therefore more easily teach through his long ministry about a much-loved – and much-used – text, uniquely interpreted with the laying on of the pastor's hand during its recitation at baptism. Neither Luther nor Calvin has any use for schemes that identify the gifts of the Spirit with specific petitions: instead, both stress the work of the Holy Spirit in the life of the believer as a manifestation of the coming kingdom, a feature we have seen in the Eastern Fathers, starting with Gregory of Nyssa, and which we shall see again.

## The Roman Catholic Counter-Reformation

In the face of the Reformation to Western Catholicism, a Council was held at Trent which met intermittently from 1545 to 1563, of which there were many fruits, which (for our purposes) amount to a Catechism (1566), a Missal (1570) and a Ritual, for pastoral offices, including baptism (not until 1614).[23] The Catechism of 1566 was a major achievement and set the tone of Roman Catholic teaching in the period from then onwards.[24] Intended for the parish clergy only, it set out Catholic teaching in every respect and provided material for sermons and instruction. Right at the end comes a lengthy treatment of prayer, which leads into a commentary on the Lord's Prayer that relies heavily on the teaching of the Fathers, particularly Augustine, and also in large measure Thomas Aquinas. There are seven petitions, and it ends with 'Amen', but no sevenfold scheme (whether of the beatitudes, the gifts of the Spirit, or vices) is mentioned anywhere, a considerable break with tradition. God's fatherhood is based on creation, providence and redemption (following Aquinas), and the heavenly dwelling means guardian angels. But God is no human construct, so his name, kingdom and will do not belong to his intrinsic nature, but are extrinsic (a summary of the Fathers and the later medieval writers). We hallow the name by praying for the conversion of unbelievers; the kingdom is of nature (what everyone experiences), grace (what believers experience) and glory (what we hope is to come), and it concerns the Church, for whose propagation we must pray, as well as the conversion of sinners; the will brings us into conflict with ourselves and the world, with our inordinate desires, mistaken requests and the weakness of our own wills. The words 'on earth as in heaven' apply to the name and the kingdom, not just the will – an unusual interpretation at the time, which, as we have seen, follows Origen, the *Opus Imperfectum* attributed to John Chrysostom, and Meister Eckhart, and which, as Carmignac points out, was frequently omitted in editions of the Catechism.

The second part of the prayer is subordinate to the first, since it concerns our own welfare, the needs of our souls and bodies, a subtle echo of Augustine's heavenly/earthly divisions. Daily bread means, first of all, our bodily needs (for which it is right that we should pray), as well as spiritual food, which includes the eucharist, in which context there is a recommendation about daily communion. Forgiveness brings us to the cross, and our own sins, which we need to acknowledge, and be ready to forget injuries, and make use of the sacrament of penance; temptation is about human frailty, the assaults of the flesh, and direct encounter with the devil; we do not pray to be exempt, but rather to survive, know God's help, and be strengthened; deliverance from evil means (following Aquinas) glorifying God; and 'Amen' is interpreted (following Jerome) as the 'seal' on the prayer.

In many respects, this Catechism summarizes patristic and medieval writings and holds the line on the place of the Universal Church in the kingdom, the eucharist in daily bread, and the role of penance in forgiveness. There is a measure of breadth in its rich clauses, though one can detect more of Augustine and Aquinas between its lines than other writers, with the sense of the shape of the prayer in its narrative (Augustine) and conceptual (Aquinas) direction. In the Ritual of 1614, there is little quarter in the baptism service with Reformation demands for simplicity or even the vernacular; the prayer, followed by the Creed, is recited as in the medieval books in its traditional position, as originally part of the rite for making a catechumen. In the Missal of 1570, the Lord's Prayer similarly appears in its traditional position, after the eucharistic prayer, with its introductory words, but with 'sed libera nos a malo' as a response at the end, followed by 'Amen' said quietly by the priest and leading straight into the embolism, 'deliver us, Lord'.[25] There is nothing new in any of these liturgical directions.

In the same year that the Catechism appeared, a Carmelite nun from Avila, Spain, probably of Jewish descent, called Teresa, produced an apparently modest work of devotion based on the Lord's Prayer, entitled *The Way of Perfection*.[26] Rowan Williams has described it as 'perhaps Teresa's most consciously mischievous book . . . a conversation between Teresa and her sisters carried on before a rather suspicious audience'. Its real purpose was to set in motion the more radical reform of the Carmelites against a background of suspicion about reform in general and woman religious writers in particular. Teresa of Avila (1515–1582) is one of the outstanding figures of the Counter-Reformation, and although *The Way of Perfection* is not in the same league as *The Interior Castle* and some of her other works, what she has to say about the Lord's Prayer brings us face to face with a rare talent for observation, humour and the occasional sharp remark about the perils of the religious life. The opening chapters are about prayer in general; 'believe me, sisters, if you serve God as you should, you will find no better relatives than those whom His Majesty (i.e. God) sends you' (ch. 9); and 'be very careful about your interior thoughts, especially if they have to do with precedence' (ch. 12).

When considering the opening invocation (ch. 27), she writes: 'what son is there in the world who would not try to learn who his father was if he had one as good, and who offers as great majesty and dominion, as ours?' Of hallowing the name (ch. 30), 'what is it that sends our faith to sleep, so that we cannot realize how certain we are, on the one hand, to be punished, and, on the other, to be rewarded?' Of the kingdom (ch. 31), 'there is a saying that, if we try very hard to grasp all, we lose all'. Of the doing of the will (ch. 32), 'the aim of all my advice to you in this book is that we should surrender ourselves wholly to the Creator, place our will in His hands and detach ourselves from the creatures'. Of daily bread (ch. 34), which for Teresa is primarily eucharistic, and enables her to give the sisters advice on how to meditate at length after receiving the sacrament, 'entreat

Him not to fail you but to prepare you to receive Him worthily'; and 'delight to remain with Him; do not lose such an excellent time for talking with Him as the hour after Communion'. Of forgiveness (ch. 36), 'I cannot believe that a soul which has approached so nearly to Mercy Itself and has learned to know itself and the greatness of God's pardon will not immediately and readily forgive, and be mollified and remain on good terms with the person who has done it wrong.' Of temptation (ch. 38), 'it is as well that we should recognize our imperfections, so that we can see how far we are from possessing the virtue of poverty, which we must beg and obtain from God'. And of deliverance from evil she has this to say (ch. 42): 'if you have learnt how to say the Paternoster well, you will know enough to enable you to save all the other vocal prayers you may have to recite'.

The simplicity and depth of Teresa's prose are a striking contrast to the more analytical and comprehensive treatments that we have seen from others. She is able to base the whole journey of faith, in all its essentials, around this prayer. The sacrament of the eucharist is at the heart of her work. The prayer draws the believer from the world of cares and delusions into a time of self-knowledge, and from there nourishes and sustains, then enables forgiveness to take place, only for the journey once more to begin. But it is not a reassuring process. For those who think religious life, of whatever kind, should be a set of rules that must not be broken, Teresa provides a challenging counterpoint.

Francis de Sales (1567–1622) became Bishop of Geneva in 1602, in the heart of one of the central bases of the Protestant Reformation. He administered the diocese from Annecy and became well known as a writer, correspondent and preacher, his most famous work perhaps being his *Introduction to the Devout Life* (1609), a copy of which was in the library of the Anglican divine Thomas Ken (1637–1711). At the end of the thirty-six volumes of his works are a devotional exposition and a paraphrase of the Lord's Prayer which is generally regarded as authentic, even though the text itself is Italian; de Sales was known to have based many of his personal prayers on the Pater Noster.[27] He begins by breaking the prayer down into several sections and sub-sections, based on the sevenfold structure. He then provides the paraphrase, an extended meditation, poring over every word. In the opening, among the many possibilities for prayer is when he reflects on Jerome's *supersubstantialem* as an alternative to the (official) *quotidianum* of the bread: 'Our "supersubstantial" bread, who is his holy Son in the Blessed Sacrament, so that we may have the memory and the under-standing of his love which he has brought to us and the things he has done and suffered for us, which are infinite.' Many themes in the paraphrase are familiar: angels doing God's bidding, inner struggling with self-will, the eucharist, the merits of Christ's passion and the prayers of the Virgin Mary in forgiveness; and all without a hint of anti-Protestant polemic.

These three different works typify the development of teaching from the preceding centuries. The Catechism provides a compre-hensive focus; the service-books of the Council of Trent set out to draw together into some kind of order the disparate liturgical practices of previous centuries through a central authority; and Teresa of Avila and Francis de Sales provide different kinds of paths, with Teresa looking at how a religious community functions, and de Sales looking instead into his own soul.

## The English Prayer Books and their aftermath, Anglican and Reformed

The English Reformation inevitably brought with it the need to find a common text for the Lord's Prayer. It equally inevitably raised the question of how the prayer should be used in public worship. From agreed text in the Prayer Books of 1549 and 1552 we move into the conflict that resulted from the Genevan party in the Church of England through the reign of Elizabeth I. Fed by their experiences of Protestant worship in exile in such centres as Frankfurt and Zurich during the reign of the Roman Catholic, Queen Mary Tudor (1553–1558), they rejected the Prayer Book's frequent use of the prayer, along with many other prac-tices. The Civil War in the following century brought to a head tensions that were about the monarchy, government and the

Church, leading to the abolition of episcopacy and the adoption of Prayer Book in both Scotland and England, and the *Westminster Directory* (1645) as the form of worship for both countries. After the Restoration of the monarchy with Charles II in 1660, the Prayer Book returns, with some revisions, in 1662.

As we have seen, the text of the Lord's Prayer was already in circulation in various vernacular versions. As the move towards an English Reformation gathered pace in the 1530s, expressed by Henry VIII's Act of Succession in 1534, two translations of the Bible appeared, one by William Tyndale (*c*.1494–1536) in 1534 and the other by Miles Coverdale (1487/8–1569) in 1536. Whereas Coverdale's translation was based on the Vulgate, Luther's German version and Tyndale's, Tyndale's version came from the Greek and Hebrew, relying on Erasmus's text of 1516. Tyndale, betrayed in Antwerp, paid with his life for translating the Scriptures. Coverdale, on the other hand, survived, because in 1538 Henry VIII bowed to pressure from the reforming party in the Church and ordered a Bible to be placed in every parish church. The version was the so-called 'Great Bible' (largely the work of Coverdale), which was not issued until the following year. The two translations of the Lord's Prayer are as follows:

| Tyndale (1534) | Coverdale (1536) (variants only) |
| --- | --- |
| Our Father who art in heaven | |
| Hallowed be thy name. | |
| Let thy kingdom come. | Thy kingdom come |
| Thy will be fulfilled | |
| As well in earth as it is in heaven. | Upon earth as it is in heaven |
| Give us this day our daily bread. | |
| And forgive us our trespasses, | And forgive us our debts, |
| Even as we forgive our trespassers. | As we forgive our debtors. |
| And lead us not into temptation: | |
| But deliver us from evil. | |
| For thine is the kingdom | |
| And the power, and the glory | |
| For ever. Amen. | |

(The 'Great Bible' (1539) has 'Let thy kingdom come' (as Tyndale), and the briefer 'thy will be done', but with Tyndale's 'as well in earth'.)

The versions show a remarkable similarity, the differences confined to the kingdom and the will petitions. But there is no single, agreed biblical translation, an issue that was to remain in the English-speaking world until 1611. We note the inclusion of the doxology, in the version that was to figure in the English translation of the 1560 Geneva Bible, and thereby gain usage in Scotland. However, the move from 'debts' (which was the commonest translation in later medieval versions) to 'trespasses' as in Tyndale's version was given a boost in three publications: *The Instruction of a Christian Man*, an unofficial publication (nicknamed 'The Bishops' Book') in 1537; in the 1538 *Primer* (unofficial book of devotion in the vernacular); and the public formulary *A Necessary Doctrine and Erudition for any Christian Man* (nicknamed 'The King's Book' because it was promulgated with royal authority) in 1543. The 'King's Book' was issued by Henry VIII as a way of countering the Protestant features of 'The Bishops' Book'. The version in the 'Bishop's Book' and the 1538 *Primer* reads, 'thy kingdom come *unto us*'. Both, however, had one line which Archbishop Thomas Cranmer (1489–1556) wanted to alter but which Henry refused to do – 'let us not be led' as the beginning of the temptation petition. Here, Henry showed his knowledge of the long tradition of interpretation of the Lord's Prayer stretching back to Augustine and the other North Africans, and his personal preference was for '*suffer* us not to be led'.[28]

'The Bishops' Book' and 'The King's Book' had their influence, the latter superseding the former in authority. They were not official service-books. But with the publication of *The Litany* (1544), we encounter for the first time an authorized Reformation service in English for the Church of England. But all we have is the opening of the prayer, 'Our Father, which art in heaven', and the conclusion, 'suffer us not to be led into temptation. [Henry's text] But deliver us from evil. Amen.' The musical version produced by John Merbecke in 1550 indicates that the final petition and the 'Amen' takes the form of a response by the congregation, thus adopting Catholic practice.[29] At this stage, we had the relatively new technology of printing, royal authority and the search for a lasting, liturgical version of the prayer that is not taken from one, single version of the Bible. It was not, however, until Henry had died (1547) and Edward VI was on the throne, that the first Prayer Book (1549) appeared, and at long last with the definitive version of the prayer, which was to become standard in many parts of the English-speaking world for centuries to come, and in which 'lead us not into temptation', Cranmer's preference, replaces Henry's 'suffer us not to be led':

> Our Father which art in heaven,
> Hallowed be thy name.
> Thy kingdom come.
> Thy will be done in earth,
> As it is in heaven.
> Give us this day our daily bread.
> And forgive us our trespasses,
> As we forgive them that trespass against us.
> And lead us not into temptation,
> But deliver us from evil. Amen.[30]

So much for the text – what of the context? As is so often the case, this is what provides the key to the use of the prayer. Unlike the Continental Reformers, Cranmer follows a more medieval approach. In the 1549–1552 Prayer Books, the Lord's Prayer appears in every service, and at the daily offices of Morning and Evening Prayer, and at Holy Communion it appears twice, once near the start (following medieval devotional practice), and once in the heart of the service; at the daily office at the beginning of the series of prayers following the Creed, and at Holy Communion, either in its traditional place, after the Consecration (in 1549), or straight after receiving communion (where it was moved in 1552). It also figures prominently at baptism (in 1549 before, and in 1552 immediately after, in line with the position adopted then at communion). Not only is Cranmer unique among the Reformers for the lavish provision he makes for the prayer, he is unique about the way it is recited. Medieval custom also lingered. In 1549 before communion the priest introduced the prayer ('As our Saviour Christ hath commanded and taught us, we are bold to say', from the Roman rite) and then recited (or chanted) it, the congregation coming in with 'the Answer', 'But deliver us from evil. Amen.' In 1552, however, congregational recitation of the prayer replaced this practice. Long ago, John Dowden tried to unravel Cranmer's complex directions. The people are supposed to say the prayer with the priest in the second position at daily prayer and communion 'repeating him after every petition', whereas the first recitation at the start is by the priest alone. In practice, this meant that on a Sunday morning, the congregation will have used the prayer in one way or another five times, if there was a communion (twice at Mattins, once in the litany, and twice at the eucharist), or, if there was no communion, four times, the first part of the eucharist being celebrated as 'Ante-Communion' on non-sacramental Sundays.[31]

What, however, of Cranmer's theology? Ashley Null in a recent study has shown how his soteriology had shifted as far back as 1532, during his time in Nuremberg, when he moved from a position that could be described as 'Erasmian Humanism' towards a Protestant Augustinianism that saw the redeemed human being's life of faith as primarily a response to a gift already given. Stephen Gardiner (*c*.1497–1535), Bishop of Winchester, who eventually came out against Cranmer, saw the difficulties in this position; he laid them at the door of the Lord's Prayer in a sermon preached at St Paul's Cross on the First Sunday in Lent 1540, in which he uses the petition for mutual forgiveness to illustrate differences between his own (Catholic) approach and that of Cranmer and the other English Reformers: whereas for Gardiner, forgiveness of those who have wronged us is like fasting, praying and weeping, and is part of our preparation for receiving divine forgiveness, according to the latter view, that forgiveness is the necessary fruit of having first been justified by God. Gardiner, as Null points out, trusted the will rather more than the Reformers, Cranmer included.[32] In his biography of Cranmer, Diarmaid MacCulloch has stripped much of the romantic rust that has been attached to his subject's theological persona over the years, and has revealed him as part of European Protestantism.[33] Conservative as Cranmer is over the use of the Lord's Prayer, he could be said to reflect a theological anthropology that underpins the doctrine of justification, whether in responding to absolution at the start of the daily offices, or to the sacramental gifts at baptism and communion. As we shall see, however, what Cranmer may or may not have thought is one thing: how his liturgical legacy was developed is another.

· Alongside these debates, a tradition of devotional and theological interpretation was already developing. William Tyndale wrote an exposition of the Sermon on the Mount in 1533 in which he interpreted the kingdom as a warning against rulers not to do anything contrary to God's word, daily bread as 'all manner of sustenance', and the doxology as an ascription of all power to God, with a protest against absolute power in secular rulers. Hugh Latimer (*c.*1485–1555), Bishop of Worcester, popular preacher and Marian martyr, delivered a series of seven pithy sermons in 1552, in which temptation and evil are drawn together; John Bradford (*c.*1510–1555), another Marian martyr, wrote extensively on prayer, producing a lengthy meditation and paraphrase; and the Catechism of Thomas Becon (1512–1567), Chaplain to Cranmer and a Canon of Canterbury in the reign of Elizabeth I, also contains a lengthy treatment.[34] All these expositions reflect the need for direct, devotional teaching, stressing the grace of God, and each one of them refers to evil as personal, although they vary over the shape of the prayer, Tyndale and Becon with seven petitions (following Augustine and Luther), Latimer and Bradford with six (the Eastern Fathers and Calvin); all of them (with the exception of Latimer, who provides his own at the conclusion of the last sermon) include the doxology in what was to become the 1662 Prayer Book form, 'for thine is the kingdom, the power and the glory, for ever and ever. Amen.'

After the reign of Mary Tudor (1553–1558), when the Prayer Book had been outlawed and England officially restored to the Papacy, returning exiles who had worshipped in the Reformed centres in Frankfurt and Switzerland found the Prayer Book as issued under Elizabeth I insufficiently Protestant. The Lord's Prayer was a case in point, for it touched upon the relationship between set and free prayer. English translations of the Geneva Bible (from the 'Breeches Bible' of 1560 onwards) translated Matthew 6:7 as 'when you pray use not vain repetitions', even though Theodore Beza (1519–1605), Calvin's successor at Geneva (and both Tyndale and Coverdale) translated it as 'babble ye not' (the consensus of New Testament scholarship today).[35] The two versions have different nuances; to babble is to speak incoherently, whereas vain repetitions could be taken as a thinly veiled attack on repeated set forms of prayer. To make matters more difficult, Geneva Bibles were printed with explanatory notes, often of a polemical kind. Next to this verse was printed, 'he commandeth us to beware of men babbling and superfluous repeats'; next to the prayer itself, 'Christ bindeth them not to the words, but to the sense, and form of prayer'; and next to the doxology, 'the conclusion excludeth man's merits and reacheth us to ground our prayers only on God'. In other words, there must be no repetition of prayers, the Lord's Prayer is not a set liturgical text but a guide to prayer, and the doxology is about ensuring that we do not rely on any human institution or human merit. All this is carefully expressed Protestant polemic.

There is a clash here between what the Prayer Book enjoined and what popular Calvinists wanted. It centres on the difference between the Lord's Prayer as traditionally used (and now adapted, in vernacular translation) in the Prayer Book, and Calvin's view of it as a quotation from Scripture that should serve as a guide to how we should pray. Things came to a head in 1572 with the two *Admonitions to Parliament*, which were followed by an acrimonious dispute between Thomas Cartwright (1535–1603), a leading reformist, and John Whitgift (*c*.1532–1604), at the time Cambridge professor and later Archbishop of Canterbury. The 'Admonitioners' wanted more than a Genevan use of the Lord's Prayer; they were after the abolition of episcopacy and a fully fledged Genevan service-book. There also developed a more radical wing from a younger generation of 'Independents' (later to become Congregationalists), such as

Henry Barrow (*c*.1550–1593) and John Penry (1559–1593), who refused to use the prayer at all, and who were hanged for their religious views in consequence. The tradition lived on in figures such as John Robinson (*c*.1575–1625), and John Smyth (*c*.1570–1612), who went to Amsterdam and who was in effect the pastor of the first Baptist Church. In his *Pattern of True Prayer* (1605), Smyth writes lyrically on the Lord's Prayer; 'I had rather speak five words to God in prayer from understanding, faith and feeling, than say the Lord's Prayer over a thousand times ignorantly, negligently or superstitiously.'[36]

Before we look at other writers, however, the tale of the Lord's Prayer through the next century needs to be told. The main result of the Hampton Court Conference held at the start of James I's reign in 1604 was not a revision of the Prayer Book that would pacify its critics but the publication of a royally promulgated translation of the Bible in 1611. The Authorized Version avoided the margin notes of the Genevan Bible, which were said to cause irritation both to Elizabeth I and to King James, but opted for 'vain repetitions' at Matthew 6:7, 'debts' and 'debtors' (as Coverdale and the Geneva Bible at Matthew 6:12), and the doxology in the version 'thine is the kingdom and the power and the glory for ever' (as both Tyndale, Coverdale, the Great and Geneva Bibles); this was also the version used by Knox in the 1564 *Book of Common Order*. In 1619, a hybrid Genevan version of the Prayer Book was issued for use in Scotland in which the Lord's Prayer appears under royal pressure in the Prayer Book version but only once, at Morning Prayer (in the earlier position), and with the doxology; it does not come in any other service, except in the catechism, which precedes Confirmation; communion, when celebrated, would follow Morning Prayer.[37] Charles I's far less successful attempt to provide a set liturgy for the northern kingdom came in 1637, with the attempted imposition of a Prayer Book on the Kirk, one of the events which gave rise to the start of the Civil War; the doxology is now added to both recitations at Morning Prayer, at Evening Prayer, and before Communion, where it is to come in the traditional position, as in the 1549 Prayer Book, with the introductory words,

'As our Saviour Christ hath commanded and taught us . . . '[38] The 1645 *Westminster Directory*, however, takes a much more restrictive and Genevan line, permitting the prayer's use in connection with the intercession following the sermon, 'because the Prayer which Christ taught his Disciples is not only a Pattern of Prayer, but itself a most comprehensive Prayer, we recommend it also to be used in the Prayers of the Church'.[39] When we come finally to the 1662 Prayer Book, the number of times the prayer is to be used is the same as before (but with its insertion, appropriately, in the Confirmation Service). However, critics are heeded in two ways; there is a trend away from directing the people to recite it clause by clause after the priest, and the doxology is added at the end of the first recitation at the daily offices, and after communion. But whereas Cranmer's Collects that refer to God with the relative pronoun 'which' are changed to 'who' in order to keep up with movement in language, conservatism over the Lord's Prayer leaves the text intact, with 'Our Father, *which* art in heaven'.[40]

What are we to make of these conflicts and changes? Richard Hooker (*c*.1554–1600) in his *Laws of Ecclesiastical Polity*, the fifth volume of which was published in 1598, was put in the position of having to defend against Genevan enthusiasts many of the Prayer Book practices, including the complex ways of reciting the prayer, which in the end did not stand the test of time. Among the points made against the Prayer Book was the fact that only a third of prayers seem to be about earthly benefits, to which Hooker retorts that 'our Saviour in his platform (i.e. the Sermon on the Mount) hath appointed but one petition amongst seven' – referring to daily bread. He sees the function of the prayer either as an introduction ('as a guide') or a conclusion ('as a complement which fully perfecteth whatsoever may be defective in the rest'). He vigorously defends its use after communion, 'when together we have all received those heavenly mysteries wherein Christ imparteth himself unto us, and giveth visible testification of our blessed communion with them'.[41] Just as influential at the time in England, as Spinks has shown, was William Perkins (1558–1602), a popular preacher at Cambridge, whose views were more overtly Calvinist; near the start of his treatise on the Lord's Prayer, he follows Calvin in six petitions and the doxology; he opts for the Augustinian view of evil as a force, though he is aware of the Greek interpretation; and he virtually quotes the margin note of the Geneva Bible when he states that 'Christ is not to bind us to the words'.[42]

It is in the sermons of Lancelot Andrewes (1555–1626) that we find perhaps the fullest treatment at the time. Published in 1611, the same year as the Authorized Version (in which he took a prominent part over the first books of the Old Testament), Andrewes' nineteen sermons read more simply than the elaborate Court Sermons for which he is famous.[43] By this time Bishop of Ely, he was a regular preacher in the presence of King James. His sermons combine profound biblical scholarship and pastoral sensitivity. The first eight are introductory, following a pattern we have already seen with many writers, in which he defends the use of a set text; for example, he remarks (Sermon 6) that 'if a man did make a prayer, he would begin at daily bread; but Christ in this prayer teacheth us "first to seek the kingdom of God"'. The uniqueness of the prayer is expressed (Sermon 7) when he describes it as 'the prayer of charity', because it is Christ's, in contrast to all others, which are, 'the prayers of nature'.

Andrewes is aware of the prayer's shape, regarding the first (hallowing the name) as about God alone, and the remaining six about us, a new structure of which the first three concern what is good (kingdom, will, bread), and the remaining three (forgiveness, temptation, deliverance) are about removing evil from us; here he adapts Luther's approach, following Albert the Great. Of the heavenly Father, he insists (Sermon 8) that 'there must be an imitation, and we must set ourselves forward to our heavenly country'. Hallowing the name (Sermon 9) 'arises from the duty which man oweth unto Him', rather than God being 'desirous of any vainglory'. Like Calvin, he distinguishes (Sermon 11) between the will of God that we may resist (the short term) and that which we cannot resist (the long term). Daily bread (Sermon 13) is not eucharistic; but he distinguishes between the Latin *quotidianum*, as daily, the Greek, *epiousion*, as 'apt and meet for our substance', the Syriac, meaning for our necessity, and the Hebrew, meaning in due season; and, as usual with Andrewes, it means all four. When it comes to the last three petitions, he distinguishes between past evil (our sins), future evil (temptation), and the last evil of all (eternal punishment). At the start of Sermon 17, he summarizes the best of Western reflection on the final two petitions by suggesting that 'when we pray that we be not led into temptation, we desire that we do no evil; when we pray that we may be delivered from evil, our desire is that we may suffer no evil': aware of the differences between East (Chrysostom) and West (Augustine), Andrewes (like Perkins) opts for Augustine's approach as offering 'the most enlarged meaning'. Sermon 18 draws the Trinity into the doxology, where Christ's is the kingdom, the Spirit has the power, and the Father the glory. These sermons have many echoes of Andrewes' private devotions (the 'Preces Privatae'),[44] which also contain short paraphrases on the prayer; in one of them, there is a veiled reference to the eucharist under 'daily bread' – 'give what things are for health, peace, sufficiency; give angels' food unto eternal salvation'.

Some of this is echoed in *The Great Exemplar* of Jeremy Taylor (1613–1667), the first devotional life of Christ in English, published in 1649, the year of Charles I's execution. The 'Discourse on Prayer', which probably started life as a sermon, has a stronger emphasis on our freedom in relation to the will of God than either Luther or Calvin; 'the bread of our necessity' (the Syriac interpretation) is also 'a bread which came down from heaven, a diviner nutriment of our souls, the food and wine of angels'. In 1685, Thomas Ken (1637–1711) as Bishop of Bath and Wells wrote his *Exposition on the Church Catechism*, in which he likewise alludes to earthly and spiritual needs, and includes 'the bread of life, the bread that came down from heaven, the body and blood of thy most blessed Son, to feed our souls to life eternal'. The eucharist is slowly returning to the daily bread.

But what of the shape of the prayer? Taylor follows Calvin with a sixfold scheme but brings a fresh perspective. 'In the first petition ("hallowed by thy Name") the soul puts on the affections of a child, and divests itself of its own interest, offering itself up wholly to the designs and glorifications of God. In the second ("thy Kingdom come") it puts on the relations and duty of a subject to her legitimate Prince, seeking the promotion of his regal interest. In the third ("thy will be done . . .") it puts on the affection of a spouse, loving the same love and choosing the same objects; delighting in unions and conformities.' When it comes to the second part of the prayer, Taylor writes as follows:

> In these last petitions, which concern ourselves, the soul hath affections proper to her own needs; as in the former proportion, to God's glory (cf. Calvin). In the first of these ('give us today') the affection of a poor indigent and necessitous beggar; in the second ('forgive . . .') of a delinquent and penitent servant; and in the last ('lead us not . . .') the person in affliction or danger.[45]

Seventeenth-century literature abounds in devotional and expository material on the Lord's Prayer, demonstrating the gradual evolution of a distinctively Anglican approach, typified by Andrewes himself, with the influences of both Luther and Calvin, as well as a ready sympathy with the (regularly quoted) Fathers of the Church. Many of them were more Calvinist in their theology, such as Henry King (1592–1669), Bishop of Chichester, who preached a course of eleven sermons at St Paul's Cathedral some time between 1623 and 1628, and the lengthy exposition by one of the Westminster Assembly divines, Thomas Watson (†1686).[46] But one of the most influential was the Catechism of Henry Hammond (1605–1660), published *c*.1644, and which, in spite of its critique of the Commonwealth religious settlement, went into many subsequent editions. Hammond distinguishes between the 'prayer of the heart, and of the tongue', discusses head-on the question of 'vain repetitions', in which he defends set forms of prayers, and (following Calvin) divides the prayer into six petitions, but works out a many-layered series of meanings, including for daily bread and evil (personal as well as impersonal); and he assumes the use of the doxology, fully aware of Jewish (and Greek) liturgical practice.[47]

## Conclusion

The three centuries which make up this creative but turbulent era see many changes as well as continuities:

- Roman Catholicism retains the prayer in the same positions in the liturgy as in the late Middle Ages, but in the Catechism of the Council of Trent tacitly shelves the elaborate sevenfold schemes of the preceding centuries.

- The Reformation draws the prayer into vernacular liturgical use, with lively debate about its function. In the teaching of Luther and Calvin, both of them reliant (positively as well as negatively) on patristic and medieval predecessors, it achieves another kind of central place.

- For Luther, followed by Cranmer, it remains at the heart of liturgical worship, in Luther's case illuminated by an array of teaching that could be described as 'liturgical theology', in the best traditions of the Eastern and Western Fathers, which is paralleled, too, in such seventeenth-century Anglican writers as Lancelot Andrewes, Jeremy Taylor and Henry Hammond.

- In Calvin, we have the systematic theologian whose writings on this prayer could be as appropriately read in meditation as in study. The sevenfold structure of Augustine, so carefully worked out through the Middle Ages, and already under strain in such writers as Albert the Great and Thomas Aquinas, heaves under Theodoric of Paderborn, and finally breaks down under Calvin's expert treatment.

- At the Reformation, old East, with its ancient tongues, meets new West; and the time-honoured consensus gives way to a fragmented scene of theological, devotional and liturgical reconstruction. In comparative terms, Cranmer's position for the Lord's Prayer immediately after baptism is paralleled in the East in *Apostolic Constitutions* VII, John Chrysostom preaching in Constantinople in 399, and Armenian practice; and his position after communion is paralleled in the East Syrian liturgy.

- A powerful ally of centralization, Roman Catholic, Protestant, Anglican, is the technology of printing, which helps to disseminate not only vernacular translations of the Bible (e.g. Tyndale, Coverdale, Geneva), and official teaching of the Church (Council of Trent Catechism), but also service books (Book of Common Prayer, Book of Common Order, Missal).

- In the end, the 'text' continues to assert itself in new 'context', with unresolved issues of translation, and a rich variety of teaching, not least about its shape; followers of Augustine and Luther (like Andrewes) opt for seven petitions, followers of much of the East and Calvin (like Hammond and Taylor) opt for six; and evil is personal (Tyndale and Taylor) or impersonal (Luther, Perkins, Andrewes and Roman Catholics), or both (Calvin and Hammond). A mark of the seventeenth-century Anglican writers is their use of a Calvinist framework, with a patristic approach to the prayer's liturgical function.

- The text, however, divides between the liturgical, which has to have some stability in order to sustain its own memory, and the versions in the various Bible translations. This issue is to become more acute in the late twentieth century.

What, finally, of musical settings? Martin Luther adapted the medieval chant for a liturgy where music was, and still is, central. John Merbecke, as we have seen, adapted the chant further for the Prayer Book in 1550. Polyphonic settings, however, had begun to appear in the Catholic Church, with such composers as Josquin Desprez in the fifteenth century and Palestrina in the sixteenth, effectively turning the prayer into a motet, a tradition that continued with Jacob Handl in the seventeenth. The English choral tradition produced versions of the Prayer Book texts that were used at the daily offices, such as those by John Stone (with the Henrician 'let us not be led') and John Sheppard in the seventeenth century; but the late Elizabethan composer John Farmer wrote a setting of a metrical text of the prayer which was probably originally intended as a motet as well. Polyphony embraces divergent traditions, and once again, text and context continue to intertwine.

# 8

# Into Modernity and Beyond

The period from the eighteenth century to the present day is far more disparate than the preceding three centuries. It would be foolish to pretend to be able to offer anything approaching a comprehensive picture of how the Lord's Prayer was used and expounded in the various Christian churches. The explosion of ideas instanced by the Western Reformation placed the prayer under a spotlight it had not hitherto experienced. Some of these changes built on inherited patterns, such as Calvin's attraction to the paraphrase tradition, which in the later Middle Ages had been an important aspect of private devotion, and which now became the substance of his liturgy; but, as we saw with John Knox in Scotland, the prayer survived into liturgical use. We shall see that conservatism increase in the Reformed tradition, with a ready acceptance of the prayer's hold on public worship. Lutherans remained specially attached to the prayer as a central feature of piety and worship, which is explored by such different figures as Nikolai Grundtvig in nineteenth-century Denmark and Helmut Thielicke preaching in Stuttgart during the bombing raids at the end of the Second World War. The 'Radical' Reformation tradition experiences changes, with the popular Baptist Charles Spurgeon preaching from the prayer in nineteenth-century England.

Many of our authors and preachers have been aware of the issues of interpretation in the prayer, which go beyond questions of the meaning of *epiousion*, temptation, and whether the doxology should be there or not. Every age and tradition has left its own particular stamp on the prayer. As we shall see, the abiding fruits of biblical scholarship in the twentieth century have been a proper attention to the eschatological focus of the prayer, which Karl Barth thought both Luther and Calvin underplayed;[1] the Jewish setting and wider biblical background of the prayer; and the care that should be taken over questions of translation.

Are there any discernible shifts in this period? Selection of material has been difficult enough hitherto; it now becomes virtually impossible. Leonardo Boff in Latin America and Alexander Schmemann broadcasting into the Soviet Union can walk side by side with Evelyn Underhill in England and Dietrich Bonhoeffer in Germany. But while each writer retains something of the 'flavour' of their tradition, there is a discernible move towards consensus over the prayer's use, and the need for agreement among and between churches on new translations becomes an issue, in the light of the liturgical changes during the latter part of the twentieth century. After the Second Vatican Council, the Roman Catholic Church at last abandons recitation of the prayer by the priest only, and adds the doxology, spurred on by ecumenical concerns, which (most radical of all) now permit their own people to pray the Lord's Prayer with non-Roman Catholics; Anglicans move towards a single recitation of the prayer at each service, invariably with the doxology; and the prayer has a fully accepted life in most parts of the Reformed tradition. The increasingly secular context of many of the churches in the West has its signs of renewal (an increasing emphasis on baptism and baptismal catechesis, with the new version) as well as its survivals (Church of England bishops leading the prayer, in its traditional version, each day in the House of Lords).

## The eighteenth century

Like every century we have so far seen, the eighteenth century is a mixture, and is certainly, in England at least, not the caricature of a dull, rationalist era from which Norman Sykes rescued it some time ago.[2] The conflicts of the preceding century produced something of a reaction; but the scene is more varied, as the four English figures will show, and there was some marginal interest in the ancient liturgies, leading in some quarters to pressure towards restoring the prayer to its patristic position in the eucharist, before communion, instead of afterwards.

First, Susanna Hopton (1627–1709), who was married to a Welsh judge, and who was able to return with him to England at the Restoration, wrote a number of devotional works. But because she was a woman, this had to be done pseudonymously. In her *Collection of Devotions*, published eight years after her death, we see something of the love of tradition of much seventeenth-century Anglican writing, the searching quality of the eighteenth century's quest for 'reasonable belief', as well as the innate gifts of a woman. Her lengthy devotion 'On the Lord's Prayer' is a paraphrase, in the style of the medieval and Reformation compositions, and reads like a female, Anglican version of Francis de Sales. Her opening reflections on the heavenly Father are worth quoting in full:

*Our Father which art in heaven.*

O My Father, tender in love, tender in thy care and providence over me, all-sufficient in thy power and provisions for me, and so to everyone, and the more so by being so unto us all. Blessed be thy name, that commanding us by thy Son to say *Our Father*, thou dost thereby knit us all together in thee, and makest us all Brethren unto thy Son, and to all saints, angels, and men, rich and poor, in thee. Most holy Father, I depend on thee, I trust in thee, I believe on thee. O do thou support, sustain, and provide for me in all things. Make me tender of thine honour, obedient to thy will, and in all things a dutiful child, and be thou pleased to continue a most merciful and gracious Father unto me, who, though thou art everywhere by thy presence, yet hast thy residence more especially in heaven, and because thou wouldest have me heavenly-minded when I call upon thee, commandest me to call thee *heavenly Father*. O my dear *heavenly Father*, I do lift up my heart unto thee to give me heavenly affections when I call upon thee. Fill, I beseech thee, my understanding with light, and my soul with love, that as the angels in heaven do hallow thy name, and pray it may be hallowed by all, so I may both with them hallow it, and fervently pray with the angels' petition: *Hallowed be thy name.*[3]

Her emphasis is, as one would expect with a personal prayer, on redemption rather than creation; as in the rest of the paraphrase, there is a confident contrast between the weak human being and the loving Father; and she also combines a strong sense of union with the angels and the need for 'understanding' and 'light', two eighteenth-century virtues. There are six petitions (following Calvin and Taylor) and evil is impersonal.

Thomas Wilson (1663–1755) was a prolific writer and Bishop of Sodor and Man from 1697 until his death fifty-eight years later. During that time, he vigorously encouraged church life, and in 1707 published his *Principles and Duties of Christianity*, which effectively became the first Manx Catechism; he took an (unusual) interest in the Moravian Church, with its stress on fellowship and witness. He had his own collection of personal devotions, published posthumously in 1781 as *Sacra Privata*, which contains no fewer than nine paraphrases on the Lord's Prayer, a sure sign of his attachment to it. Usually sprinkled liberally with biblical quotations, nearly all have the doxology, and two either use or suggest 'debts' as a variant at the petition for forgiveness.[4] They bring us close to the devotional mind of a learned cleric and missionary bishop, as his thoughts on 'thy kingdom come' in the second paraphrase show:

Establish thy kingdom in my heart, O God. I own thee for my king; do thou make and own me for thy faithful subject. Grant that by my ministry thy kingdom may be enlarged: – that I may be thy subject out of choice, and ever yield thee willing obedience. Inflame my heart with an hearty desire of enlarging thy kingdom. Increase thy flock, O great shepherd, for the honour of thy great name. May I preserve thy kingdom within me, the government of thy Spirit. Bring me into subjection to thyself, by thy grace.

We see here a number of strands: devotional submissiveness, ministerial dedication, missionary zeal, and the tradition, explicit in some of the Eastern Fathers, starting with Gregory of Nyssa, and implicit in Luther and Calvin, of identifying the kingdom with the work of the Spirit, and throughout all the texts, following Taylor, 'daily bread' is regarded as 'the bread of necessity'. Like Hopton, there are six petitions (usually), and evil is interpreted impersonally.

A different wind blows through what John Wesley (1703–1791) has to preach in 1748 on the Sermon on the Mount.[5] A classic Wesley sermon, it represents much of the inclusive evangelicalism associated with him. Wesley was brought up with his brother, Charles, in Epworth Rectory, near Lincoln, and in 1726 went to Oxford as a student, where he helped form a 'holy club', nicknamed 'Methodists' after their strict rule of life. Twelve years later, he underwent a conversion experience at a meeting in London, and thereafter committed himself to a life of itinerant preaching, often outdoors, to reach the unchurched. The tensions between his organization and the Church of England came to a head when in 1784 he ordained Thomas Coke as 'superintendent' of the growing Methodist community in the United States of America.

The Sermon is an exposition of Matthew 6:1–15, which therefore sets the Lord's Prayer within its biblical context, as one would expect of a series on the Sermon on the Mount; Augustine, John Chrysostom and Martin Luther took a similar approach. Near the start, Wesley strikes a common note in his preaching – 'purity of intention', which he took from the *devotio moderna* represented by Thomas à Kempis. For Wesley, and also for writers such as Thomas Ken in the seventeenth century, 'right intention' is central not only to all praying but all faithful living, and he goes on to assert that 'purity of intention is equally destroyed by a view to any temporal reward whatever'; this, like many of the points made in the rest of the sermon, is echoed in his *Explanatory Notes Upon the New Testament*, first published seven years later in 1755, where he speaks of 'the language of the heart'. On 'vain repetitions' he sides (gently) with those critical of set texts, although Wesley's liturgical project amounted to a simplification (not a curtailment) of the Prayer Book;[6] 'do not use abundance of words without any meaning . . . The thing here reproved is not simply the length, no more than the shortness of our prayers.' He defines the prayer in terms that go back to the Fathers – 'there is nothing which we have need to ask God, nothing which we can ask without offending him, which is not included either directly or indirectly in this comprehensive form'. And he describes it in terms of 'the preface, the petitions, and the doxology or conclusion', like many seventeenth-century writers following Calvin and much of the East, in identifying six (not seven) petitions.

The heavenly Father is 'Creator' and 'Preserver', the God of all creation – 'uncreated night', an expression he is fond of, which has been identified from a metrical version of Psalm 46 (author unknown) in a letter from John to his brother Charles in 1726.[7] The hallowing of the name takes us into 'his Trinity in Unity and Unity in Trinity'; the kingdom 'comes to a particular person when he "repents and believes the gospel" (Mark 1:15)'; his eschatological point of reference is a direct quotation from the Prayer Book Burial Office, in the prayer for the kingdom in all its fullness ('beseeching thee . . . shortly to accomplish the number of thine elect, and to hasten thy kingdom'). The will is done both 'willingly' and 'perfectly' by the angels, not grudgingly, or heroically. Daily bread is 'a supply for our own wants' as well as 'the things pertaining to life and godliness'. Forgiveness is about letting go of a debt or loosening a bond, as sin 'has no dominion over those who "are under grace" (Romans 6:14, 15)'. He follows Calvin, but in gentler vein, over temptation and deliverance; temptation can cover people 'as a cloud' (suggesting confusion and deceit), but 'those who are the children of God by faith are delivered' out of the devil's hands. Following the Authorized Version, and well-established Anglican practice, Wesley includes the doxology, but even though the sermon is based on the Bible, he uses the Prayer Book doxology, rather than the 1611 version. There is an unusual realistic optimism about this sermon, a note struck by the 'creation soteriology' of its opening. The concluding paragraph on the doxology, in which Wesley shows that his understanding of the kingdom is universal, and not limited to any particular group, is as follows:

> The conclusion of this divine prayer, commonly called the doxology, is a solemn thanksgiving, a compendious acknowledgment of the attributes and works of God. 'For thine is the kingdom' – the sovereign right of all things that are or ever were created; yea, thy kingdom is an everlasting kingdom, and thy dominion endureth throughout all ages. 'The power' – the executive power whereby thou governest all things in thy everlasting kingdom, whereby thou dost whatsoever pleaseth thee, in all places of thy dominion. 'And the glory' – the praise due from every creature for thy power, and the mightiness of thy kingdom, and for all thy wondrous works which thou workest from everlasting, and shalt do, world without end, 'for ever and ever! Amen'. So be it!

In true Wesley fashion, a nine-stanza metrical version of the prayer is appended to the sermon, which follows each of the petitions in turn. The fifth stanza reflects on the doing of the will; it invokes the Spirit and has a wider vision than many of the expositions we have so far seen:

> Spirit of grace, and health, and power,
>   Fountain of light and love below,
> Abroad thine healing influence shower,
>   O'er all the nations let it flow.
> Inflame our hearts with perfect love,
>   In us the work of faith fulfil;
> So not heaven's hosts shall swifter move
>   Than we on earth to do thy will.[8]

The *Lectures on the Catechism* by Thomas Secker (1693–1768) take us from the world of prayer into direct teaching. Before studying at Oxford, Secker took a doctorate in medicine at Leiden in 1721; Bishop of Bristol in 1735 and Oxford in 1737, he was made Archbishop of Canterbury in 1758. Secker admired Methodists, though he suspected some of their enthusiastic excesses. Not in the same league as Wesley as a preacher or thinker, he has something of the 'sobriety' of much Anglicanism of the time. Three of these lectures concern the Lord's Prayer, which he sees as consisting of six petitions, with evil (unusually) as personal, and he includes the doxology.[9] In dealing with the coming of the kingdom, he distinguishes between 'this natural kingdom' and 'a moral and spiritual one, founded on the willing obedience of reasonable creatures to those laws of righteousness, which he hath given them'; he makes a distinction between 'our temporal wants' (daily bread) and 'our spiritual ones' (forgiveness), which are more important, because 'our pardoning others is no more than a qualification, requisite to our receiving that final pardon from God'. Secker's aim is to combine the gospel of grace with reasonable belief.

The eighteenth century saw a remarkable divergence of liturgical practice. This includes the following: the decline of the prayer in the Kirk; Baptists who rarely used the prayer, even at baptism itself; Anglican Evangelicals like Samuel Walker (1714–1761), who simplified the Prayer Book services in his Truro parish, with the Lord's Prayer only once, after the confession at morning service. The Scottish Episcopal liturgy was remodelled in 1764 along patristic lines, with a full eucharistic prayer followed by the intercession, leading into the Lord's Prayer, with 'who art' instead of 'which art', a sign of things to come; much of this (but not the change of words at the beginning) bore fruit in the 1789 Book of Common Prayer of the Episcopal Church in the United States. Perhaps one of the most influential – in the longer term – of all customs was iconography. Seventeenth-century parish churches in England frequently had their east ends decorated with panels on which the Decalogue was painted; in the eighteenth, these often became triptychs, with the Lord's Prayer and Creed on either side. Such a use of iconography must have had a considerable cumulative effect on generations of worshippers, and also formed something of a contrast to the art of the medieval period.[10]

## The nineteenth century

The nineteenth is sometimes regarded as the century of the Romantic Movement, following on from the Enlightenment of the eighteenth. While the two merge in and out of each other, the Romantic Movement brought a greater sense of confidence about the past (particularly the medieval and ancient past) as creative legacies both in art and theology. It also helped to draw together thinking and feeling, so that emotion could be seen as revelatory about the human condition.[11] In the four different examples we shall be looking at, the prayer continues to meet new questions and new situations.

John Keble (1792–1866), after several years as a don at Oriel College, Oxford, was Vicar of Hursley, near Winchester, from 1836 until his death thirty years later. He was one of the leading lights of the Tractarian Movement, cooperating with John Henry Newman (before he became a Roman Catholic) and others in writing some of the 'Tracts for the Times'. He exemplifies many of the features of the Tractarians, a deep love of the fullness of Anglican tradition, both in itself and as part of the whole Church Catholic. In his *Sermons, Academical and Occasional*, put together after Newman's conversion in 1845 in order to reassure wavering Anglicans of their Church's authenticity as a 'branch' of the Catholic Church, he concluded the preface with a short litany-paraphrase on the Lord's Prayer.[12] This devotional gem epitomizes many of the aspirations of the 'Catholic Revival' of Anglicanism in alerting Christians to their wider inheritance, and the imperative not to acquiesce in disunity. It is a harbinger of the ecumenical movement of the following century.

– Our Father, which art in heaven: One God, the Father Almighty, One Lord Jesus Christ, One Holy Ghost, proceeding from the Father and the Son; have mercy upon us, thy children, and make us all One in thee.
– Hallowed be thy name: Thou who art One Lord, and thy name One; have mercy upon us all, who are called by thy name, and make us more and more One in Thee.

- Thy kingdom come: O King of righteousness and peace, gather us more and more into thy kingdom, and make us both visibly and invisibly One in thee.
- Thy will be done in earth, as it is in heaven: Thou declared unto us the mystery of thy will, to 'gather together in One all things in Christ, both which are in heaven and which are on earth'; conform us, O Lord, to that holy will of thine, and make us all One in thee.
- Give us this day our daily bread: Thou in whom we being many are One bread and One body; grant that we, being all partakers of that one bread, may day by day be more One in thee.
- And forgive us our trespasses as we forgive them that trespass against us: Thou, who didst say, *Father, forgive them,* for those who were rending thy blessed body, forgive us the many things we have done to mar the unity of thy mystical body, and make us, forgiving and loving one another, to be more and more One in thee.
- And lead us not into temptation: As thou didst enable thine apostles to continue with thee in thy temptations; so enable us, by thy grace, to abide with thee in thy true Church, under all trials, visible and invisible, nor ever to cease from being One in thee.
- But deliver us from evil: from the enemy and false accuser; from envy and grudging; from an unquiet and discontented spirit; from heresy and schism; from strife and debate; from a scornful temper, and reliance on our own understanding; from offence given or taken; and from whatever might disturb thy Church, and cause it to be less One in thee: Good Lord, deliver and preserve thy servants forever.

There is much here: invocation of the Trinity; the repeated address to Christ; the explicit reference to the eucharist (and nothing else) in daily bread; the temptation to give up on the Church; the catalogue of evils, inspired by the 'deprecations' in the Prayer Book Litany – 'from all evil and mischief . . . Good Lord, deliver us' and doubtless, too, the embolism prayer, not used in Anglican worship; and above all, the repeated prayer for union in Christ, which is the context of Keble's message at this point, and a theme dear to his heart. Keble has turned the ecumenical imperative which is the Lord's own prayer (cf. John 17:20) into an eloquent but concise prayer of personal devotion and intercession, within a Trinitarian framework. It belongs to no particular age, except that there is a medieval flavour to its overall setting; and one notes the Augustinian seven petitions, with evil as impersonal. Although Keble preached a series of thirty-three sermons on baptism during his parish ministry, not once does he deal with the Lord's Prayer, for that belongs to the whole Church.[13]

What, then, of sermons? F. D. Maurice (1805–1872) was born in Lowestoft, the son of a Unitarian minister, who joined the Church of England as an adult, along with his mother and siblings, but unlike them, he was not able to embrace Calvinist Evangelicalism. Maurice is difficult to label for he was strongly loyal to the Prayer Book and to social reform. As Chaplain to Lincoln's Inn (one of the 'Inns of Court') from 1846 until 1860 while holding a chair at King's College, London, he was enabled for a time to have a rich but unrestricting preaching ministry. Because of his liberal views, he was deprived of the professorship in 1853, but was given a Cambridge chair in 1866.

It is no coincidence that Maurice should have decided to preach a course of sermons on nine successive Sunday afternoons in the spring of 1848, for it was a time of revolution in Europe. On 23 February, the Wednesday before the third of these sermons, the barricades went up in Paris, Louis Philippe abdicating the next day, and the Second Republic was declared; first thing on the morning of Sunday 27th, Louis Napoleon left Charing Cross Station, London, for Paris, eventually arriving the next day. On 12 January, there had been a revolt in Palermo; on 18 March the Croat troops of the Austro-Hungarian Empire were expelled from Milan; and on 10 April, the day after the last of these sermons, a 'Chartist' demonstration took place in London, for which F. D. Maurice (unsuccessfully) volunteered himself as a special constable.

These sermons are therefore charged with an atmosphere of uncertainty and a conviction in the immutability of the King of heaven, as well as the increasing need to apply the gospel in a society that was, in the cities, increasingly alienated from the churches in general, and the Church of England in particular. In many ways, Maurice is one of the first thinkers to try to confront secularism in its early stages. His sermons are not always easy to follow, but they contain some fine passages. In Sermon 1 he remarks: 'the Paternoster . . . may be committed to memory quickly, but it is slowly learnt by heart'. Of the hallowing of the name (Sermon 2), he says, 'upon our thoughts of God it will depend, in one time or another, whether we rise higher or sink lower as society and as individuals' – preached on the Sunday after the Paris revolution, and doubtless with the events in France in 1789 in mind. Of the kingdom (Sermon 3) he says that 'we have reached this petition of the Lord's Prayer at a time which would seem to give it special emphasis and significance'. The doing of the will (Sermon 4) provokes the observation that 'the Cross is at once the complete utterance of the Prayer and the answer to it' – following Christ is costly.

The petition for bread (Sermon 5) enables him to ease any harsh sense of obligation with the thought that 'we may be very slow in listening to calls on duty, and the reason may be that we regard Him who calls us an Exactor, not a Giver'. On forgiveness (Sermon 6, for which he uses Matthew's 'debts') he remarks, 'Yes, debts are trespasses: we have not only forfeited an obligation, but committed a sin: we have broken a law which was not formed on earth, and cannot be repealed on earth. But at this point of despair hope begins.' Of temptation (Sermon 7), Maurice sees the hand of God: 'praying so, that which seemed to be poison becomes medicine; all circumstances are turned to good; honey is gathered out of the carcass; death itself is made the minister of life'. More direct still on deliverance from evil, seen as personal (Sermon 8) he says: 'I will pray in the certainty that He is maintaining a conflict with the self-will which is the curse and dislocation of the world, and that every plague, pestilence, insurrection, revolution, is a step in the history of that conflict, tending towards the final victory.' And the doxology (Sermon 9) enables him to ascribe all glory to God alone.

Later in 1848, in a course of sermons on the Prayer Book, Maurice took the opportunity (again on the Lord's Prayer) to remark that 'Churches were not built as signs of exclusion, but of reconciliation'. Here is an ecclesiology somewhat distant from the 'Church = Kingdom' of some of the Catholic exponents of the prayer in preceding centuries. For Maurice, ecclesiology was given in reality but provisional in its application as a witness to the kingdom. He was determined not to let any of his congregations overlook the events of the day; and yet perhaps his preaching is able to leap out of its 1848 context, in order to address another fragile age.

We now move to the preaching of Nikolai Grundtvig (1783–1872) in Denmark. There can be few countries where a pastor achieved a reputation for pioneering new forms of education (the 'Folk High Schools'); for delving into the nation's past (he studied manuscripts of the Anglo-Saxon *Beowulf* in the British Museum on a scholarship from the Danish King); and for writing 1,583 hymns. However, his reputation was hard-built: distinguished theological student, he fought the rationalism of the time, insisting on a proper Lutheran renunciation of evil in the baptism service when there was pressure to remove it. The bulk of his career was spent (from 1839 until his death) at the Vartov Hospital, Copenhagen, where, like Maurice at Lincoln's Inn, he was able to develop a wider preaching ministry unencumbered by parochial constraints. Grundtvig is in some ways as difficult to label as Maurice. He is both a traditional Lutheran and a very contemporary man; he loves history and has a wide vision of the Church Catholic, and yet he is very Danish. For Grundtvig, like a good Lutheran, the Lord's Prayer was central to the Christian's life, because of its central place in the liturgy. He wrote several metrical versions; the best-known in Denmark are those which allude to the prayer in the context of faith in general and baptism in particular. But he only preached once on it, on the 15th Sunday after Trinity, 1851, on the Gospel for the day (Matthew 6:24–34).

Grundtvig begins by drawing attention to the tension in a life centred on trying to 'serve two masters', and from there moves towards the Lord's Prayer (in Danish referred to in one word, *Fadervor*, easily used in his hymnody in consequence). For him, the *Fadervor* is not only the focus but the means whereby this tension can be dealt a blow, exposed for what it is, and the Christian enabled to look towards the heavenly Father. To seek the kingdom of God and his righteousness means the baptismal movement away from the false world of delusion to the real world of God. True to the spirit of Luther, Grundtvig emphasizes that it is Christ who prays the prayer; in some respects, Grundtvig is more Lutheran than Luther himself, for he turns the prayer into more than a 'testament', seeing it as an effective means towards the Christ-centred end. For him, 'Abba Father' is more than a corroborative quotation from Paul's Letters (cf. Romans 8:14–16; Galatians 4:6); it *is* the cry of Jesus himself (cf. Mark 14:36). Divine sonship means first realizing that we are indeed God's children, and then knowing the assurance that we are heirs of the kingdom. Then he turns the prayer outwards to the life that we reject in consequences, 'our sins and debts, our trials and everything that is evil'; and he ends on a favourite note, daily growth in the Christian life, so that we do not forget the *Fadervor* when we praise the One who is good and whose mercy endures for ever, in the heavenly kingdom.[14]

Much of this is summarized in a hymn that begins, 'Rely only on your *Fadervor*', about which Christian Thodberg has written in relation to Grundtvig's understanding of baptism. Like the sermon, it has a patristic emphasis on baptism, adopted sonship, and the privilege of saying the Lord's Prayer. It contains the following stanza:

If thus you pray your *Fadervor*
The Spirit with the Father's voice
Entitles you to be a child with Jesus,
So that you are at home in God's house:
For only God's true children have a mouth

To call God their Father
From the ground of the heart.

The expression 'ground of the heart' (*af hjertens grund*) may be
compared with Wesley's 'purity of intention' and 'language of
the heart'. Grundtvig is perhaps the preacher and writer who
combines 'thinking' and 'feeling' with equal strength in the
search for the knowledge of God. He more than others in his
time (or tradition) emphasizes the eschatological character of
the prayer. And it is due to his influence that the 1912 Danish
baptism rite has the Lord's Prayer, with the hand-laying, straight
*after* baptism (not as Luther before it) – a position, as we have
seen, analogous to Syrian and Armenian practice, and the
Anglican Prayer Book tradition from 1552.[15]

Our final nineteenth-century figure is Charles Spurgeon (1834–
1892), who became a Baptist in 1850, and soon after began a
preaching ministry. He was appointed minister of a congregation
in Southwark which became so large that a new church had to be
built, the Metropolitan Tabernacle. His theological position was
conservative evangelical, which involved him in controversies
not only with fellow Evangelicals in the Church of England over
baptismal regeneration but with other Baptists as well; he left the
Baptist Union in 1887. There are two sermons, one undated, the
second preached on 30 April 1884 for the Baptist Missionary
Society. He begins the first sermon, on 'Lead us not into temptation' (Matthew 6:13), by alluding to 'a book of addresses to
young people' which contained an exposition of the prayer; and
it is clear from what Spurgeon says that it was, in turn, inspired by
Jeremy Taylor's interpretation in *The Great Exemplar* (1649),
for it speaks of the subject in relation to the monarch in relation
to the kingdom, the beggar asking for bread; but there are some
adjustments elsewhere. From such a context, Spurgeon, conservative Baptist that he is, regards the Lord's Prayer as a beloved
part of the Christian repertoire; but that does not convey or
ensure anything. Inward regeneration comes first, hence the need
for watchfulness against temptations of all kinds, and these he
lists in different categories, mental, physical and spiritual. The

second sermon, on the doing of the will (Matthew 6:10), spreads the text through the Gospel: 'He taught us this prayer, (and) used it himself in the most unrestricted sense' (alluding to Gethsemane). He draws attention to the fact that heaven is mentioned twice in the prayer – the heavenly Father, and the doing of the will as in heaven: 'between earth and heaven there is but a thin partition'. And he applies the doing of the will to the missionary task, with confidence.[16]

Different as these writers are, three of them (Keble, Grundtvig and Spurgeon) represent the movement towards recovery of tradition that is one of the features of the Romantic Movement: Keble's medieval-style litany, with its sacramental focus in Tractarian Anglicanism; Grundtvig's radical patristic–Lutheran sense of the prayer as effective expression of divine sonship; and Spurgeon's embracing of the prayer as an authentic part of the Christian life from a tradition that began as openly hostile to its use in any other context than as a quotation from Scripture.

Alongside these (and other) movements, the prayer was becoming the focus of liturgical activity as well, including in the Church of England. There were pressures towards Prayer Book revision, and these can be traced through the nineteenth century in two directions: High-Church desire to enrich the liturgy, and Evangelical desire to simplify it. In 1852, the 'Convocations' (meetings of the bishops and representative clergy of the Provinces of Canterbury and York) began to meet for proper business, instead of as a formality. This led to proposals in 1852 and 1856 by High Churchmen such as Benjamin Webb and John Mason Neale to render optional on certain occasions the penitential introduction to Morning and Evening Prayer (and by implication, first recitation of the Lord's Prayer). This would eventually bear fruit in proposals for Prayer Book revision in England in 1927 and 1928 (neither of which were passed by Parliament, though they were widely used), and Scotland in 1929; they also omitted the first recitation at the eucharist and moved the second recitation to before communion (instead of after it) with the doxology. But perhaps the most daring Anglican innovation came from the USA, where the Episcopal

Church produced a revised Prayer Book in 1928 which at last grappled with the question of language. What has since been called the 'modified traditional' form of the prayer changes not only 'which art' to 'who art' (as Scottish 1764), but 'in earth' to 'on earth', and 'them that trespass' to 'those who trespass'; but the doxology mixes Prayer Book and Authorized Version, with 'For thine is the kingdom *and* the power, and the glory, for ever and ever.' In the Church of Scotland, the Church Service Society, formed in 1865 in order to stimulate interest in the renewal of worship in the Kirk, began to produce a series of service-books, which they called the *Euchologion*, whose first edition appeared in 1867. The Lord's Prayer was claimed for its rightful place, according to the 1564 *Book of Common Order*, but there were moves to introduce the Prayer Book version (with 'trespasses') alongside the old Kirk version (with 'debts').[17] Among the works of writing that helped to inform debate about the role of the Lord's Prayer in the worship of the ancient Church was an important study by F. H. Chase published in 1891, which, while more confident than some of the scholarship that has appeared since, set the prayer in a wider frame of reference, as part of catechesis, a focal point in worship, and embodying a rich tradition of interpretation.[18]

## The twentieth century

We start with a series of Retreat Addresses delivered in 1936 by Evelyn Underhill (1875–1941) and published as *Abba: Meditations based on the Lord's Prayer*.[19] Brought up conventionally 'Church of England', she struggled with her faith and her position as a gifted woman in the world of theological teaching. Attracted to Roman Catholicism, the Anti-Modernist policy of Pope Pius X ensured her remaining within Anglicanism. She became more and more interested in the mystical aspect of religious faith, encouraging the publication of late medieval writings such as *The Cloud of Unknowing* (1912). Publicly embracing the Church of England in 1921, she became well known as a giver of retreats and lectures; she was made a Fellow of King's College, London in 1927.

She divides her addresses into an introduction, followed by eight others: The Father, The Name, The Kingdom, The Will, Food, Forgiveness, Prevenience, and Glory. This cleverly suggests the shape in an Augustinian way, heavenly followed by earthly, but in amalgamating temptation and deliverance into 'Prevenience', she follows the East, Calvin, many seventeenth-century Anglican writers and Wesley. She begins by warning against 'the cheap fussiness of the anthropocentric life' that has 'even invaded our religion. There, too, we prefer to live upon the surface and ignore the deep.' Of the heavenly Father she speaks of the crowds following Christ, contrasting them with 'those whom he was going to incorporate into his rescuing system' – an unusual way of describing the Church. And of the shape of the prayer she writes along the lines of Aquinas: 'men have three wants, which only God can satisfy. They need food, for they are weak and dependent. They need forgiveness, for they are sinful. They need guidance, for they are puzzled. Give–Forgive–Lead–Deliver.'

As she goes through the prayer, she offers a number of gems: 'if the transforming power of religion is to be felt, its discipline (i.e. hallowing the name) must be accepted'; 'the kingdom is the holy, not the moral; the beautiful, not the correct; the perfect, not the adequate; charity not law'; ' "Thy will be done" always means being ready for God, God's sudden No over against our eager and well-meaning Yes'; 'perhaps because of his borderline status, his embryonic capacity for God, man is kept in constant memory of his own fragility' (the need for food); 'theology claims that original sin . . . causes especially four kinds of spiritual damage, ignorance, malice, weakness and claimful desire'; 'if a realistic and full acknowledgement of sinfulness . . . comes late in the prayer, later still comes this complete down-fall of self-sufficiency and acceptance of our true situation'; 'behind every closed door which seems to shut experience from us, He is standing; and within every experience which reaches us, however disconcerting, His unchanging presence is concealed'. Underhill knew about suffering, both from her own spiritual struggles and as a volunteer nurse caring for the troops returning from the Front during the Great War, which makes her Augustinian treatment of sin and evil all the more impactful. These addresses exude a rare depth, and they are gently laced with quotations or citations from her favourite writers, including Teresa of Avila and John of the Cross.

Karl Barth (1886–1968) by contrast writes as a forceful Reformed theologian. Born at Berne in Switzerland, he studied there, as well as at Berlin, Tübingen and Marburg. After a pastoral ministry in Switzerland during the Great War, he began to question the optimism as well as the method of the prevailing liberal theology, a process that was worked out in his famous Commentary on Romans, published in 1919. Here he returns to the heart of the Reformation, emphasizing the sovereignty of God, sinful human nature and the centrality of eschatology. He was appointed professor at Göttingen in 1921. Deeply critical of the Nazi dictator, he encouraged the formation of the 'Confessing Church', which withdrew from the state-controlled Evangelical Church; in 1935 he had to leave Germany, moving back to Switzerland, for a professorial chair at Basle. His theological work was vast, of which the *Church Dogmatics* were his crowning achievement. After the Second World War, he turned more and more to the issue of prayer, as McKim points out, and the place of theology and the theologian within it; this resulted in a series of seminars given at Neuchâtel between 1947 and 1949, when they were published in French; an English translation was produced in 1952, with a fiftieth anniversary edition that has recently appeared, together with additional essays by Saliers (who edited them), Hesselink and Migliore, as well as McKim himself. These sparkling seminars (in published form entitled, 'The interpretation of The Lord's Prayer according to the Reformers') contain an exposition that also embodies much of his theological position.[20]

Barth sets out to provide what Saliers calls a 'synoptic' approach to Calvin and Luther. He begins with an ecclesiological statement that echoes Calvin, the Church as 'those who are gathered by Jesus Christ', and goes straight into adoptive sonship, 'by thy Word and thy Spirit' which is 'accomplished at Christmas, on Good Friday and at Easter and made effective at our baptism'. In the vivid tradition of the Reformers, he states that 'when we call God our Father, we are not using symbols, but are experiencing the full reality of the words "father" and "son"'. Such an approach turns on its head the language of analogy – Barth's 'analogy of faith' makes God's fatherhood even more fatherly than our own fathers, and our sonship of God more filial than we are children of our earthly parents. The prayer is made up of six petitions (he follows Calvin), and it is divided into two parts, as the first four of the Ten Commandments are about God and the remaining six are about us. Following Luther, Barth insists that Jesus is praying this prayer – we do not do so on our own – 'we must take our part in God's activity'; and the hallowing of the name means good preaching (again following Luther, but this time mentioning him). He criticizes both the Reformers for not drawing out the eschatological aspects of the prayer when it comes to kingdom – a feature that was strong in Grundtvig. It is like a table that is concealed by a covering and is waiting to be revealed, which the Spirit (emphasized by both Luther and Calvin) is there to carry; Barth mentions the 'Spirit' variant in the textual tradition that we saw in Gregory of Nyssa and Maximus the Confessor. His discussion on the kingdom is taken much further in *The Christian Life*, published posthumously, which was part of a projected, extended exposition of the prayer which he did not finish: many of the themes recur, including references to Luther and Calvin; the prayer for the coming of the kingdom is 'pure prayer', because it cannot be omitted, because we turn to God, and because it has to be heard.

Barth goes on in these seminars to reflect on daily bread, giving a nod to Luther over the list of bodily needs to which it can refer, but he also speaks of spiritual needs – bread as 'the earthly symbol of God's grace'. Calvin and Luther are both brought into his discussion on human forgiveness, which he describes as 'a lovely thing and almost a physical necessity'. Temptation includes minor trials as well as the 'great eschatological testing'; here Barth touches on the tension between what may have been meant by the original text and how the Church understands this petition in more general difficulties as well. Evil for him is 'the evil one' and personal. And although (like Calvin) he recognizes that the doxology does not belong to the original text, it is a necessary liturgical addition. Barth's stark preaching of the gospel of grace seeps through his treatment of the Lord's Prayer, with its careful blending of the two great Reformers, and as a Reformed (not a Lutheran), Barth was part of a tradition that had learnt to use the Lord's Prayer in public worship in the generations since Calvin. For him, being able to pray together should mean being able to receive communion together; worship and life are closely bound, for this prayer has important ethical dimensions – it is not just words. As Migliore points out, for Barth the Lord's Prayer represents a 'theology of freedom' – for the faithful believer to live the life of grace.

A not uncritical follower of Barth was Dietrich Bonhoeffer (1906–1945), who was born in Wroslaw (then Breslau, part of Germany), from where the family moved to Berlin in 1912. The son of a professor of psychiatry, Bonhoeffer grew up in a household that sang hymns around the piano at festivals but did not go to church. He had clerical forebears, and in the end he decided to study theology, first at Tübingen, and then at Berlin. Here he wrote a doctoral dissertation in 1927 about the nature of the Church, which tried to combine the insights of sociology from Ernst Troeltsch (1865–1923) and the dialectical theology of Karl Barth, a project that did not endear him to his conventional teachers. After pastoral appointments in Barcelona and London, he returned to Germany and, along with Barth and others, signed the 'Barmen Declaration' (1934), which set in motion the anti-Hitler 'Confessing Church'. He set up a seminary for training pastors at Finkelwalde, Pomerania, whose corporate life and daily worship were influenced by his experience of theological colleges in England. Out of this in 1937 came *The Cost of Discipleship* (*Nachfolgung*, more simply, in the original German), whose central theme is a succinct, demanding exposition of the Sermon on the Mount as the heart of Christian living. Six pages are devoted to what he calls 'the hiddenness of prayer', following 'the hidden righteousness' (Matthew 6:1–14).[21]

Prayer is God's activity in us (cf. Luther), and therefore 'excludes all reflection and premeditation', for it is 'the supreme instance of the hidden character of God'. Bonhoeffer is similarly pithy about each petition, which the following selections show: of the heavenly Father, 'the call of Jesus binds the disciples into a brotherhood'; the hallowing of the name, 'may God protect his holy gospel being obscured and profaned by false doctrine and unholiness of living' (an adaptation of Luther aimed at compromised Christians and an anti-Christian government); 'the kingdom of God is still exposed to suffering and strife'; '(Christ's) followers must also pray that the will of God may prevail more and more in their hearts every day and break down all defiance'; 'as long as the disciples are on earth, they should not be ashamed to pray for their bodily needs' (cf. Luther); 'every day Christ's followers must acknowledge and bewail their guilt'; 'the disciple is conscious of his weakness, and does not expose himself unnecessarily to temptation in order to test the strength of his faith'; 'the last petition is for deliverance from evil (i.e. impersonal, following Luther) and for the inheritance of the kingdom of heaven'; and, of the doxology, 'the disciples are renewed in their assurance that the Kingdom is God's by their fellowship in Jesus Christ, *on whom depends the fulfillment of all their prayers*'.

Bonhoeffer follows Luther rather more than Calvin, and (unlike Barth) adopts Luther's sevenfold structure rather than Calvin's six. 'Discipleship' is stressed throughout. In *The Prayer-Book of the Bible: An Introduction to the Psalms* (1940), the last of his works to be published in his lifetime, he saw the Lord's Prayer as the embodiment of the gospel itself, the summation of all prayer. He ends by quoting Luther's preface to the Neuburg Hymn-Book of 1545:

Our dear Lord, who hast taught and given us the Psalter and the Lord's Prayer to pray, give us also the spirit of prayer, and the grace that we may with joy and sincerity pray with a true faith and without ceasing; for we are in need of it; and thus he commanded and desires from us: to Him the praise and honour and thanksgiving. Amen.[22]

Bonhoeffer paid the final price for his involvement with those who were conspiring against Hitler, by being hanged in April 1945 in the final weeks of the War. By one of those ironies of history, a very Lutheran series of sermons was being preached around the same time during the Allied bombing raids on Stuttgart by another great theologian and pastor, Helmut Thielicke (1908–1986), whose sermon on 'thy will be done' was interrupted by the blasts of attack from the skies; he resumed preaching after everyone moved to a nearby school for safety, as the old Hospitallers' Church where the congregation had gathered as usual was destroyed.[23]

The Second World War is the spiritual cauldron in which Bonhoeffer along with Thielicke and many others had their faith and teaching refined. It has also alerted the world to the need for Christians to come to terms with the existential realities behind the truth that Christianity arose out of Judaism, and the place of the Holocaust of millions of Jews (and others) who were systematically murdered in the death camps of the Third Reich. It is appropriate, therefore, in order to pay theological courtesy to our common ancestry, that a little space is devoted to the writing of Primo Levi (1919–1987), an Italian Jew who was born in Turin, and who, in spite of the anti-Jewish laws in force in Italy by the time, was still able to graduate from the Faculty of Science at Turin in 1941.

After fighting against the Fascists in Northern Italy in 1943 he was sent to Auschwitz in February 1944 and remained there until January 1945, an experience that was (understandably) to shape the rest of his life. One of his favourite characters was Panurge, who appears in a novel entitled *Gargantua et Pana-gruel*, and asks 'for bread in all the living and dead languages'; he is 'all of us, is Man. He is not exemplary, he is not perfection, but he is humanity.'[24] That request for bread takes Levi back to daily life at Auschwitz, with its daily humiliations, daily hunger, daily deaths, and the sense of life's utter pointlessness. In his *Se Questo E' Un Uomo* ('But what is a Man?'), published in 1989, he returns to the Auschwitz experience with a reflection on food. 'We have learnt the value of food; now we also diligently scrape the bottom of the bowl after the ration and we hold it under our chins when we eat bread so as not to lose the crumbs.' For Levi, there was no way of getting over these days, weeks and months in his life. Not a religious person, Levi was unable to 'lament', in the Jewish liturgical sense; nor was he praying in the conventional sense for 'daily bread'. Yet he clearly yearned for it. What he represents is the religionless void into which humanity can be plunged by constant exposure to the inhumanity of others. Grundtvig's desire to turn the petitions in the second part of the Lord's Prayer outwards to embrace what we are not, to reach the negativities of our nature at its weakest (and worst?), perhaps has something to say in how the desire for 'daily bread' is really to be seen, in both material and spiritual terms – as if they can really be separated from each other.

Next, we come to Leonardo Boff (1938–) an ex-Franciscan theologian from Brazil who left the Roman Catholic priesthood not so much because of his theological views as because of his political opinions, which included open criticism of the lack of democracy in government and church. What he has to say about the Lord's Prayer informs the actions and words which his authorities have found exceptionable. Boff studied in Europe at Oxford, Louvain, Würzburg and Munich before returning to Petropolis as a professor. One of the main exponents of liberation theology, Boff brings to the Lord's Prayer, about which he wrote an exposition in 1979,[25] the experience of deep poverty in Latin America. In such a context, the prayer is described as 'the prayer of integral liberation', which is the subtitle of his book.

Like Calvin and Barth, Boff sees the prayer in two sets of three petitions; 'three optatives are addressed heavenward; three petitions are made for the earth. Faith has two eyes: one that looks up to God and contemplates his light; another that is turned toward the earth and discerns the tragedy of darkness.' God is the heavenly Father 'even in the darkness of internal night or the grief over nameless sufferings'. Hallowing the name is about all life: 'as long as we remain locked into a conception of God who helps and a religion as something good for human balance, we cannot break out of that vicious circle of our own egotism and meet with God'. The kingdom understandably pre-occupies Boff: 'what distinguishes human beings from animals is not so much intelligence as imagination' (referring to our capacity to destroy as much as to build); and 'these hopes (of the kingdom) become more fervent in direct proportion to the cruelty of this world's contradictions'. Doing the will 'is an invitation and not a pre-emptive command'.

Like Bonhoeffer, Boff writes of daily bread that 'we should never feel ashamed of our needs'. Forgiveness is about the fact that 'God is primarily the God of sinners and relieves us of the burden of a heavy conscience.' Temptation tears him into agony: 'this anxiety and this suffering cannot be healed by any medicine or therapy', but only by God. Deliverance from evil (which Boff would prefer to have viewed in personal terms) has a woefully incarnate form: 'evil has never been experienced in a vague, abstract form, nor have grace and goodness'. And he writes of the 'Amen' in a way that sums up all his thinking: 'being able to say Amen implies being able to trust and be confident and certain that everything is in the hands of the Father; he has already con-quered mistrust and fear, despite everything'. The tone of Boff's writing is more in the mould of Bonhoeffer than anything else we have read. That is no coincidence, given the fact that each is addressing an unprecedented context of suffering and trial. This 'despite everything' says it all; there is angst in Boff's heart, and one can almost hear him ask the question, 'does this prayer really work?' – a prayer Boff would have experienced in the daily offices of his church, and before communion at mass.

What of the text, and its liturgical use? After the Second Vatican Council (1962–1965), a comprehensive reform of the Roman liturgy was set in motion. The focal point of the Lord's Prayer in Roman Catholic worship was clarified at baptism and the eucharist. Already the experience of 'Dialogue Masses' (with parts of the liturgy led in the vernacular by someone other than the priest) had produced an expectation that it should no longer be recited by the celebrant alone, but by everyone. There was therefore much discussion. Should the embolism be kept, as a venerable tradition going back many centuries? Should there be a doxology, as was the (almost) universal custom in the East, and in the churches of the Reformation? And, if so, how should the embolism figure in the process? In the end, a compromise was reached; the embolism was simplified, with a focus on the coming kingdom (reflecting the eschatological focus of biblical scholarship), and this would be followed by the doxology, ending in Amen.[26] In the rites of Christian initiation, which were much influenced by patristic scholarship, the adult rite includes an optional 'Presentation (the patristic "handing over") of the Lord's Prayer' before baptism, at which the Gospel-text is Matthew 6:9–13, introduced with the words, 'this is how our Lord taught his disciples to pray', which is followed by a homily on the prayer. Such a scenario finds its inspiration in Augustine, Chromatius of Aquileia, Peter Chrysologus and Caesarius of Arles. At children's baptism, the Lord's Prayer comes at the end, before the blessing, unless it takes place during the eucharist; there was no obvious desire to make more of it in that context, nor in the Anglican rites of baptism in the ensuing years, so that the path which began in 1552 and continued in 1662, with the prayer said by all immediately after baptism, was abandoned, arguably a serious loss.[27]

These radical changes reflected the build-up of biblical, patristic and liturgical scholarship. While the embolism continues to delay the prayer's ending (it was not designed for reciting aloud), the ecumenical gesture of including the doxology, as well as joining the rest of Christianity in having everyone recite the prayer, is not without significance. A custom of varying the introductory words has also grown up, a modest variant of some of the non-Roman early medieval rites, Celtic, Gallican and Spanish. However, the question of translation became a pressing one[28] and in the English-speaking world, it had ecumenical as well as international ramifications. In 1966 the modified traditional form from the 1928 American Episcopal Prayer Book (but with the Prayer Book doxology) emerged as a text around which different churches could unite (Roman Catholics had been using it for some time); and it became the mainstream alternative to the later 'modern versions'. It won wide acceptance and became standard throughout the Roman Catholic English-speaking world, agreed by the International Committee on English in the Liturgy (ICEL), and approved by Rome.[29] Its ecumenical equivalent, building on the Church of England's *Modern Liturgical Texts* (1968), the International Consultation on English Texts (ICET), went one stage further and proposed in 1970 a fresh translation:

> Our Father in heaven,
> holy be your Name,
> your kingdom come,
> your will be done,
> on earth as in heaven.
> Give us today our daily bread.
> Forgive us our sins
> as we forgive those who sin against us.
> Do not bring us to the test
> But deliver us from evil.
> For the kingdom, the power, and the glory are yours
> now and for ever. Amen.[30]

This reappeared in a revised version of texts in the following year and was much debated in consequence, with a change made in the second line to 'hallowed be your name' and in the ninth line to 'Save us from the time of trial', which appeared in a revised version in 1975. The first change ensured the retention of an old word that implied process rather than result; the second change softened the specific character of the temptation alluded to, which reflected the consensus of biblical scholarship around the question of eschatological trial.[31] As Anglicans around the world gradually became accustomed to new texts, they were often printed in parallel columns (as happened in the Church of England from 1987 onwards) with the 'modified traditional' version which was still easier on the ear for those brought up on the old Prayer Book version.[32] However, the Church of England altered the ninth line to the more traditional 'lead us not into temptation' before the introduction of the *Alternative Service Book* (1980), and resisted pressure to revert to 'Save us from the time of trial' before the introduction of its successor, *Common Worship* (2000). The reasons were partly linguistic (what is deemed easier on the ear) and partly theological (temptation needs to be comprehensive in scope, and not supposedly limited to one particular 'time', whatever the original text is thought to mean).

All in all, the new text, with its main variants (at the name and temptation) is a re-run of the tensions that have been part of the scene long since – which may be characterized as Bible text *versus* liturgical text. To illustrate this, the following translations from five mainstream versions are worth comparison.

| RSV (1952) | NRSV (1989) |
|---|---|
| Our Father who art in heaven, | Our Father in heaven, |
| Hallowed be thy name. | hallowed be your name. |
| Thy kingdom come, | Your kingdom come. |
| Thy will be done, | Your will be done, |
|   On earth as it is in heaven. |   on earth as it is in heaven. |
| Give us this day our daily bread, | Give us this day our daily bread. |
| And forgive us our debts, | And forgive us our debts, |
|   As we also have forgiven our |   as we also have forgiven our |
|   debtors; |   debtors. |
| And lead us not into temptation, | And do not bring us to the time of trial, |
| But deliver us from evil. | but rescue us from the evil one. |
| Alternatives in notes: | Alternatives in notes: |
| the bread of tomorrow | our bread of tomorrow |
| the evil one | us into temptation |
| doxology | from evil |
| | doxology |

| NEB (1961, 1970) | REB (1989) |
|---|---|
| Our Father in heaven, | Our Father in heaven, |
| thy name be hallowed; | may your name be hallowed; |
| thy kingdom come, | your kingdom come, |
| thy will be done, | your will be done, |
| on earth as in heaven. | on earth as in heaven. |
| Give us today our daily bread. | Give us today our daily bread. |
| Forgive us the wrong we have done, | Forgive us the wrong we have done, |
| as we have forgiven those who have wronged us. | as we have forgiven those who have wronged us. |
| And do not bring us to the test, | And do not put us to the test, |
| but save us from the evil one. | but save us from the evil one. |
| Alternatives in notes: <br> our bread of tomorrow <br> from evil <br> doxology | Alternatives in notes: <br> our bread of tomorrow <br> doxology |

| NIV (1978) |
|---|
| Our Father in heaven, |
| hallowed be your name, |
| your kingdom come, |
| your will be done |
| on earth as it is in heaven. |
| Give us today our daily bread. |
| Forgive us our debts, |
| as we also have forgiven our debtors. |
| And lead us not into temptation, |
| but deliver us from the evil one. |

It will be obvious from these versions that there is much unsettled business, which centres on how to translate 'debts', 'temptation', 'evil'. They are at one in reproducing 'have forgiven' from Matthew's text – unlike the sixteenth- and early seventeenth-century versions. They hesitate over how to render 'hallowed',

215

and offer an alternative at 'daily bread' that reflects biblical scholarship; and the doxology is included as a late addition. But looking at the scene overall, the following features emerge.

- We have moved into an era where the function of the prayer – at baptism (for catechesis) and eucharist (before communion) – is increasingly a matter of agreement, as the churches together face a different kind of world, where Underhill, Barth, Bonhoeffer and Boff can walk side-by-side, and in which the riches of different traditions of interpretation and application can be shared. For example, the *Book of Common Order* of the Church of Scotland (1979 and 1994) provides eucharistic rites which make provision for the prayer before communion.

- The issue of translation, however, is unresolved, with many modern rites in the English-speaking world using two texts, the 'modified traditional' ('who art') and the ecumenically agreed version ('save us from the time of trial') side-by-side.[33] It is something of an irony that, in the atmosphere of such agreement, light years away from the sixteenth-century controversies, including the sevenfold symbolism so roundly rejected by the Reformers and not included in the Council of Trent Catechism in 1566, we should be in a position where such different texts are in use, from old Prayer Book and Genevan Scots through modified traditional to the modern versions, to say nothing of the versions in contemporary translations of the Bible.

- Much of this common work results from a re-appropriation of the rich baptismal vision of the prayer from the Fathers, as well as the increasingly common work of scholars from different traditions over the Jewish setting of the prayer. We now view the prayer in a much richer light, whether we are praying it or studying it – and can do so together.

We end with two postscripts of a potentially ecumenical kind.

The *Catechism of the Catholic Church*, a suggestion made at the 1985 Extraordinary Synod of Bishops in Rome, in order to express the teachings of the Second Vatican Council, was published in 1992, with an English translation in 1994.[34] Unlike its predecessor after the Council of Trent, the new production is intended for laity as well, and not just for priests in their teaching role, a sign of the renewed emphasis on the role of the laity in the documents of the Second Vatican Council, particularly the 'Decree on the Apostolate of Lay People' (1965). As before, the Lord's Prayer figures at the end as the basis for teaching about prayer. The style and layout are generous and expansive; there are copious references to the Fathers, including Augustine, and John Chrysostom (an ecumenical gesture towards the East), as well as to Thomas Aquinas. As 'the prayer of the Church' it belongs to the baptized, and when 'handed over' to those preparing for Christian initiation, it is seen as part of the life of the sacramentally reborn Christian. Divergences of view about the structure of the prayer are deftly dealt with: there are seven petitions, 'the first series carries us toward him', whereas 'the second series of petitions unfolds the same movement as certain eucharistic epicleses: as an offering up of our expectations that draws down upon itself the eyes of the Father of mercies'. Augustine's view persists, but in an adapted form and without the explicit Platonism of the 'heavenly' and 'earthly'. The approach is comprehensive throughout, with baptism in hallowing 'the name', the Spirit central to the work of the kingdom, and daily bread applying in the first instance to our earthly needs, then to our spiritual ones, and from there to the eucharist, as Augustine taught; when dealing with forgiveness, there is, as in the Trent Catechism, a passing reference to formal confession; and also to the Assumption of the Blessed Virgin Mary when discussing deliverance from evil; and, after the embolism ('deliver us, Lord') from the eucharist, the doxology, whose place in Eastern tradition is carefully explained at the start, appropriately concludes the prayer as an act of adoration.

Apart from such explicit Marian teaching (unusual for the Lord's Prayer) and the embolism, the 1992 *Catechism* contains

217

little of substance with which other Christians would disagree. It expresses a full approach to the prayer that does justice to many of the traditions of interpretation we have been dealing with so far. As with all such documents, and indeed all translations of the prayer, there is a provisionality about it – like the 'living text' itself.

Finally, Eastern Orthodoxy has a particularly strong voice in Alexander Schmemann (1921–1983), whose broadcast addresses on Radio Liberty into the former Soviet Union have recently been published. Schmemann was born in Tallinn, Estonia, and fled the Soviet invasion. He studied for a time at the St Sergius Institute in Paris, from 1945 to 1951, before going to the United States, where he was a professor at the St Vladimir's Seminary, Crestwood. His teaching career saw a deepening awareness of the role of the liturgy within the life of his own church, and far beyond, as he was a considerable ecumenical figure.

The style of these short addresses is simple and direct – and very Russian. Schmemann draws in figures from Russian litera-ture, such as Sviyazhsky from *Anna Karenina*, to illustrate spiritual superficiality (avoiding the heavenly Father); Pushkin's poem, 'The Memory of a Glorious Moment', to illustrate the sacredness of beauty (hallowing the name); and (twice) Dostoevsky's *The Brothers Karamazov* to illustrate guilt (for-giveness), and the reality of suffering in the world (temptation and evil). As he goes through the prayer, he tries to speak to the institutional atheism of his home country, Estonia, and the rest of the (then) Soviet world. On invoking the heavenly Father he writes, 'possibly our most horrible trait is that we regularly hide from everything that seems too exalted and spiritually meaning-ful'. Holiness requires 'an inner transformation', but this desire is 'often blocked by a certain inertia, a weakness, the pettiness of our existence'. The kingdom 'comes when my life is filled to the brim with this light, with this knowledge, with this love'. 'The worst betrayal lies in this constant substitution of our will, our *self-will*, for the will of God.'

Daily bread provokes from him the view, countering Feuerbach's materialistic 'man is what he eats', that food is both a gift and a need, and that it is both earthly and heavenly: he follows Eastern tradition in interpreting this as 'the food which is essential to us', but he does not bring in the eucharist. 'Forgiveness is not a legal action but a moral one.' Like many Eastern writers, he draws temptation and evil together, and sees the latter in personal terms: 'evil comes to us precisely as temptation, as doubt, as the disintegration of faith; the victory of darkness, cynicism, and helplessness in our soul'. Schmemann ends with the doxology on a note of hope, in the best traditions of Byzantine patristic interpretation. ' "Our Father" is more than a prayer; it is an epiphany and revelation for which we are created, that hierarchy of values which enables us to arrange everything in its place within our lives.' 'Each petition of this prayer', which Schmemann will have known in the rich liturgical chant of the Byzantine liturgy as well as his daily devotions with the Orthodox rosary, 'opens a whole layer of personal awareness, a whole revelation about ourselves.'[35]

All these different examples demonstrate the new worlds and new patterns of communication that we have entered, where the spoken word not only is printed and meets a wide audience, but can now be broadcast all over the world, and through the internet sent anywhere in the world within a short space of time. They demonstrate, too, an emerging consensus of substance about the meaning of the prayer, with a greater overall acceptance between the traditions of its rich ambiguity. These are echoed in such contrasting musical versions as that of Bernard Rose, with his hauntingly sublime setting for the Prayer Book daily offices; Maurice Duruflé's expansively plainchant-inspired setting in the questing spirit of the times; and Igor Stravinsky's Orthodox expression of deep tradition in constant development. At the end of the day, Schmemann is perhaps the most representative figure of today's world, as he confronts its materialism, engages with its secularism, utilizes its literary traditions, and all with a confidence that the Prayer of the Lord can always find new climates in which to interpret human experience – of whatever kind.

# 9

# Conclusion

## Collection of texts

In 1662, Janis Reiters, a native Latvian Lutheran scholar and pastor in Riga, put together a collection of texts of the Lord's Prayer in just over forty different languages. Although no copies have survived, a second edition appeared in 1675 in Rostock, where he earned his doctorate. Reiters was a gifted linguist who had already set to work on translations into Latvian of parts of the Bible, including the Sermon on the Mount. The selection of languages reflects Reiters' cosmopolitan Baltic setting as a base for international trade (German, in more than one form, Luther's having preeminence, Estonian, Finnish, Old Prussian, Polish, Czech, Swedish, Danish and two forms of Low German, or Dutch); his own knowledge of what must have been for him some recondite tongues (Lowland Scots, Welsh, Irish and Turkish); and the ancient biblical languages as well (Hebrew, Syriac and Greek). In his concluding commendation, Reiters has this to say: 'believing and benevolent reader, use the Lord's Prayer, which wishes you joy and promises you success, so that you may understand the similarity of languages as well as the differences between them; learn also to realize the lovely shifts of letters and change of sounds; teach your sons and daughters, and pupils, if you have them, to praise God in different languages'.[1] Reiters may have had an ulterior motive, for he was trying to persuade Latvian Lutherans to adopt his version of the prayer as a replacement (in vain as it turned out) for the version which was already in use.

Reiters' collection of texts forms a kind of backdrop to our study, not least in the dialogue between scholarship and usage that makes new versions either desirable, or possible or controversial. And it would be interesting to speculate about what he would suggest for a version of the prayer at once accurate and elegant in the language of his choice. But there are two differences. Whereas he gathered together over forty versions, we have been looking at the evolution of the main texts of early and late antiquity, and then concentrating on the development of versions in English. Second, Reiters' desire to communicate parallels of sound has been replaced by considering the different interpretations that the prayer has inspired across the centuries. Were he to attempt a similar exercise from a cosmopolitan base in our own time, the possible world-wide languages would be between four and six thousand. A laptop publication in Portsmouth, England, could embrace (on the one hand) the ancient tongues of the British Isles, Celtic (Welsh, Irish, Gaelic, Manx and Cornish), as well as medieval English, and Lowland Scots; or (on the other hand) an international collection that could include the tongues of the American continent, the Far East, to say nothing of the possibilities of the Indian subcontinent. In all of them, we suggest, similar issues would recur; short, rhythmic translation; a position in public worship highlighting its uniqueness; and a tradition of interpretation that nourishes the people of God and breaks new boundaries of thought, religious as well as secular. These are the 'givens' of our story, and the focus on the West indicates this study's limited place of origin; another venue and context would have produced another array of evidence.

### The shape of the prayer

In his study of the beatitudes, Benedict Green quotes some words of Louis MacNeice: 'in any poet's poem the shape is half the meaning'.[2] We have seen many suggestions as to the shape of the prayer. They all distinguish between the opening petitions (addressed to God) and the later petitions (about our needs). But real differences of approach surface over whether temptation and evil are separate or one and the same, which impact upon the number of petitions the prayer is supposed to contain. These views may be summarized as follows:

- *Seven petitions:* the Western tradition with Tertullian who provides Augustine with his 'three heavenly/four earthly' Platonist framework. While this scheme bypasses a few subsequent figures such as Peter Chrysologus, it comes to rule supreme in the West until the twelfth century, when Anselm of Laon suggests that the petition for bread is both heavenly and earthly, which leads subsequent writers to interpret it as exclusively heavenly; medieval eucharistic theology, as we have shown, may well lie behind this shift. Deliverance from evil as a separate petition explains why the Latin 'deliver us, Lord' prayer which follows at mass begins on the theme of evil. By the time of Aquinas a more Aristotelian approach was appearing, with the prayer seen as the quest for God, the ultimate Good, and the application of that quest to our needs in the life of grace. But Augustine is responsible for another development; the application of the sevenfold gifts of the Spirit to each petition, which is taken over, adapted, and extended into other sevenfold schemes through the Middle Ages. They do not appear in the Catechism of the Council of Trent, nor do they survive the Reformation. However, Luther retains the sevenfold structure; he regards the bread petition as for our earthly needs, and the remaining three (adapting Albert the Great) as referring to what needs to be averted, namely, sin, temptation, evil.

- *Six petitions:* the Eastern tradition, represented by John Chrysostom, Titus of Bostra, Cyril of Alexandria, and Maximus the Confessor, takes the view that temptation and deliverance are part of the same petition. This scheme rules supreme, without any distinctions of earthly and heavenly, throughout the East, right down to the present day, as exemplified by Schmemann. The doxology, a fourth-century variant in some Eastern manuscripts, doubtless the result of liturgical use, gradually spreads through most of the Eastern liturgies; some also include an embolism prayer, but they open on the theme of temptation (unlike the Western 'evil'), again reflecting the Eastern view of the basic sixfold shape of the prayer. At the Reformation, Calvin rejects the patristic and medieval Western view, and adapts the Eastern approach, with six petitions and the doxology. This results in an historic divide between Lutheran and Calvinist traditions (e.g. in their Catechisms). Such a divergence is also apparent in such Anglican writers as Andrewes (seven petitions, but with doxology) and Jeremy Taylor (six petitions, with doxology); John Wesley and Karl Barth opt for the latter approach, Wesley following Anglican intermediaries, Barth taking his lead direct from Calvin.

These are the two basic approaches that hold equal sway in the tradition. But even though the Western view has the weight of Augustine behind it, our preference is for the East and Calvin, because it better reflects the linguistic structure of the prayer, memorably described as 'three aspirations' and 'three petitions' by Austin Farrer.[3]

There is, however, one remaining question of shape that is intrinsic to the first part of the prayer: does 'on earth as in heaven' refer exclusively to the doing of the will or to the name and the kingdom? The overwhelming evidence, patristic, medieval and Reformation, associates it exclusively with the will. But there is a significant minority view that takes these words to refer to all three: Origen, the fifth-century author of the *Opus Imperfectum* (for long regarded as the work of John Chrysostom and therefore invested with his authority), Meister Eckhart and the Catechism of the Council of Trent (1566). This view is also endorsed by modern scholarship, starting with B. F. Westcott and F. J. A. Hort in their 1888 text of the Greek New Testament.[4] Typography can help. It is not just a question of ensuring that there is a comma placed between 'your will be done' and 'on earth as in heaven'. Modern versions have often been drafted to indicate this subtle change by indenting the three opening petitions, and then indenting further 'on earth as in heaven': a straight left-hand margin, so frequent in service books (and service sheets) is, unfortunately, more common in practice.

## Text and translation

As a collection such as Reiter's demonstrates, the West is influenced heavily by what becomes the standard Latin version of the Church's liturgy with its particular nuances of the Greek of Matthew 6:9–13, especially 'daily' for bread, and 'evil', rather than 'the evil one'. This holds true even when the former is interpreted comprehensively (as Augustine) to mean material, spiritual and eucharistic, and when the latter is interpreted by him in impersonal terms. Similarly, even the Greek liturgical version departs from the original, with 'as we forgive' instead of 'as we have forgiven' – a past tense which modern English translations of the Bible have taken care to reinstate.

All this highlights yet again the question of biblical text *versus* liturgical prayer. Parker's notion of the 'living text' explains this tension; there is no point, on his argument, in trying to recover a lost 'original', in the same way that liturgical scholars have sometimes tried to recreate a form of eucharistic liturgy used by the early Christians. We can only study the various texts and theories, and then try to adjudicate between them. This is one of the reasons why, for example, while we have argued for an Aramaic original lying behind Matthew's text (rather than regard the prayer as essentially Matthew's Greek composition), it makes little difference to the history of interpretation of the prayer. Matthew's Greek version was edited and translated. Both these processes are necessary risks in order for the prayer to travel into popular and liturgical use – whether the journey is next door into Syriac-speaking Christianity, to the Livs in northwest Latvia, or the Mohawk translation made in 1715 for native American use. And all along, there is the built-in tension of the need for a community's memory in the familiar text, and the reality of a wider collective memory of interpretation that may challenge details – and understandings – of that text.

The two New Testament versions (Matthew 6:9–13 and Luke

11:2–4) were merged into an edited text of the former, which then began to bear the load of translation, particularly in the second part of the prayer, when we pray for ourselves, for it is there that the difficulties (not surprisingly) lie. In our view, the Syriac *Peshitta* translation ('the bread of our need') – Jeremy Taylor's interpretation – is the most accurate and rhythmic that we have so far seen.[5] The other main alternative, 'the bread of tomorrow', suggested in some modern versions of the Bible, and echoing Jerome's evidence from the (lost) *Gospel of the Nazarenes*, reflects the eschatological origins of the prayer, but does not express the tradition of interpretation that we have seen again and again. 'Daily' has the advantages of ambiguity. It can mean both what we receive and what we need. But its frequent use in so many other less loaded contexts has the result that it has to rely on catechesis to explain why it means considerably more than is immediately apparent. It is, however, an easier option if we take the Gregory of Nyssa–Luther–Calvin line and make it refer exclusively to material need, a view from which some seventeenth-century Anglican writers retreated.

The next problem is less complex and concerns forgiveness. The Semitic image of 'debts' survived through Greek and Latin into late medieval English, from where, thanks to the Geneva Bible and the Authorized Version, it entered Presbyterian usage on both sides of the Atlantic – and beyond. Owing something to someone is, arguably, a stronger image for sin than moving onto their space, which is the image of 'trespass'. 'Sin', however, is what the word really means – and it is the best word to use. To revert the second part of this petition to Matthew's 'as we have forgiven' would also draw out something of the force of Gregory of Nyssa's exaggerated cry to God that he imitate us as we forgive others.

Temptation – testing – is perhaps the biggest problem of all. We have seen many different interpretations, some of them helped on by periphrases such as Augustine's 'do not *bring* us'. Andrewes' suggestion that not being led into temptation is about not *committing* evil whereas deliverance is about not *experiencing* it makes sense of the mainstream tradition of interpretation. But we have to attend, also, to its Semitic background: Carmignac's view that this is not about God not *leading* us into temptation, but about God not letting us *experience* temptation, comes even nearer to its heart. Attempts to render this as 'the time of trial' limit its application: the prayer is about all kinds of testing, which means that 'temptation' is a more comprehensive translation. As in other parts of the prayer, the simpler the expressions, the more resonant the meanings. We would suggest 'do not let us into temptation'. And as for the question of 'evil' *versus* 'the evil one', while the latter is more accurate, and less abstract, and has Eastern tradition behind it (even if Calvin suspended judgement on the matter), 'evil' on its own is more comprehensive, and theologically (and experientially) richer.

There is one important matter of translation in the first aspiration: should it be rendered 'holy' or 'hallowed'? 'Holy' has the advantage of being in common speech, but it is an adjective and not a verb; hallowed may be archaic, but it reflects the original Greek better for that reason. For the time being, 'hallowed' is probably going to be the best we can achieve. This could leave us with the following translation, which is based on a combination of the study of New Testament language as well as the rich literature of the interpreting tradition:

> Our Father in heaven,
>     hallowed be your name,
>     your kingdom come,
>     your will be done;
>         on earth as in heaven:
> give us today the bread of our need,
> and forgive us our sins,
>     as we have forgiven those who sin against us;
> do not let us into temptation,
>     but deliver us from evil.
> For the kingdom, the power and the glory are yours,
>     now and for ever. Amen.

# Conclusion

## The uses of the prayer

We have seen how the Lord's Prayer gradually entered the liturgy of the hours, and the eucharist, probably *via* baptismal catechesis. The usual positions are at the conclusion of the former, and between the eucharistic prayer and the distribution of communion at the latter. Such is also the contemporary consensus. But it is important not to iron out the many anomalies in the tradition. These include East Syrian repetition after communion, the traditional Lutheran eucharistic practice of placing it between the thanksgiving and the institution narrative, Calvin's preference for a publicly recited paraphrase, perhaps related to catechesis, and Cranmer's position after the main sacramental act, both at the eucharist and at baptism. This latter tendency gathers interest because of the (albeit sporadic) evidence of the late fourth century in Antioch (*Apostolic Constitutions*) and Constantinople (John Chrysostom), where the prayer is recited by the newly baptized immediately on coming up from the font, a practice that survives in the Armenian rite. In our age, the amount of interest in baptism, both in ecclesiology and pastoral practice,[6] suggests that however important good catechesis is in the life of the Church, how the Lord's Prayer is used at this foundational sacrament needs to be looked at again.

Nor should we forget the important anomalies in the devotional tradition. The farced versions in Syrian daily prayer show how text can inspire modest improvisation. The development of the paraphrase, of which there are fine examples in Anglo-Saxon usage, and in the work of such contrasting figures as Francis of Assisi and Lancelot Andrewes, is an area where new paths might emerge. The disadvantage of the paraphrase is that it becomes an end in itself; the advantage is that it can alert the praying Christian to the rich shades of meaning that familiar words can easily disguise. The anomalies spread further, and include Anselm of Laon, who in his prayer-like discourse starts with the end of the prayer (evil) and works back to the beginning towards the vision of God (heavenly Father), as well as the view of the prayer as a ladder to heaven which we find in such contrasting twelfth-century writers as Honorius of Autun and the Eastern biblical exegete, Euthymius Zigabenus.

But to whom does this prayer belong? This tension goes back to the New Testament, with Jesus giving it to the world as a guide to prayer in the Sermon on the Mount (Matthew 6:9–13), and to the disciples as a prescribed form of prayer when requested by them for help (Luke 11:2–4). Our investigation of the prayer's origins has convinced us of the importance of its Jewish background – so that it emerges from Jesus' own Jewish devotional tradition as a prayer composed by a rabbi for his followers. Even if one takes a sceptical view about its supposed dominical origin, this is still how it comes across, with its central themes of the fatherhood of God, his name, his kingdom, and his will; and daily sustenance, forgiveness and protection. And even if we (rightly) note that the coming of the kingdom and mutual forgiveness are less explicit in Jewish piety than they are in the New Testament, the prayer is still highly Semitic in both style and content. Such an approach to the prayer's origins has profound implications for its use today, particularly with Jews – who sometimes need to be reassured that daily bread does not have to refer exclusively to the eucharist. Enthusiastic baptismal catechesis is needed for believing Christians, but there is a wider context in which the prayer can be used, which would not 'dumb down' separate faith communities' strongly held beliefs when they meet to study and pray together. As J.-B. Frey wrote many years ago, the Lord's Prayer 'is the prayer of humanity'.[7]

## Interpretations of text

We have indeed seen a galaxy of interpretations. These have not just related to different contexts, such as Yuhanna ibn Saba writing in an expository manner in thirteenth-century Egypt, Amalar of Metz allegorizing on the three days' burial of Christ in the ninth, Alan of Lille writing on preaching in the twelfth century, or Susanna Hopton providing extended devotional prayers in early eighteenth-century England. They also refer to different doctrinal emphases, such as Bonaventura on free will as directed by God in the twelfth, or Karl Barth propounding the kingdom of God as a fundamental given in the Christian repertoire of belief in the twentieth. There are also, however, some issues which are to do with the analogical nature of some of these foundational images, particularly father and kingdom.

It is not just feminism which poses questions about fatherhood. In eighteenth-century England, William West warned against taking the image too literally, and identifying it too closely with negative experiences of earthly fatherhood: 'in the first place, we should be very careful not to ascribe any of the imperfections or weaknesses of earthly parents to God our heavenly Father, who is infinitely above them'.[8] Such an observation explains the use of the expression 'Good Father' in one of the new eucharistic prayers of the Church of England's *Common Worship* (2000).[9] To the radical feminist critique of patriarchal language there can only be two responses: either find an alternative (and there is nothing in principle against such a notion, given the unstable nature of the text of the prayer in any case), or make do with the traditional term as inherited, but make sure that it is explained in as broad a way as possible, perhaps expanding on divine parenthood in paraphrase style. The creating and redeeming father is not the superman, magician, policeman, domestic pet, or favourer of the few of popular religiosity. Roland Mushat Frye has written perceptively about this issue, and ends by citing Origen's warning that God 'is not to be reached by word': we must not be too literal in our theologizing – or our praying.[10] The apophatic tradition leads us towards reticence, and the Lord's Prayer, with its brevity, is about reticence too. The meaning of kingdom, on the other hand, is less of a problem, because it is a central Gospel image. There is a rich tradition of seeing it as the embodiment of the authority of God, whether among us now, or yet to come; the tension between the 'now' and the 'not yet' is so inherent in the gospel message that it takes the notion of 'kingdom' onto another plane altogether.

## Liturgical theology

Liturgical theology is how Don Saliers describes Barth's approach to the Lord's Prayer, because of the close relationship between the text prayed and the text interpreted.[11] In fact, we have been dealing with liturgical theology from the moment we began looking at the text as a prayer; it is a process that formally begins with the earliest discourse, by Tertullian, but which starts life between the lines of the Gospels of Matthew and Luke, and long before that in the Jewish devotional tradition we regard as central to the prayer's origin and scope. The three classic modern exponents of liturgical theology, Alexander Schmemann, Geoffrey Wainwright and Aidan Kavanagh, all place worship at the centre of the thinking and the praying life of the Christian community.[12] They reflect, too, the different emphases of their respective traditions. Schmemann, whose broadcast addresses on the prayer we have already seen, has an Orthodox confidence in a long tradition of worship and theology, alongside such writers as Maximus the Confessor and Germanus of Constantinople. Wainwright has a Methodist's love of song combined with a gentle suspicion of liturgical triumphalism, in the best traditions of John Wesley himself. And Kavanagh embodies a radical-traditional Roman Catholic's conviction that fine definitions are necessary equipment which have nonetheless to be left aside in order to gain access to the font, and thereafter to the altar – an overall approach comparable to Ambrose of Milan and the Jerusalem *Mystagogic Catecheses*.

Meaning, however, is not always a straightforward exercise which is somehow to be provided by a heavenly blank cheque. It is for this reason that Augustine and Calvin in their different ways stand out as profound Christian thinkers who use the Lord's Prayer in order to address the controversies of their time. For Augustine the Pelagian tendency to want to earn grace and the Donatist temptation to turn the Church into a gathering of the already entirely pure made him time and again revert to the petition for forgiveness as evidence that the Church relies on the grace of God and will never be perfect in this life. For Calvin, it was those who identified the kingdom with the Church or who associated forgiveness too closely with the sacrament of penance which made him interpret those petitions in a way that reflected both Reformation distrust of the inherited institutional Church and the doctrine of justification by faith.

The Lord's Prayer not only suggests but invites the work of the liturgical theologian. While there will be different answers from different writers and preachers in different eras (it is easier for a Protestant to see daily bread as eucharistic when frequent reception of communion is a regular feature of a Roman Catholic's life – which it certainly was not at the Reformation), the prayer's short span embraces evangelical truths, which explains Tertullian's 'summary of the gospel', early Egyptian monastic reference to 'the prayer of the gospel', and Maximus the Confessor's description as 'the symbol of adoption'. The Lord's Prayer emerges as its own 'primary theology' precisely because of its Gospel-base (and even in the looser sense, its dominical origin), from which emanate different strands of 'secondary theology' – whether in preaching, catechesis, exposition, devotional paraphrase, broadcast addresses, parish study-groups, or even website talk-ins. The most perceptive are those that explore the gospel truths in such a way as to reveal human nature for what it is and could be: for example, temptation can easily mean the temptation to do nothing, as Christians in Bangladesh have recently suggested in a study-pack on the meaning of the prayer.[13]

There is, therefore, an important ethical dimension to the prayer, hence its growing association with the Decalogue in catechesis as the Middle Ages progressed, its connection with the gifts of the Spirit and the virtues (and vices), and a recurring insistence on its challenging implication for daily living, lucidly expressed by Evelyn Underhill. And while Bonhoeffer and Boff rightly exude the social context of their respective situations, there has to come a point when we have said and done all that we can, and surrender ourselves to the will of God, as we try to use our wills in a way that shows a Christian's rightful suspicion of human instincts. The Lord's Prayer thus takes on an overarching function, as the prayer of Christ himself (cf. John 17), holding together the different insights, experiences and devotional colourings of different ages. In our own time, a globalized world presses heavily on our responsibility not only for each other but for the creation itself, for which pragmatism, in which Christianity can be seen in functional terms (in effect concerned, consumer-style, with the second part of the prayer, in isolation from the first), is clearly a less than satisfactory answer to the question of how to be fully human.[14] To pray for hallowing the name, the coming of the kingdom and the doing of the will have to take root on less reassuring ground in those multi-faceted (and textually unstable) petitions about bread for today, forgiveness for yesterday, and providence for the future.

## Text, textuality and imagination

'As our Saviour taught us, so we pray.' These words are more than a 'cue'. They point to the prayer's dominical character. They also ensure that everyone is able to join in with the opening words, 'Our Father'. But there is an inherent tension which is voiced by Luther. The Lord's Prayer for him is the prayer of Christ among us *now*, which suggests the gloss 'as our Saviour *taught* us' also means 'as our Saviour *says*'. In this way, the prayer's function comes across as 'performative holiness',[15] the work of redemption among us now, as Luther taught, the prayer of Christ in every human circumstance. Such a view explains the various devices that have been used to express the prayer's meaning, whether in the 'deliver us, Lord' embolism which has for long followed it at the Roman mass, Armenian recitation immediately after baptism, making special beads for a rosary as the prayer seeps into the subconscious, or Calvin providing a paraphrase for public (not private) use in order to prevent it becoming no more than words. Some of these issues reflect the notion of textuality, which is about the relationship between a text and its interpretation, and different approaches to literary theory, which concern the relationship of text and readership. These are complex, and multi-layered, and demonstrate the prayer's innate dynamism.

There is no such thing as a fixed text, a fixed meaning, or a fixed way of using this prayer, as we have seen from the very start of our story. Not only are there significant textual variants (over temptation in North Africa and elsewhere, and daily bread in the Syriac tradition), but the Latin text of the Roman Church produced its own need for vernacular versions and paraphrases. Much later, the technology of printing brought with it important rivals ('trespasses' in England and 'debts' in Scotland), so that the common memory occasionally invoked as a reaction to today's multiplicity of texts is not quite as uniform as it is made out to be. As David Brown has reminded us, 'imagination' is part of 'tradition'.[16] Such is the prayer's bulging 'excess of meaning' that the community of faith is left to respond prayerfully and imaginatively, just as we have done in the past – whatever the circumstances. It is only when the prayer's meaning becomes an end in itself – as in the later Middle Ages – that its focus, too intent on the Church, becomes blurred: the Spirit's work is to check as well as liberate. And yet, granted that all prayer, whatever the circumstances, is inadequate, we can still *dare* to address God as Father – and not merely 'say' it. The words of the prayer, it seems, develop their own music, whether in the popular chant of the ancient East and West, the elaborate choral settings of the Divine Office in the Byzantine, Roman, Lutheran and Anglican traditions, which try to interpret the greatness of God's mercy alongside the struggles of Christian discipleship – or even Mendelssohn's tapestry-like Sixth Organ Sonata, based on Luther's 'Vater Unser' Chorale. The music of the prayer lives on, too, in the many forms of the spoken word, as well as in the unspoken words of sign-language, where kingdom is expressed by the tips of a clawed hand touching the head, followed by palm-down hands moving forward and apart – indicating authority that engages with people.

But the question must still be asked: Is the notion of the Lord's Prayer as a text that is 'living' and 'multi-contextual' compatible with post-modernity, an era in which many no longer see any 'big picture', and which can be caricatured as describing us as no more than insignificant footnotes to things that have already happened? To the contrary, the Lord's Prayer shows itself capable of entering every human construct, whether it is the modified Platonism of Augustine, the revised Aristotelianism of Aquinas, the demands of a revitalized religious community for Teresa of Avila, the evangelical humanism of Calvin, the post-industrial revolution world of F. D. Maurice, the charred fragments of post-First World War Europe of Karl Barth, or the aggressively materialistic atheism of Soviet Russia deftly addressed by Alexander Schmemann. Perhaps Jonathan Clark[17] is justified when he challenges the apathy of 'presentism' in order to tell us that, regardless of prevailing structures of thought (or the lack of them), we can still be part of a narrative, even if we bear the memory of the twentieth century's spectacular failures. As Rowan Williams has often observed, the Lord's Prayer is a prayer of the cross, and deliverance from evil is about being free from the power of the lie – the sheer falsehood which claims that God is out to get us, and that we can somehow avoid him, when in reality he wants to nourish, redeem and liberate us. To pray for the hallowing, coming and doing of God is, therefore, to rest in our dependence on him, and only then do we pray for food for the hungry, reconciliation for the unforgiving and unforgiven, and the capacity to move trustingly into an uncertain future – a future in which dominion, power and glory only make sense when they are themselves shot through with the scars of the wounded healer of Nazareth who dared to call God his 'Abba'.

# Notes

*Chapter 1: Scope and Method*

1. Edwin Muir, *An Autobiography* (London: Methuen, 1964), p. 246; I am indebted to Alan Wilkinson for drawing my attention to this.

2. See *The Sermons of Lancelot Andrewes*, vol. v, Library of Anglo-Catholic Theology (Oxford: Parker, 1854), p. 369. (Sermon 7; cf. Sermon 5, where Andrewes refers to this prayer as 'free of all imperfections', because it is Christ's, p. 349).

3. Ernst Lohmeyer, *The Lord's Prayer* (London: Collins, 1965).

4. Joachim Jeremias, *The Prayers of Jesus*, Studies in Biblical Theology (London: SCM Press, 1967), pp. 82–107 (pp. 95–99 on *Abba*); see also James Barr, 'Abba Isn't "Daddy"', *Journal of Theological Studies* 39.1 (1988), pp. 28–47.

5. Jean Carmignac, *Recherches sur le Notre Père* (Paris: Letouzey, 1969); see also Pierre Grelot, 'L'arrière-plan araméen du "Pater"', *Revue Bénédictine* 91.4 (1984), pp. 531–556.

6. Ulrich Luz, *Matthew 1–7: A Commentary*, tr. Wilhelm C. Linss (Edinburgh: T. & T. Clark, 1990), pp. 367–389.

7. W. D. Davies and Dale C. Allison, jr, *The Gospel According to St Matthew*, vol. i, Critical and Exegetical Commentary Series (Edinburgh: T. & T. Clark, 1988), pp. 590–617 (bibliography, pp. 621–624).

8. Graham N. Stanton, *A Gospel for a New People: Studies in Matthew's Gospel* (Edinburgh: T. & T. Clark, 1992).

9. D. C. Parker, ' "As our Saviour taught us . . .": The Lord's Prayer', in *The Living Text of the Gospels* (Cambridge: Cambridge University Press, 1997), pp. 49–76; cf. also, in general, Vernon K. Robbins, *The Tapestry of Early Christian Discourse: Rhetoric, Society and Ideology* (London and New York: Routledge, 1966), especially his remarks on text and sub-text, pp. 44ff.

10. Bruce M. Metzger, *The Bible in Translation: Ancient and English Texts* (Grand Rapids: Baker Academic, 2001).

11. See Barbara Johnson, *The Critical Difference* (Baltimore: Johns Hopkins University Press, 1980), and Jonathan Culler, *On Deconstruction:*

*Theory and Criticism after Structuralism* (Ithaca, NY: Cornell University Press, 1982); see also Jonathan Culler, *Literary Theory: A Very Short Introduction* (Oxford: Oxford University Press, 1997).

12. H. Benedict Green, CR, *Matthew, Poet of the Beatitudes*, Journal for the Study of the New Testament Supplement Series 203 (Sheffield: Academic Press, 2001), pp.77–91; for the Lucan Version, see Appendix A, pp. 293–299. Green uses Austin Farrer's 'aspirations' and 'petitions', in the Church of England Liturgical Commission, *Modern Liturgical Texts* (London: SPCK, 1968), pp. 1–3; R. C. D. Jasper indicates Farrer's authorship of these choice pages in *The Development of the Anglican Liturgy 1662–1980* (London: SPCK, 1968), pp. 292–293.

13. Paul F. Bradshaw, *The Search for the Origins of Christian Worship* (London: SPCK, 1st edn 1992; 2nd rev. edn 2001, 2001 edition used hereafter); for 'text in context', however, see 1992 edn, pp.72–78. See also Bradshaw's essay, 'Continuity and Change in Early Eucharistic Practice: Shifting Scholarly Perspectives', in R. N. Swanson (ed.), *Continuity and Change in Christian Worship*, Studies in Church History 35 (Bury St Edmunds: Boydell and Brewer, 1999), pp. 1–17.

14. See Bradshaw; *Search for the Origins*, pp. 14–20; see also Anton Baumstark, *Liturgie comparée: principes et méthodes pour l'étude historique des liturgies anciennes* (Chevetogne: Editions de Chevetogne, 1953). See Robert F. Taft's groundbreaking articles, 'The Structural Analysis of Liturgical Units: An Essay in Methodology' and 'How Liturgies Grow: The Evolution of the Byzantine Divine Liturgy', in *Beyond East and West: Problems in Liturgical Understanding*, 2nd rev. edn, enlarged, Edizioni Orientalia Christiana (Rome: Pontifical Oriental Institute, 2001), pp. 187–232.

15. Ingemar Furberg, *Das Pater Noster in der Messe*, Bibliotheca Theologiae Practicae 21 (Lund: Gleerups, 1968).

16. Maria-Barbara Von Stritzky, *Studien zur Überlieferung und Interpretation des Vaterunsers in der frühristlichen Literatur*, Münsterische Beiträge zur Theologie 57 (Münster: Aschendorff, 1989).

17. W. O. E. Oesterley, *The Jewish Background of the Christian Liturgy* (Oxford: Clarendon Press, 1925), pp. 151–154.

18. M. Brocke, J. J. Petuchowski and W. Strolz (eds), *Das Vaterunser: Gemeinsames Beten von Juden und Christen* (Freiburg-im-Breisgau: Akademieverlag, 1974); ET, Jakob Petuchowski and Michael Brocke (eds), *The Lord's Prayer and Jewish Liturgy* (New York: Seabury, 1978).

19. See, for example, Paul F. Bradshaw and Lawrence Hoffmann, *The Making of Jewish and Christian Worship* (Notre Dame, IN: University of Notre Dame Press, 1991); and E. Kessler, J. Pawlikowski and J. Banki (eds), *Jews and Christians in Conversation: Crossing Cultures and Generations* (Cambridge: Orchard Academic, 2002).

# Notes

20. See Carmignac, *Recherches*, pp. 283–292; he had already outlined this suggestion in ' "Fais que nous n'entrons pas dans la tentation": la portée d'une négation devant un verbe au causatif', *Revue Biblique* 72.2 (1965), pp. 218–226.

21. David Tracy, *The Analogical Imagination* (London: SCM Press, 1981), p. 18.

## Chapter 2: From the Bible to the Third Century

1. For the eucharistic prayer, see, for example, Thomas J. Talley, 'The Eucharistic Prayer of the Ancient Church according to Recent Research: Results and Reflections', *Studia Liturgica* 11 (1976), pp. 138–158; see also Bradshaw, *Search for the Origins*, pp. 118–143.

2. The literature on this subject is prodigious; see in particular, Millar Burrows, 'Thy Kingdom Come', *Journal of Biblical Literature* 74.1 (1955), pp. 1–8; T. W. Manson, 'The Lord's Prayer', *Bulletin of the John Rylands Library* 38.1–2 (1955–1956), pp. 99–113, 436–448; Robert Leaney, 'The Lucan Text of the Lord's Prayer (Lk/xi/2–4)', *Novum Testamentum* 1.2 (1956), pp. 103–111; R. F. Cyster, 'The Lord's Prayer and the Exodus Tradition', *Theology* 64 (1961), pp. 377–381; M. D. Goulder, 'The Composition of the Lord's Prayer', *Journal of Theological Studies* NS 14 (1963), pp. 32–45; J. Blenkinsopp, 'Apropos of the Lord's Prayer', *Heythrop Journal* 3 (1962), pp. 51–60; and R. E. Brown, 'The Pater Noster as an Eschatological Prayer', in *New Testament Essays* (New York: Doubleday, 1982), pp. 217–253.

3. *Didache* 8:2–3; see W. Rordorf and A. Tuiller (eds), *La doctrine des douze apôtres*, Sources Chrétiennes 248 (Paris: Cerf, 1978), p. 174.

4. Tertullian, *De Oratione* 1: see *The Ante-Nicene Fathers*, vol. iii (Edinburgh: T. & T. Clark, 1997), p. 681.

5. See J. L. Houlden, 'Lord's Prayer', *The Anchor Bible Dictionary*, vol. iv (London: Doubleday, 1992), p. 357 (for whole article, see pp. 357–362).

6. *On Prayer* 18.3; see Origen, *Prayer: Exhortation to Martyrdom*, trans. John O'Meara, Ancient Christian Writers 19 (London: Longmans, 1954), p. 66.

7. For Stanton on Matthew, see *A Gospel for a New People*; for Evans on Luke, see C. F. Evans, *St Luke* (London: SCM Press, 1990), pp. 441–480; for Brown, see 'The Pater Noster as an Eschatological Prayer', p. 222; for Green on Luke, see *Matthew, Poet of the Beatitudes*, pp. 293–299.

8. See Luz, *Matthew 1–7*, pp. 380–382.

9. Tom Wright, *The Lord and His Prayer* (London: SPCK, 1996), p. 76;

see also C. F. D. Moule, 'An Unsolved Problem in the Lord's Prayer', in *Forgiveness and Reconciliation: Biblical and Theological Essays* (London: SPCK, 1998), pp. 190–204; Luz takes a similar line, *Matthew 1–7*, pp. 384–5.

10. On Paul, see Gordon P. Wiles, *Paul's Intercessory Prayers: The Significance of the Intercessory Prayer Passages in the Letters of St Paul* (Cambridge: Cambridge University Press, 1974), p. 55 n. 2. On the *Didache*, see Huub van de Sandt and David Flusser, *The Didache: Its Jewish Sources and its Place in Early Judaism and Christianity*, Compendia Rerum Iudiacarum ad Novum Testamentum III.5 (Assen: Royal Van Gorum; Minneapolis: Fortress, 2002), p. 293 (see also whole discussion of the Lord's Prayer, pp. 291–296); I am indebted to Graham Stanton for drawing my attention to this.

11. See Karlheinz Müller, 'Das Vater Unser als jüdisches Gebet', in A. Gerhards, A. Doeker and P. Ebenbauer (eds), *Identität durch Gebet* (Munich: Ferdinand Schöningh, 2003), pp. 159–204; and Alfons Deissler, 'The Spirit of the Lord's Prayer in the Faith and Worship of the Old Testament', in Petuchowski and Brocke, *The Lord's Prayer and Jewish Liturgy*, pp. 3–17.

12. Birger Gerhardsson, *The Shema in the New Testament: Deuteronomy 6:4–5 in Significant Passages* (Lund: Nova Press, 1996).

13. J.-B. Frey, 'Le pater est-il juif ou chrétien?', *Revue Biblique* 12.3–4 (1915), pp. 556–563; he ends by maintaining the Lord's Prayer 'est vraiement la prière de l'humanité'; see also Robert Aron, 'Les origines juifs du pater', *La Maison-Dieu* 85 (1966), pp. 36–85.

14. For Jewish prayers, see the essays by Jakob Petuchowski ('Jewish Prayer Texts of the Rabbinic Period' and 'The Liturgy of the Synaogogue'), Baruch Graubard ('The Kaddish Prayer'), Simon Lauer ('"Abinu Malkenu": Our Father, Our King!') and Joseph Heinemann ('The Background of Jesus' Prayer in the Jewish Liturgical Tradition'), in Petuchowski and Brocke, *The Lord's Prayer and Jewish Liturgy*, pp. 21–44, 45–58, 59–72, 73–80, 81–89). On the *Kaddish* in particular, see David Telsner, *The Kaddish: Its History and Significance* (Jerusalem: Tal Orot Institute, 1995), esp. texts on pp. 42–57 (text quoted here from pp. 42–43); see also Ismar Elbogen, *Jewish Liturgy: A Comprehensive History* ET and updated R. P. Schiedin (Philadelphia: Jewish Publication Society, 1993), pp. 80–84; C. K. Barrett (ed.), *The New Testament Background: Selected Documents*, rev. edn (London: SPCK, 1987), p. 206; and Gordon J. Bahr, 'The Use of the Lord's Prayer in the Primitive Church', *Journal of Biblical Literature* 84.2 (1965), pp. 153–159. See also Bradshaw and Hoffman, *The Making of Jewish and Christian Worship*; and Louis Jacobs, *A Jewish Theology* (New York: Behrman House, 1973), pp. 183–198, for important insights on the development of Jewish theology in relation to worship and prayer. I have also been greatly helped by Andrew Tremlett, 'The Influence of Jewish

# Notes

Spirituality in the Lord's Prayer', essay submitted for Certificate in Theology, Oxford University, 1987.

15. See texts in Petuchowski and Brocke, *The Lord's Prayer and Jewish Liturgy*, pp. 30–35, 39–40; an earlier text of the *Amidah*, with the eighteen blessings only, appears on pp. 27–30.

16. William Barclay, *The Lord's Prayer* (Berkhamsted: James, 1998), pp. 11–12 (*Aboth* 2.13) and 16 (*Jer. Ber.* 7a).

17. *Didache* 8.3.; See Paul F. Bradshaw, *Daily Prayer in the Early Church*, Alcuin Club Collections 63 (London: SPCK, 1981), p. 26.

18. See Ephraim Urbach, *The Sages: The World and Wisdom of the Rabbis of the Talmud* (Cambridge, MA, and London: Harvard University Press, 2001).

19. See *The Ante-Nicene Fathers*, vol. iii, pp. 681–691; see also E. Dekkers, J. G. Ph. Borleffs, R. Willems, R. F. Refoulé, G. F. Diercks and A. Kroymann (eds), *Tertulliani Opera, Pars I: Opera Catholica*, Corpus Christianorum Series Latina 1 (Turnhout: Brepols, 1954), pp. 255–274; on the Old Latin version of the New Testament, see Bruce Metzger, *The Text of the New Testament: Its Transmission, Corruption and Restoration* (Oxford: Oxford University Press, 1964), pp. 72–73; see also the (Montanist-era) *De fuga in persecutione* II.5, where he reads *sed erve nos a maligus*, 'but rescue us from the evil one'.

20. Geoffrey Lampe, '"Our Father" in the Fathers', in Peter Brooks (ed.), *Christian Spirituality: Essays in Honour of Gordon Rupp* (London: SCM Press, 1975), pp. 11–12 (see whole essay, pp. 11–31).

21. Hilary of Poitiers, *In Mat.* 5.2.; see J. Doignon (ed.), *Hilaire de Poitiers: Sur Matthieu*, vol. i, Sources Chrétiennes 254 (Paris: Cerf, 1978), p. 472.

22. See *The Ante-Nicene Fathers*, vol. v (Edinburgh: T. & T. Clark, 1995), pp. 447–457; M. Simonetti and C. Moreschini (eds), *Sancti Cypriani Episcopi Opera* (Pars II), Corpus Christianorum Series Latina 3A (Turnhout: Brepols, 1976), pp. 90–113; see also Lampe, '"Our Father" in the Fathers', pp. 15–18; Kenneth Stevenson, *Abba Father: Understanding and Using the Lord's Prayer* (Norwich: Canterbury Press, 2000), pp. 142–148.

23. See Simonetti and Moreschini, *Sancti Cypriani Episcopi Opera*, pp. 91, 97, 98 (twice), 99.

24. Ibid., p. 90; cf. Robert F. Taft, SJ, 'The Lord's Prayer in the Eucharist: When and Why?', *Ecclesia Orans* 14 (1997), pp. 137–155.

25. See Origen, *Prayer: Exhortation to Martyrdom*, pp. 65–140 (text) and 212–228 (notes), and pp. 8–10 (introduction); see also, in general, Joseph Wilson Trigg, *Origen: The Bible and Philosophy in the Third-Century Church* (London: SCM Press, 1983), pp. 156–163. See also Lampe, '"Our Father" in the Fathers', pp. 18–21; and Harold Buchinger, 'Gebet and Identität bei Origenes', in Gerhards, Doeker and Ebenbauer (eds), *Identität durch Gebet*, pp. 307–333.

26. On Jerome's use of *supersubstantialem*, see Chapter 4.

27. Polycarp, *Ep.* 7 and 8, in *Early Christian Writings*, Penguin Classics (Harmondsworth: Penguin, 1968, 1987), pp. 121–122; Irenaeus, *Adversus Haereses* IV.17.1, in *The Ante-Nicene Fathers*, vol. i (Edinburgh: T. & T. Clark, 1996), p. 544. See also F. E. Vokes, 'The Lord's Prayer in the First Three Centuries', in F. L. Cross (ed.), *Studia Patristica*, vol. x, Texte und Untersuchungen 107 (Berlin: Akademieverlag, 1970), pp. 253–260, pp. 255–258.

28. Clement of Alexandria, *Paedogogia* I.8.73; *Stromateis* IV.7.66, VII.13.1, and *Adumbra in I Pet. 3:15*, in *The Ante-Nicene Fathers*, vol. ii (Edinburgh: T. & T. Clark, 1994), pp. 228, 421, 546.

29. Dionysius of Alexandria, *PG* 10.1601.

30. See, for example, Paul F. Bradshaw, Maxwell E. Johnson and L. Edward Phillips (eds), *The Apostolic Tradition: A Commentary*, Hermeneia Series (Minneapolis: Fortress, 2002); Sebastian Brock and Michael Vasey (eds), *The Liturgical Patterns of the Didascalia*, Grove Liturgical Study 29 (Bramcote: Grove, 1982). Paul F. Bradshaw, *The Canons of Hippolytus*, Alcuin/GROW Liturgical Study 2 (Bramcote: Grove, 1991); Grant Sperry-White, *The Testamentum Domini: A Text for Students, with Introduction, Translation and Notes*, Alcuin/GROW Liturgical Study 19 (Bramcote: Grove, 1991); and S. G. Hall, *Melito of Sardis: Peri Pascha*, Oxford Early Christian Texts (Oxford: Clarendon Press, 1979).

31. See *Acts of Thomas* 12.144, in J. K. Elliott, *The Apocryphal New Testament* (Oxford: Clarendon Press, 1993), p. 502 (see also introduction, pp. 439–447, together with patristic citations, p. 439). Vokes misrepresents the address of the prayer (and also confuses the Lucan textual variants, as referring to the petition for the hallowing of the Name, in Gregory of Nyssa and Maximus), 'The Lord's Prayer in the First Three Centuries', pp. 258–259; the text of the *Acts* gives no such impression, see M. R. James, *Apocryphal New Testament* (Oxford: Oxford University Press, 1924), p. 427. On the baptism rite in general, see E. C. Whitaker, *Documents of the Baptismal Liturgy* (London: SPCK, 1970), pp. 13–19; on the nuptial blessing-prayer, see Korbinian Ritzer, *Formen, Riten und religiöses Brauchtum der Eheschliessung in den christlichen Kirchen des ersten Jahrtausends*, Liturgiewissenschaftliche Quellen und Forschungen 38 (Münster: Aschendorff, 1962, 1982), pp. 54–57 (discussion), 207–209 (text).

32. See Jeremias, *The Prayers of Jesus*, pp. 82–107, and Green, *Matthew, Poet of the Beatitudes*, pp. 77ff.; and H. D. Betz, *The Sermon on the Mount*, Hermeneia series (Minneapolis: Fortress, 1995), p. 349 (see whole discussion, pp. 370–383).

33. Tertullian, *On Baptism*, in *The Ante-Nicene Fathers*, vol. iii, pp. 669–679.

# Notes

34. See Eberhart and Erwin Nestlé and Barbara and Kurt Aland (eds), *Novum Testamentum Graece*, 27th edn, revised (Stuttgart: Deutsche Bibelgesellschaft, 1993) p. 13.

35. See Bradshaw *et al.*, *The Apostolic Tradition*, p. 47, for a discussion of this (on the whole eucharistic prayer, see pp. 37–48).

## Chapter 3: The Patristic East

1. See, in general, Bradshaw, *Search for the Origins*; and Robert F. Taft, 'Historicism Revisited', in *Beyond East and West*, pp. 15–30; the classic wedge-driver was Gregory Dix, *The Shape of the Liturgy* (London: Dacre, 1945), pp. 141ff.; see also Massey H. Shepherd, *Liturgical Expressions of the Constantinian Triumph*, Dumbarton Oaks Papers 21 (Washington DC: Dumbarton Oaks Center for Byzantine Studies, 1967).

2. Text in Carmel McCarthy, *Saint Ephrem's Commentary on Tatian's Diatessaron: An English Translation of Chester Beatty Syriac MS 709 with Introduction and Notes* (Oxford: Oxford University Press, on behalf of Manchester University Press, 1993), pp. 118–119. I am indebted to Sebastian Brock for much assistance, both here and elsewhere, over the Syriac tradition and interpretation.

3. See Bradshaw, *Search for the Origins*, pp. 113–114; W. J. Swaans, 'Apropos des "catéchèses mystagogiques" attribuées à Cyrille de Jérusalem', *Le Muséon* 55 (1942), pp. 1–43; C. Beukers, ' "For our Emperors Soldiers and Allies": An Attempt at Dating the Twenty Third Catechesis by Cyrillus of Jerusalem', *Vigiliae Christianae* 15 (1961), pp. 171–184; E. J. Yarnold, 'The Authorship of the Mystagogic Catecheses Attributed to Cyril of Jerusalem', *Heythrop Journal* 19 (1978), pp. 143–161; Alexander James Doval, *Cyril of Jerusalem, Mystagogue: The Authorship of The Mystagogic Catecheses*, Patristic Monograph Series 17 (Washington: Catholic University of America Press, 2001); and Juliette Day, 'The Mystagogic Catecheses of Jerusalem and their Relationship to the Eastern Baptismal Liturgies of the Fourth and Early Fifth Centuries', London University Ph.D. dissertation, 2003. See Edward Yarnold, SJ, *The Awe-Inspiring Rites of Initiation* (Edinburgh: T. & T. Clark, 1994), pp. 67–69; and A. Paulin, *Saint Cyrille de Jérusalem Catéchète*, Lex Orandi 29 (Paris: Cerf, 1959); see also Leo P. McCauley and Anthony A. Stephenson (tr.), *St Cyril of Jerusalem*, vol. i, Fathers of the Church 61 (Washington DC: Catholic University of America Press, 1969), pp. 1–65.

4. See in general, Enrico Mazza, *Mystagogy: A Theology of Liturgy in the Patristic Age* (New York: Pueblo, 1989). For Cyril, see Auguste Piédagnel (ed.), *Cyrille de Jérusalem: Catéchèses Mystagogiques*, Sources Chrétiennes 126 (Paris: Cerf, 1966), pp. 160–169 (Piédagnel rejects the view that they are the work of John of Jerusalem, but assigns them to the

later years of Cyril); and *The Works of St Cyril of Jerusalem*, vol. ii, Fathers of the Church 64 (Washington DC: Catholic University of America Press, 1970), pp. 198–202; see also Lampe, '"Our Father" in the Fathers', pp. 21–23; see also Yarnold, *Awe-Inspiring Rites*, pp. 67–97; Mazza, *Mystagogy*, pp. 150–164. On Egeria, see John Wilkinson, *Egeria's Travels*, newly translated with supporting documents and notes (Warminster: Aris and Phillips, 1999), where there is no mention of the Lord's Prayer, although there are references to baptismal preaching, pp. 162–163, where, however, only the Creed is mentioned. For an attempt to accuse the author of Origenism, see E. Bihain, 'Une Vie arménienne de S. Cyrille de Jérusalem', *Le Muséon* 76 (1963), pp. 319–348. See also in general H. M. Riley, *Christian Initiation: A Comparative Study of the Interpretation of the Baptismal Liturgy in the Mystagogical Writings of Cyril of Jerusalem, John Chrysostom, Theodore of Mopsuestia, and Ambrose of Milan*, Studies in Christian Antiquity 17 (Washington: Catholic University of America Press, 1974).

5. Furberg argues (unsuccessfully, in our view) that the Lord's Prayer concludes the eucharistic prayer in the Mystagogic Catecheses, the 'Amen' coming at the very end, *Pater noster*, p. 17.

6. *Hom. in or. dom.* I–V, in Hilda C. Graef (ed.), *St Gregory of Nyssa: The Lord's Prayer; The Beatitudes*, Ancient Christian Writers 18 (New York: Newman Press, 1954), pp. 7–17 (Introduction), pp. 21–84 (text), and pp. 180–193 (notes); see also Lampe, '"Our Father" in the Fathers', pp. 23–27 (quote on p. 23); and see Stevenson, *Abba, Father*, pp. 162–167, and notes, pp. 193–194.

7. See Graef, *St Gregory of Nyssa*, p. 52, and p. 187 n. 69; and Carmignac, *Recherches*, pp. 89–91.

8. *Or. Cat.* 5 (evil), 24 (catching the devil), in Henry Bettenson (ed. and tr.), *The Later Christian Fathers* (London: Oxford University Press, 1970), pp. 130–131, 142.

9. See J. N. D. Kelly, *Golden Mouth* (London: Duckworth, 1995); see also Yarnold, *Awe-Inspiring Rites*, pp. 150–164; and Mazza, *Mystagogy*, pp. 105–149.

10. *Hom. in Mat.* XIX.6–10, in *Nicene and Post-Nicene Fathers* (First Series), vol. x (Edinburgh: T. & T. Clark, 1991), pp. 134–137; see also Lampe, '"Our Father" in the Fathers', pp. 27–29.

11. See *Hom. de diab.* II.6, in *Nicene and Post-Nicene Fathers* (First Series), vol. ix (Edinburgh: T. & T. Clark, 1996), p. 190; *Hom. in Rom. 12:20* 7, ibid., p. 190; *Hom. de statuis* XX.7, 17, ibid., pp. 477, 478; and XXI.17, ibid., p. 488; *Hom. in 1 Cor.* XXIII.6, ibid., vol. xii (1989), p. 135 (preached in Antioch, 392–3); *Hom. in Eph.* XVII, ibid., vol. xiii (1994), p. 129 (preached in Antioch, 395–7); *Hom. in Tim.* VI, ibid., p. 427 (preached in Antioch); *Hom. in Philemon*, ibid., p. 549; *Hom. in Joh.*

XXXIX.4, ibid., vol. xiv (1996), p. 142 (preached in Antioch, 391); and *Hom. in Gen*. XXVII.8, *PG* 53.251 (part of the very first course of sermons preached by John as a newly ordained presbyter in Antioch, Lent 386). See also Frans Van de Paverd, *Zur Geschichte der Messliturgie in Antiocheia und Konstantinopel gegen Ende des Vierten Jahrhunderts*, Orientalia Christiana Analecta 187 (Rome: Pontificium Institutum Orientalium Studiorum, 1970), pp. 143, 229–230, 232, 368–369, 371–374, 402, 526–527.

12. See Carmignac, *Recherches*, pp. 320–333.

13. *Hom. de statuis* III.2, in *The Nicene and Post-Nicene Fathers* (First Series), vol. ix, p. 355.

14. *Hom. in Col*. VI, in *The Nicene and Post-Nicene Fathers* (First Series), vol. xiii, p. 287; cf. the reference to baptism and repentance in *Hom. in Joh*. XXXIV, ibid., vol. xiv, p. 121.

15. *Hom. de capto Eutropio* I.5, in *The Nicene and Post-Nicene Fathers*, vol. ix, p. 252. See also Kelly, *Golden Mouth*, pp. 145ff.

16. Text in *PG* 56.711–715; see J. van Banning, SJ, *Opus Imperfectum in Matthaeum*, Corpus Christianorum Series Latina 87B (Turnhout: Brepols, 1988), pp. v–xvi, on the origins; and 'Il Padre Nostro nell' *Opus Imperfectum in Matthaeum*', in *Gregorianum* 71/2 (1990), pp. 293–313, which includes a defence of the author's 'orthodoxy', and a discussion of the work's subsequent influence in the later medieval period. I am grateful to van Banning for sight of the proofs of his reconstructed text, which (for our purposes) does not radically differ from *PG* 56.711–715.

17. A. Mingana (ed.), *Christian Documents Edited and Translated with Critical Apparatus*, vol. vi: *Commentary of Theodore of Mopsuestia on the Lord's Prayer and on the Sacraments of Baptism and the Eucharist* (Cambridge: Heffer, 1933), pp. 1–16; see also Yarnold, *Awe-Inspiring Rites*, pp. 165–250; Clemens Leonhard, 'The Lord's Prayer Between Ethics and Liturgy', in Gerhards, Doeker and Ebenbauer (eds), *Identität durch Gebet*, pp. 335–367 (Leonhard does not think the prayer was used in Theodore's eucharist). On the dating, Mazza (*Mystagogy*, p. 61) accepts the Antioch ministry, as does Yarnold (*Awe-Inspiring Rites*, p. 150); but H. Lietzmann believed it to be Mopsuestia, see 'Die Liturgie des Theodor von Mopsuestia', in *Kleine Schriften*, vol. iii (Berlin: Akademieverlag, 1962), p. 19, an opinion upheld by Thomas Finn, *The Liturgy of the Baptism in the Baptismal Instructions of St John Chrysostom*, Studies in Christian Antiquity 15 (Washington: Catholic University of America Press, 1967), p. 12. Mazza, *Mystagogy*, pp. 45–104.

18. Rowan Greer, *Theodore of Mopsuestia: Exegete and Theologian* (London: Faith Press, 1961), p. 85, where Greer sees Theodore's treatment of the prayer as a summary of his entire theology.

19. Joseph Sickenberger, *Titus von Bostra: Studien zu dessen Lukashomilien* (Leipzig: Hinirich, 1901), pp. 197–202.

20. See R. M. Tonneau, *S. Cyrilli Alexandrini Commentarie in Lucan* (Pars Prior), Corpus Scriptorum Christianorum Orientalium 140: Scriptores Syri 70 (Louvain: Durbecq, 1953), pp. 194–217; the text in *PG* 72.686–696 is not thought to be as authentic as the Syriac.

21. *Epistularum Liber IV* 24, *PG* 78.711–714.

22. See letter to Theodosius the Wise, where he also takes this wider interpretation, *Epistularum Liber II* 281, *PG* 78.712.

23. Simon Weber (tr.), *Ausgewählte Schriften der Armenischen Kirchenväter*, Bibliothek der Kirchenväter 58 (Munich: Kosel and Pustet, 1927), vol. ii, pp. 273–275 (Introduction), 277–285 (text); see also Serop Jamourlian, 'Il commento al "Padre Nostro" di Ełišē-Vardapat', *Bazmavep* 155 (1997), pp. 207–274; text discussed, pp. 237–247, analysed, pp. 247–253, with conclusions, pp. 254–261, and appended Armenian text, pp. 261–268; see also R. W. Thomson (to whom I am grateful for much assistance here), *Elishe: History of Vardan and the Armenian War*, Harvard Armenian Texts and Studies 5 (Cambridge, MA: Harvard University Press, 1982).

24. See R. H. Connolly, *The Liturgical Homilies of Narsai*, Texts and Studies 111 (Cambridge: Cambridge University Press, 1909), pp. 25–26 (Homily XVII (A), before communion), and pp. 59–60 (Homily XXI (C), after communion); see also pp. lix, lxi (comparison with Liturgy of Addai and Mari), and pp. 81–82 (notes); on his life, see A. Vööbus, *A History of the School at Nisibis*, Corpus Scriptorum Christianorum Orientalium 266: Subsidia 26 (Louvain: Durbecq, 1965), pp. 63, 120.

25. See George C. Berthold (tr.), *Maximus Confessor: Selected Writings*, Classics of Western Spirituality (New York: Paulist Press, 1985), pp. 99–125; Peter Van Deun, *Maximi Confessoris Opuscula Exegetica Duo*, Corpus Christianorum Series Graeca 23 (Turnhout: Brepols; Leuven: Leuven University Press, 1991), pp. 32–73; text also in *PG* 90.871–910; see also Nicholas Madden, 'The Commentary on the Pater Noster: An Example of the Structural Methodology of Maximus the Confessor', in F. Heinzer and C. Schonborn (eds), *Maximus Confessor: Actes du Symposium sur Maxime le Confesseur, 2–5 Septembre, 1980*, Paradosis 27 (Fribourg: Presses Universitaires, 1982), pp. 147–155.

26. *Mystagogia* 18 and 20, see *PG* 91.695–696.

27. See Basil of Caesarea, *Interrogatio* 252, *PG* 31.1251–1252; and John of Damascus, *De Fide Orthodoxa* 4, *PG* 94.1151–1152; and John Moschus, *Pratum Spirituale* 210, *PG* 87.3.3101–3102; cf. also Pseudo-Clementine, Homily 17.2 (probably fourth-century Arian), which refers to the petition for the deliverance from evil in terms of 'the devil', *PG* 2.423–424.

28. Juliette Day, 'Adherence to the *Disciplina Arcani* in the Fourth Century', *Studia Patristica*, vol. 35 (Louvain: Peeters, 2001), pp. 266–270.

29. Robert F. Taft, SJ, *The Liturgy of the Hours in East and West: The*

# Notes

*Origins of the Divine Office and its Meaning Today* (Collegeville: Liturgical Press, 1986), pp. 63–64; see also A. Veilleux, *Pachomian Koinonia*, vol. ii, Cistercian Studies 46 (Kalamazoo: Cistercian Publications, 1981), pp. 199–200; and *La Liturgie dans le cénobitisme pachomien au quatrième siècle*, Studia Anselmiana 57 (Rome: Herder, 1968), pp. 307ff.

30. See Taft, *Liturgy of the Hours*, p. 199.

31. See *Apostolic Constitutions* VII.24.1–2, in W. Jardine Grisbrooke (ed. and tr.) *The Liturgical Portions of the Apostolic Constitutions: A Text for Students*, Alcuin/GROW Liturgical Study 13–14 (Bramcote: Grove, 1991), pp. 52–53; and M. Metzger, *Les Constitutions Apostoliques*, vol. iii, Sources Chrétiennes 336 (Paris: Cerf, 1987), pp. 50–53; on the origins, see Metzger, *Les Constitutions Apostoliques*, vol. i, Sources Chrétiennes 320 (Paris: Cerf, 1985), pp. 54–62, 104–105; accepted by Grisbrooke, *Liturgical Portions of the Apostolic Constitutions*, pp. 5–8; and Bradshaw, *Search for the Origins*, p. 85: but see I. M. Hanssens, *La Liturgie d'Hippolyte*, Orientalia Christiana Analecta 155 (Rome: Pontificium Institutum Studiorum Orientalium, 1959), p. 52.

32. See Taft, *Liturgy of the Hours*, pp. 221–223.

33. See ibid., pp. 232–234; see full texts in A. J. MacLean, *East Syrian Daily Offfices* (London: Rivingtons, 1894), pp. 1–2, start of Vespers, same version near the end, p. 11, and at the start of the Vigil Office, p. 83, and near the end of Mattins, p. 106; another version appears for use on Sundays in Lent at the vigil, pp. 206–207, a text attributed to various sixth/seventh-century figures.

34. See Taft, *Liturgy of the Hours*, pp. 254, 256.

35. See ibid., pp. 263–265, 267–268.

36. See ibid., pp. 274, 282; see also A. Longo, 'Il testo integrale della *Narrazione degli abati Giovanni e Sofronio* attraverso le Hermeneiai di Nicone', *Rivista di studi bizantini e neoellinici* 12–13 (1965–1966), pp. 223–267.

37. Thomas Finn, *Early Christian Baptism and the Catechumenate: Italy, North Africa and Egypt*, Message of the Fathers of the Church 6 (Collegeville: Liturgical Press, 1992), p. 16.

38. See above n. 14. See also the *Mystagogic Homily of Proclus of Constantinople* (434–446), which refers to the Lord's Prayer at baptism, but not in a way that enables a precise context to be determined; see F. J. Leroy, *L'Homilétique de Proclus de Constantinople*, Studi e Testi 247 (Vatican: Biblioteca Apostolica, 1967), p. 193 (whole homily, pp. 184–194).

39. See *Apostolic Constitutions* VII.45.1–2 and III.18.1–2, in Grisbrooke, *Liturgical Portions of the Apostolic Constitutions*, pp. 70, 65; and Metzger, *Les Constitutions Apostoliques*, vol. iii, pp. 106–107, and *Les Constitutions Apostoliques*, vol. ii, Sources Chrétiennes 329 (Paris: Cerf, 1986), pp. 158–161.

40. See, for example, Maxwell Johnson, *Liturgy in Early Christian*

*Egypt*, Alcuin/GROW Liturgical Study 33 (Bramcote: Grove, 1995), pp. 1–16; but see some of the cautions registered about 'Cathedral' (as opposed to 'Evangelical' and 'Monastic') Baptism in Juliette Day, *Baptism in Early Byzantine Palestine: 325–451*, Alcuin/GROW Liturgical Study 43 (Bramcote: Grove, 1999).

41. See Armenian texts in translation in Whitaker, *Documents of the Baptismal Liturgy*, p. 64, where the newly baptized also recites a prayer, similar in scope to that contained in *Apostolic Constitutions* VII.2; on the Syriac liturgical texts, see Sebastian Brock, 'A Remarkable Syriac Baptismal Ordo (BM Add. 14518)', *Parole de l'Orient* 2 (1971), pp. 372, 375, 377, in a ninth-century text reflecting earlier practice, where the prayer appears shortly after baptism (whole article, pp. 365–378); 'Studies in the Early History of the Syrian Orthodox Baptismal Liturgy', *Journal of Theological Studies* NS 23.1 (1972), p. 8 (chart) and pp. 61–3, where it comes after the chrismation following baptism, with an introductory prayer, though sometimes it is a prayer that comes afterwards, like *Apostolic Constitutions* VII.2 (the manuscripts Brock is dealing with date from the eighth century) (whole article, pp. 16–64); for the Syrian Orthodox rites, see texts in H. Denzinger, *Ritus Orientalium*, vol. i (Würzburg: Stahl, 1863), pp. 278–279, 287, 308, 315; and Gabriele Winkler, *Das armenische Initiationsrituale: entwicklungsgeschichtliche und liturgievergleichende Untersuchung der Quellen des 3. bis 10. Jahrhunderts*, Orientalia Christiana Analecta 217 (Rome: Pontificium Institutum Studiorum Orientalium, 1982), pp. 451–452, where the Lord's Prayer appears in all four principal manuscripts, after the reading of Matthew 3:13–17, the narrative of Jesus' baptism in the Jordan, which comes straight after the baptism itself.

42. See text in Denzinger, *Ritus Orientalium*, vol i, p. 356; and the important study by Augustin Mouhanna, *Les Rites de l'initiation dans L'église maronite*, Orientalia Christiana Analecta 212 (Rome: Pontificium Institutum Orientalium Studiorum, 1980), pp. 88, 108–109, 141, 150, and 221–224; I am grateful to John Baldovin for assistance here.

43. On the 387 homilies, see *Cat. Bap.* III.9, in A. Piédagnel (ed.) *Jean Chrysostome: Trois Catéchèses Baptismales*, Sources Chrétiennes 366, (Paris: Cerf, 1990), pp. 238–241; see Finn, *Early Christian Baptism and the Cathechumenate: West and East Syria*, p. 80, where he translates from Antoine Wenger's edition (*Cat. Bap.* II.29), *Jean Chrysostome: Huit Catéchèses Baptismales*, Sources Chrétiennes 50 (Paris: Cerf, 1957), pp. 149–150; see also Thomas M. Finn, *The Liturgy of Baptism in the Baptismal Instructions of St John Chrysostom*, Studies in Christian Antiquity 15 (Washington, DC: Catholic University of America Press, 1967), esp. pp. 38–39 (Lord's Prayer only for the baptized), pp. 66–67 (rejecting the theory that the daily instruction was on the Lord's Prayer, preferring the view that it was based on the Creed), and pp. 186–189 (discussion of the Lord's Prayer in the baptism rite).

# Notes

44. Whitaker, *Documents of the Baptismal Liturgy*, pp. 69–82 (which translates the eighth-century Barberini 336 manuscript); see also Jacobus Goar, *Euchologion, sive Rituale Graecorum* (Venice: Javarini, 1730), pp. 287–303; see also Stefano Parenti and Elena Velkovska (eds), *L'Eucologio Barberini gr. 336*, Bibliotheca 'Ephemerides Liturgicae' Subsidia 80 (Rome: Edizioni Liturgiche, 1995), pp. 108–119.

45. See R. J. S. Barrett-Lennard, *The Sacramentary of Sarapion of Thmuis: A Text for Students, with Introduction, Translation, and Commentary*, Alcuin/GROW Liturgical Study 35 (Bramcote: Grove, 1993), p. 28; Grant Sperry-White (ed.), *The Testamentum Domini: A Text for Students with Introduction, Translation, and Notes*, Alcuin/GROW Liturgical Study 19 (Bramcote: Grove, 1991); and Paul F. Bradshaw (ed.), *The Canons of Hippolytus*, ET Carol Bebawi, Alcuin/GROW Liturgical Study 2 (Bramcote: Grove, 1987).

46. See texts in F. E. Brightman, *Liturgies Eastern and Western*, vol. i: *Eastern* (Oxford: Clarendon Press, 1896), pp. 58–60 (Greek James), 99–100 (Syriac James), 135–136 (Greek Mark), 181–182 (Coptic Mark), 234–235 (Ethiopic), 295–296 (East Syrian), 339–340 (MS Barberini 336, Basil and John Chrysostom), 444–445 (Armenian); on the Coptic rite, see Geoffrey J. Cuming, *The Liturgy of St Mark*, Orientalia Christiana Analecta 234 (Rome: Pontificium Institutum Studiorum Orientalium, 1990), pp. 50–52(early texts), 137–138 (commentary); for current use, see for example, *The Divine Liturgies of Saints Basil, Gregory and Cyril* (2001), pp. 180–190 (Basil), 266–268 (Gregory), 350–353 (Cyril [= Mark]); and pp. 369–420 (additional seasonal forms); for MS Barberini 336, see Stefano Parenti and Elena Velkovska, *L'Eucologia Barberini gr. 336*, Bibliotheca 'Ephemerides Liturgicae' Subsidia 80 (Rome: Edizioni Liturgiche, 1995), pp. 17 (Basil), 38 (Chrysostom) and 286 (Presanctified). See also I. M. Hanssens, SJ, *Institutiones Liturgicae De Ritibus Orientalibus*, vol. iii (Rome: Pontificia Universitas Gregoriana, 1932), pp. 488–493, and comparative chart, p. 504; on the Egyptian position, after the fraction, see Johnson, *Liturgy in Early Christian Egypt*, pp. 32f.; see also Faustus of Byzantium's evidence for its use before communion in the Armenian rite in the late fifth century, Taft, 'The Lord's Prayer', pp. 141–142 n.31.

47. See Robert F. Taft, SJ, *A History of the Liturgy of St John Chrysostom: The Pre-Communion Rites*, Orientalia Christiana Analecta 261 (Rome: Pontificio Istituto Orientale, 2000), pp. 130ff.

48. No mention is made of the prayer in the writings of Ps.-Denys, *PG* 3.369–485; I am indebted to Andrew Louth for assistance here.

49. See, for example, Didymus the Blind, *De Trinitate* 111.39, *PG* 39.977–982; cf. 'Das Vater Unser ist für Chrysostomus das eigentliche "Gebet der Gläubigen"', Georg Wagner, *Der Ursprung der Chrysostomusliturgie*, Liturgiewissenschaftliche Quellen und Forschungen 59 (Münster: Aschendorff, 1973), p. 124 (see discussion, pp. 122–125); see also R. G.

Coquin, 'Le thème de la *parrhēsia* et ses expressions symboliques dans les rites d'initiation à Antioche', *Proche-Orient Chrétien* 20 (1970), pp. 3–19.

## Chapter 4: The Patristic West

1. See R. De Latte, 'Saint Augustin et le baptême: étude liturgico-historique du rituel baptismal des adultes chez Saint Augustin', *Questions Liturgiques* 56.4 (1975), pp. 177–224; and 'Saint Augustin et le baptême: étude liturgico-historique du rituel baptismal des enfants chez Saint Augustin', *Questions Liturgiques* 57.1 (1976), pp. 41–55.

2. See *De Sacramentis* V.4.20–30 (cf. VI.5.24, when he is dealing with the different parts of the eucharist), in Henry Chadwick (ed.), *Saint Ambrose: On the Sacraments*, Studies in Eucharistic Faith and Practice (London: Mowbrays, 1960), pp. 42–45 (cf. pp. 52–53); also in B. Botte, OSB (ed.), *Ambroise de Milan: Des Sacrements, des Mystères, Explication du Symbole*; Sources Chrétiennes 25bis (Paris: Cerf, 1994), pp. 128–137, 150–153 (see also pp. 16–17, 30); Botte takes the view, based on a doxology with which the fifth address concludes, that the Lord's Prayer ended with a doxology at Ambrose's time (p. 106) (supported by Archdale A. King, *Liturgies of the Primatial Sees* (London: Longmans, 1957), p. 398); but there seems little ground for this assumption; see G. G. Willis, 'St Gregory the Great and the Lord's Prayer in the Roman Mass', in *Further Essays in Early Roman Liturgy*, Alcuin Club Collections 50 (London: SPCK, 1968), pp. 179–182; see also Whitaker, *Documents of the Baptismal Liturgy*, pp. 127–132, for discussion of Ambrose and selection from these addresses; see also Mazza, *Mystagogy*, pp. 14–44, for general discussion of Ambrose as mystagogue, and Yarnold, *Awe-Inspiring Rites*, pp. 98–149; see also Craig Alan Saterlee, *Ambrose of Milan's Method of Mystagogic Teaching* (Collegeville: Liturgical Press, 2002), p. 182.

3. *De Sacramentis* V.4.24–26, in Chadwick, *Saint Ambrose*, pp. 43–44; and Botte, *Ambroise de Milan,* pp. 132–135.

4. See *Commentarium in Matthaeun* I.6, *PL* 26.44–45; see also J. N. D. Kelly, *Jerome* (London: Duckworth, 1975), esp. pp. 222–225; on *mahar*, see ch. 2; see also in general Philip Burton, *The Old Latin Gospels: A Study of Their Texts and Language*, Oxford Early Christian Studies (Oxford: Oxford University Press, 2000); see pp. 94 (temptation petiton), 135 (*sanctificetur* as translation of *hagiasthētō*), and 196 (Jerome's translation of *epiousion*).

5. Text in *PL* 26.44; see also *Commentarium in Hiezechielem* VI.18.5/9, in F. Gloire (ed.), *Sancti Hieronymi Presbyteri Opera*, Pars I: *Opera Exegetica* 4, Corpus Christianorum Series Latina 75 (Turnhout: Brepols, 1964), p. 239; see also Carmignac, *Recherches*, pp. 127–128:

6. *Dialog. contra Pel.* III.15, in *Nicene and Post-Nicene Fathers* (Second Series), vol. vi (Edinburgh: T. & T. Clark, 1996), pp. 480–481; see also Kelly, *Jerome*, pp. 319–321.

# Notes

7. *Sermo* XL and *Tractatus* XVIII on Matthew 6:9–13, in R. Étaix and J. Lemarié (eds), *Chromatii Aquileiensis Opera*, Corpus Christianorum Series Latina 9A (Turnhout: Brepols, 1974), pp. 171–173; and pp. 329–335.

8. See the various editions of his *Confessions*, his spiritual autobiography, written *c.*398–400, e.g. Henry Chadwick (tr.), *Saint Augustine: Confessions* (Oxford: Oxford University Press, 1991); see also the classic biography, Peter Brown, *Augustine of Hippo: A Biography* (London: Faber, 1967).

9. For *De Sermone Domini in Monte* II.4.15–39, see *The Nicene and Post-Nicene Fathers* (First Series), vol. vi (Edinburgh: T. & T. Clark, 1996), pp. 38–47; and A. Mutzenbecher (ed.), *Augustini De Sermone in Monte*, Corpus Christianorum Series Latina 35 (Turnhout: Brepols, 1967), pp. 104–130. For *Letter* 130 (to Proba), see *Nicene and Post-Nicene Fathers* (First Series), vol. i (Edinburgh: T. & T. Clark, 1994), pp. 465–466; for the Sermons, see Edmund Hill (tr.), *The Works of Saint Augustine: Sermons III* (New York: New City Press, 1999), pp. 95–108 (*Sermo* 56), pp. 109–117 (*Sermo* 57), pp. 118–125 (*Sermo* 58); see 117 n. 8 on versions of the third petition (cf. *De dono perseverantiae* 3.6 PL 45.997) and pp. 126–131 (*Sermo* 59); and for the *Encheiridion*, 7 (on Creed and Lord's Prayer in general), 115 (on Matthew's version), and 116 (Luke's version), see *The Nicene and Post-Nicene Fathers* (First Series), vol. iii (Edinburgh: T. & T. Clark, 1993), pp. 238–239, and 274; and for the first part of the prayer, mainly taken from *De Sermone Domini in Monte*, see Lampe, ' "Our Father" in the Fathers', pp. 29–31. See also the important study by M. G. Jackson, 'The Lord's Prayer in St Augustine', in E. A. Livingstone (ed.), *Studia Patristica*, vol. xxvii (Louvain: Peeters, 1993), pp. 311–321; J. Moffat, 'Augustine on the Lord's Prayer', *Expositor* 18 (1919), pp. 259–272; Suzanne Poque, *Augustine d'Hippone: Sermons Pour La Pâque*, Sources Chrétiennes 116 (Paris: Cerf, 1966), pp. 65–69; P.-P. Verbraken, 'Les Sermons CCXV et LVI de saint Augustin "De Symbolo" et "De Oratione Dominica" ', *Revue Bénédictine* 70 (1958), pp. 5–40; 'Le Sermon LVIII de saint Augustin pour la tradition du Pater', *Ecclesia Orans* 1 (1984), pp. 113–132; 'Le Sermon 57 de saint Augustin pour la tradition de l'Oraison dominicale', in *Homo Spiritalis: Festgabe für L. Verheijen* (Würzburg: Akademieverlag, 1987), pp. 411–424.

10. See Brown, *Augustine*, pp. 149ff.

11. See T. van Bavel, ' "Inferas–inducas": à propos de Mtth. 6, 13 dans les oeuvres de saint Augustin', *Revue Bénédictine* 69.1–2 (1959), pp. 348–351, although he overlooks the difference between the Gospel text and the liturgical text (cf. *De dono perseverantiae* 6.12, PL 45.1000).

12. See *Sermone Domini in Monte* I.4.11, in *Nicene and Post-Nicene Fathers* (First Series), vol. vi, pp. 6–7.

13. See Ambrose, *De Sacramentis* III.2.8–10, IV.2.6–8, and *De Mysteriis* VI.41–42, in Botte, *Ambroise de Milan*, pp. 96, 140, 178.

14. 'First Letter to Proba', *Ep*. 130.22, in *Nicene and Post-Nicene Fathers* (First Series), vol. i, p. 466 (cf. p. 463); cf. *Epp*. 131, 150 and 188, ibid., pp. 469–470, 503–504, and 548–552.

15. *Encheiridion*, see above n. 9; cf. *Tractatus in Johannem* 98.5, in *Nicene and Post-Nicene Fathers* (First Series), vol. vii (Edinburgh: T. & T. Clark, 1991), p. 378.

16. See De Latte, 'Saint Augustin et le baptême', pp. 199ff. See William Harmless, *Augustine and the Catechumenate* (New York: Pueblo, 1995), esp. pp. 286–293; and, in general, A.-M. La Bonnardière, 'Pénitence et réconciliation des pénitents d'après saint Augustin', *Revue des Etudes Augustiniennes* 13 (1967), pp. 31–53, esp. pp. 47ff., on 'daily' forgiveness through recitation of the prayer.

17. *Ep*. 149.16, *PL* 33.636–637, quoted by Taft, 'The Lord's Prayer', p. 137.

18. *Sermo* 213.9 (before 410), 261.10 (? 418), in *The Works of St Augustine: Sermons*, vol. III/6 (New York: City Press, 1993), pp. 145–146, and vol. III/7 (New York: City Press, 1993), p. 213.

19. *Sermo* 135.8 (417–418), in *The Works of St Augustine: Sermons*, vol. III/4 (New York: City Press, 1992), p. 350 (apostles also sinned); *De Peccatorum Meritis et Remissione* 11.10.13 (411/412), ibid., vol. I/23 (New York: City Press, 1997), p. 89 (everybody sins); *Sermo* 114A.5 (428–429), ibid., 11/4 (New York: City Press, 1992), p. 196 (not to be omitted); *De Peccatorum Meritis et Remissione* 11.4.4, ibid., pp. 82–83 (evil remains in our flesh); *De natura et gratia* 67.70 (415), ibid., p. 261 (people pray the Lord's Prayer right up to their last breath), and 67.80, ibid., p. 267 (evil can be resisted, but only by divine grace); *De Correctione Donatistarum* IX.39, in *The Nicene and Post-Nicene Fathers* (First Series), vol. iv (Edinburgh: T. & T. Clark, 1996), p. 647; on the Second Council of Milevis and the Sixteenth Council of Carthage, see Carmignac, *Recherches*, pp. 232–233.

20. *Responsio ad Julianum* III.21.48 (41) in *The Works of St Augustine*, vol. I/24 (New York: City Press, 1998), p. 366.

21. See Willis, 'Gregory the Great and the Lord's Prayer in the Roman Mass', p. 179; *Sermo* 228.3, in *The Works of St Augustine: Sermons*, vol. III/6, pp. 258; *Sermo* 352.7 (398), in ibid., vol. III/10 (New York: City Press, 1995), p. 328.

22. Jackson, 'The Lord's Prayer in St Augustine', pp. 320–321.

23. *Conferences* IX.18–25, see *Nicene and Post-Nicene Fathers* (Second Series), vol. xi (Edinburgh: T. & T. Clark, 1991), pp. 393–396; and E. Pichery (ed.), *Jean Cassien: Conférences VIII–XVII*, Sources Chrétiennes 54 (Paris: Cerf 1958), pp. 55–62.

24. See Adalbert de Vogue, *La Règle du Maître*, vol. i, Sources Chrétiennes 105 (Paris: Cerf, 1964), pp. 300–317; and Timothy Fry (ed.), *The Rule of St Benedict in Latin and English with Notes* (Collegeville: Liturgical Press, 1981), pp. 3–64.

# Notes

25. *La Règle du Maître*, p. 300; he uses 'dare' on two further occasions, pp. 304 and 316.

26. For the citations to Cyprian, see pp. 301, 303, 304, 306, 307, 310.

27. On the *oratio in monasterio*, see *La Règle du Maître*, pp. 315–316, for which cf. Jean Deshusses and Bénôit Darragon (eds), *Concordances et Tableaux pour l'Étude des Grands Sacramentaires*, vol. i, Spicilegii Friburgensis Subsidia 9 (Fribourg: Editions Universitaires, 1982), p. 214, where the prayer is listed against two other books, the late eighth-century Sacramentary of Gellone, as well as the early ninth-century 'Supplement' to the Gregorian Sacramentary.

28. *Sermones 67–72*, in Alexander Olivar (ed.), *Sancti Petri Chrysologi: Collectio Sermonum*, Corpus Christianorum Series Latina 24A (Turnhout: Brepols, 1981), pp. 402–405 (67), 406–411 (68), 412–418 (69), 420–423 (70), 424–428 (71), and 429–433 (72), with introduction pp. 400–401); see also Sermons 67 and 70 (in English translation) in George E. Ganss, SJ (tr.), *Saint Peter Chrysologus: Selected Sermons; and Saint Valerian: Homilies*, Fathers of the Church 17 (New York: Fathers of the Church, 1953), pp. 115–119 and 119–123; see also Kenneth Stevenson, 'The Six Homilies on the Lord's Prayer of Peter Chrysologus', forthcoming in Maxwell E. Johnson and L. Edward Phillips (eds.), *Studia Liturgica Diversa: Essays in Honor of Paul F. Bradshaw* (Portland: Pastoral Press, 2004), pp. 65–70.

29. *Sermo 147*, see G. Morin (ed.), *Sancti Caesarii Arletensis Sermones* (Pars I/2), Corpus Christianorum Series Latina 104 (Turnhout: Brepols, 1953), pp. 602–604; and also *Saint Caesarius of Arles: Sermons*, vol. ii, Fathers of the Church 47 (Washington: Catholic University of America, 1963), pp. 311–315.

30. See William E. Klingshirn, *Caesarius of Arles: The Making of a Christian Community in Late Antique Gaul*, Cambridge Studies in Medieval Life and Thought (Cambridge: Cambridge University Press, 1994).

31. *Sermon 130.5*, in *Sancti Caesarii Arletensis Sermones* and *Saint Caesarius of Arles: Sermons*.

32. *Expositio*, PL 88.313–322.

33. *De officiis ecclesiasticis* I.15.3–5 (the whole prayer), 18.7 (daily bread), PL 83.753, 756.

34. *Annotationes de cognitione baptismi* 133–135, PL 96.166–167; 134 (ibid. 167) deals with prayer in general; see also Whitaker, *Documents of the Baptismal Liturgy*, pp. 113–115.

35. *In Matthaei Evangelii Expositio* I, PL 92.32–33; *In Lucae Evangelii Expositio* III, PL 92.472–473; the two expositions differ little, except that Bede points out the differences in the two versions.

36. *In Psalm 118* 1.15, in Marc Milhou (ed.), *Hilaire de Poitiers: Commentaire sur le Psaume 118:I*, Sources Chrétiennes 344 (Paris: Cerf,

1988), pp. 124–125; see also A. J. B. Higgins, ' "Lead us not into temptation": some Latin Variants', *Journal of Theological Studies* 46 (1945),
p. 182 (whole article, pp. 179–183).

37. See also the important evidence assembled by G. G. Willis, 'The
Lord's Prayer in Irish Gospel Manuscripts', *Studia Evangelica*, vol. iii,
Texte und Untersuchungen 88 (Berlin: Akademieverlag, 1964), pp. 282–
288; on 'et ne passus fueris', see Burton, *The Old Latin Gospels*, p. 94.

38. See Bradshaw, *Search for the Origins*, pp. 161–184; cf. also his
important article which applies even more to this period, 'The Gospel and
the Catechumenate in the Third Century', *Journal of Theological Studies*
50.1 (1999), pp. 143–152; see also Taft, 'The Lord's Prayer', p. 151 n. 72,
for the suggestion that Peter Chrysologus' references to 'the womb'
(*Sermones* 67.11; 68.3, 11; 69.6; 70.3) may mean catechumens already
reciting the prayer publicly, a practice which Augustine would not have
countenanced.

39. See R. F. Taft, 'The Inclination Prayer before Communion in the
Byzantine Liturgy of St John Chrysostom', *Ecclesia Orans* 3 (1986),
pp. 51–54 (whole article pp. 29–60); see also Optatus of Milevis, *Contra
Parmenianum Donatistam* II.20, in Mireille Labrousse, *Optat de Milève:
Traité Contre les Donatistes*, Sources Chrétiennes 413 (Paris: Cerf, 1996),
pp. 282–283; see also Furberg, *Pater Noster*, p. 25.

40. See Ambrose, *De Virginibus* III.4.18, in *Nicene and Post-Nicene
Fathers* (Second Series), vol. x (Edinburgh: T. & T. Clark, 1989), p. 384; on
the daily office, see Graham Woolfenden, *Daily Prayer in Christian Spain*,
Alcuin Club Collections 77 (London: SPCK, 2000), pp. 43–44; Taft,
*Liturgy of the Hours*, pp. 133, 161–162.

41. *Rule of St Benedict* 13.12–13; see Fry, *Rule of St Benedict*, p. 209.

42. See D. Sherwin Bailey, *Sponsors at Baptism and Confirmation*
(London: SPCK, 1952), p. 37.

43. For texts, see L. C. Mohlberg, L. Eizenhöfer and P. Siffrin (eds),
*Liber Sacramentorum Romanae aeclesiae ordinis anni circuli (Sacramenta-
rium Gelasianum)*, Rerum Ecclesiasticarum Documenta Series Maior:
Fontes IV (Rome: Herder, 1960), p. 186; and Michel Andrieu, *Les Ordines
Romani du Haut Moyen Âge*, vol. ii, Spicilegium Sacrum Lovaniense 23
(Louvain: Spicilegium Sacrum Lovaniense, 1971), pp. 437–440 (see also
discussion of this rite, pp. 394–395); texts also in Whitaker, *Documents of
the Baptismal Liturgy*, pp. 177–178 (Gelasian Sacramentary), p. 68 (*Ordo
Romanus* XII); there is also a briefer form for use at the Pentecost Vigil,
p. 192; on the dating of these works, see Cyrille Vogel, *Medieval Liturgy:
An Introduction to the Sources*, tr. and rev. William Storey and Niels
Rasmussen (Washington: Pastoral Press, 1986), pp. 64, 164–165. Similar
texts are to be found in L. C. Mohlberg (ed.), *Missale Gallicanum Vetus*,
Rerum Ecclesiasticarum Documenta Series Maior: Fontes III (Rome:

# Notes

Herder, 1958), pp. 23–25, which is an eighth-century document consisting of two manuscripts, the second of which contains the masses for Lent and Easter, and which shows signs of Gallican usage. On this rite in general, see Antoine Chavasse, *Le Sacramentaire Gélasien*, Bibliothèque de Théologie, Série IV (Paris: Desclée, 1957), pp. 160–161, and J. D. C. Fisher, *Christian Initiation: Baptism in the Medieval West*, Alcuin Club Collections 47 (London: SPCK, 1965), pp. 4 and 10.

44. See Bradshaw, 'The Gospel and the Catechumenate'; Kenneth Stevenson, 'Animal Rites: The Four Living Creatures in Patristic Exegesis and Liturgy', *Studia Patristica*, vol. xxxiv, pp. 482–486, for a discussion of this rite in relation to the 'exposition of the gospels' (whole article, pp. 470–492); Pierre de Puniet, 'Les trois homélies catéchétiques du Sacramentaire Gélasien', *Revue d'Histoire Ecclésiastique* 6 (1905), pp. 15–32; his theory that it was written by Leo the Great (†461) is an open question.

45. See Taft, *Liturgy of the Hours*, p. 107, citing Aurelian of Arles, *Rule of Monks* 57.11–12.

46. See Michel Andrieu, *Les Ordines Romani du Haut Moyen Âge*, vol. iii, Spicilegium Sacrum Lovaniense 24 (Louvain: Spicilegium Sacrum Lovaniense, 1974), pp. 151–152 (*Ordo Romanus* 16), 189 (*Ordo Romanus* 17); texts also in Hermann Schmidt, *Hebdomada Sancta*, Volumen Alterum (Rome: Herder, 1957), p. 507 (*Ordo Romanus* 16, *c*.680–775), p. 509 (*Ordo Romanus* 17, *c*.790).

47. C. Munier (ed.), *Conciliae Galliae: A.314–A.506*, Corpus Christianorum Series Latina 148 (Turnhout: Brepols, 1963), p. 125.

48. *Ep.* 12, in *Nicene and Post-Nicene Fathers* (Second Series), vol. xiii, (Edinburgh: T. & T. Clark, 1989), pp. 8–9, p. 9; for a full discussion of this letter, see Willis, 'Gregory the Great and the Lord's Prayer in the Roman Mass', pp. 177–188; see also Taft, 'The Lord's Prayer', pp. 137–155; and Joseph-Andreas Jungmann, *Missarum Sollemnia*, vol. iii, Théologie Historique 21 (Paris: Aubier, 1954), pp. 200–218.

49. *De Miraculis S. Martini* 11.30, *PL* 71.954–955; this is corroborated by Ps.-Germanus, *De Liturgia Gallicana* 1.21, *PL* 77.138–139.

50. See Jean Deshusses, *Le Sacramentaire Grégorien: ses principales formes d'après les plus anciens manuscrits*, Spicilegium Friburgense 16 (Fribourg: Editions Universitaires, 1971), p. 91; Willis's suggestion that the embolism was written by Gregory the Great because of the presence of St Andrew, to whom Gregory's old abbey in Rome was dedicated, in pride of place alongside Peter and Paul ('Gregory the Great and the Lord's Prayer in the Roman Mass', p. 188) is negated by Deshusses' edition, where it is clear that Andrew does not appear in the earliest (or best) manuscripts; the manuscripts which have 'Amen' at the end are Deshusses' O (Beauvais, second half of ninth century), P (copied in Rome for Paris Cathedral, third quarter of ninth), R (Paris, St Denis, second half of ninth), S (Cambrai, for

St Vedast of Arras, second half of ninth), U (Stavelot, second half of ninth), V2 (Cologne Cathedral, before end of ninth), W (Essen, first quarter of ninth) and X (Senlis, second half of ninth); for the Gellone variant, see A. Dumas, OSB, *Liber Sacramentorum Gellonensis*, Corpus Christianorum Series Latina 159 (Turnhout: Brepols, 1981) 1947, p. 255 (in the mass); but the other form appears at 553, p. 72 (pre-baptismal catechesis) and 2287, p. 328 (baptism rite).

51. See G. F. Warner, *The Stowe Missal*, Henry Bradshaw Society 32 (1906), p. 35 (order for the communion of the sick); H. M. Bannister, *Missale Gothicum* Henry Bradshaw Society 54 (1916), pp. 2, 6 (Christmas Masses), 10 (St Stephen), 19 (Circumcision), 28 (Epiphany), 43 (St Andrew), 50, 53 (start of Lent), 62 (Holy Week), 64 (Maundy Thursday), 131, 133, 135, 136–7, 138, 140–141 (Ordinary Sundays); see also Bannister, *Missale Gothicum*, Henry Bradshaw Society 54 (1917), p. 3 (note); W. C. Bishop and C. L. Feltoe, *The Mozarabic and Ambrosian Rites: Four Essays in Comparative Liturgiology*, Alcuin Club Tracts 15 (London: Mowbrays, 1924), pp. 40–42, 73, 83; and Marius Férotin, OSB, *Le Liber Mozarabicus Sacramentorum et les Manuscrits Mozarabes* (réimpression de l'édition de 1912 et bibliographie générale de la liturgie hispanique, préparée et présentée par Anthony Ward, SM, et Cuthbert Johnson, OSB), Bibliotheca 'Ephemerides Liturgicae' Subsidia 78: Instrumenta Liturgica Quarreriensia (Rome: Edizioni Liturgiche, 1995), *passim*; there are 167 in all. See also F. E. Warren, *The Liturgy and Ritual of the Celtic Church* (Oxford: Clarendon Press, 1881), pp. 98 (introduction, in varying forms), 164 (*Book of Deer*, ninth/tenth century), 169 (*Book of Dimma*, ninth century), 172–173 (*Book of Armagh*, early ninth century), 177 (St Gall Ms 1394, ninth century), 223–224 (*Stowe Missal*): all these are in offices for the sick.

## Chapter 5: The Later East

1. For texts, see P. Meyendorff (ed. and tr.), *St Germanus of Constantinople: On the Divine Liturgy* (Crestwood, NY: St Vladimir's Seminary Press, 1984), pp. 100–103; on the Maximus quotation, *Mystagogy* 20 (*PG* 91.695–696), see Chapter 3. For a full discussion of the provenance of the manuscripts of this work, its significance, and authorship, see R. Bornert, *Les Commentaires Byzantins de la Divine Liturgie du VIIe au XVe Siècle*, Archives de l'Orient Chrétien 9 (Paris: Institut Français d'Études Byzantines, 1966), pp. 124–180; see also, in general, Hans-Joachin Schulz, *The Byzantine Liturgy* (New York: Pueblo, 1980); see also Taft, *A History of the Liturgy of St John Chrysostom*, pp. 129–30.

2. Parenti and Velkovska, *L'Eucologio Barberini gr. 336*, pp. 17 (Basil), 38 (Chrysostom), 46 (Vespers), 286 (Presanctified).

3. *PG* 98.444–446; see Meyendorff, *Germanus of Constantinople*, p. 12; on the identification of this particular manuscript, see Bornert, *Commentaires Byzantins*, p. 133 and n. 1.

4. *PG* 140.461–462; on Nicholas of Andyda, see Bornert, *Commentaires Byzantins*, pp. 181–206.

5. Text in *PG* 86.2.3329–3336.

6. Text in *PG* 123.203–206.

7. Text in *PG* 123.853–856.

8. Text in *PG* 129.233–242.

9. Text in *PG* 150.447–448.

10. Text in *PG* 155.739–740.

11. Text in André de Halleux, *Martyrius (Sahdona): Oeuvres Spirituelles*, vol. ii, Corpus Scriptorum Christianorum Orientalium 214–215: Scriptores Syri 90–91 (Louvain: Corpus Scriptorum, 1961), pp. 51–54 (in both Syriac and French translation versions).

12. *Horae Semiticae V: The Commentaries of Isho'dad of Merv*, vol. i (Cambridge: Cambridge University Press, 1911), pp. 37–40.

13. Text in R. H. Connolly and H. W. Codrington, *Two Commentaries on the Jacobite Liturgy*, Text and Translation Society (London: Williams and Norgate, 1913), pp. 12 (baptism), 19 (eucharist).

14. Text in Connolly and Codrington, *Two Commentaries*, pp. 73–85.

15. Noted by editors, p. 73 n. 2.

16. See Simon Evans, ' "Womb of the Spirit": The Liturgical Implications of the Doctrine of the Spirit for the Syrian Baptismal Tradition', University of London Ph.D. dissertation, 1999.

17. The references are to *Mystagogic Catechesis* 23.14 and 17.

18. See Peter Cowe (ed.), *Commentary on the Divine Liturgy by Khosrov, Anjewac'i* (New York: St Vartan Press, 1991), pp. 202–205 (text), 3–18 (biography); and P. Vetter, *Chosroae Magni Episcopi Monophysitici Explicatio Precum in latinam versam* (Freiburg-im-Breisgau: Herder, 1880), pp. 48–50; Brightman, *Liturgies Eastern and Western*, pp. 445–446.

19. I. Sedlacek and I. B. Chabot (eds), *Dionysius Bar Salibi: Commentarii in Evangelia*, Corpus Scriptorum Christianorum Orientalium 77 (Louvain: Durbecq, 1953), pp. 172–174.

20. *The Precious Pearl* 33; text in Jean Périer (ed. and tr.), *Jean Ibn Saba: La Perle Précieuse*, Patrologia Orientalis 16.4 (Paris: Firmin-Didot, 1922), pp. 683–707.

21. See, for example, the brief style and content of Nicholas Bulgaris, in the seventeenth century, in W. E. Daniel (tr.) and R. Raikes Bromage (ed.), *The Holy Catechism of Nicolas Bulgaris* (London: Masters, 1893), pp. 224–228.

## Chapter 6: The Medieval West

1. *Rule of St Benedict* 50.1–4; see Fry, *Rule of St Benedict*, pp. 252–255.

2. On the prayer repeated in private devotion, André Duval, 'Rosaire', in *Dictionnaire de Spiritualité* (89–90) (Paris: Beauchesne, 1988), 937–967; and John D. Miller, *Beads and Prayers: The Rosary in History and Devotion* (London: Burns and Oates, 2002), pp. 61–62.

3. See Marcia L. Colish, 'Peter Lombard', in G. R. Evans (ed.), *The Medieval Theologians* (Oxford: Blackwell, 2001), pp. 168–183; on the marriage liturgy, see Kenneth Stevenson, *Nuptial Blessing: A Study of Christian Marriage Rites*, Alcuin Club Collections 64 (London: SPCK, 1982), pp. 68–71; and Jean-Baptiste Molin and Protais Mutembe, *Le Rituel du Mariage en France du XIIe au XVIe Siècle*, Théologie Historique 26 (Paris: Beauchesne, 1974), esp. *Ordo* V, pp. 289–291, from the abbey of Bury St Edmunds, the first known rite to direct public consent in this way.

4. See also H. E. J. Cowdrey, 'Pope Gregory VII (1073–1085) and the Liturgy', *Journal of Theological Studies* (forthcoming); for Gregory, the use of the Roman rite was a matter of loyalty to Rome, the Visigothic being regarded as decadent; see also King, *Liturgies of the Primatial Sees*.

5. *Commentarium in Matthaeum* 2, PL 107.817–823.

6. See Alice L. Harting-Correa, *Walahfrid Strabo's Libellus de Exordiis Incrementis Quarundam in Observationibus Ecclesiasticis Rerum: A translation and Liturgical Commentary* (Leiden: Brill, 1996), pp. 116–119, 126–127, 144–145 (text); and pp. 259, 265–266, 280 (notes).

7. *Expositio in Matthaeum*, PL 114.876.

8. *Expositio in Matthaeum* 12, PL 106.1314–1316.

9. *Commentarium in Matthaeum* 5, PL 168.1428–1434.

10. *Commentarium in Matthaeum* 1.6, PL 165.115–118.

11. Text of *Allegories*, with second exposition on the deadly sins, attributed to Hugh of St Victor, PL 175.763–789; text of *Expositio* (without the material on the deadly sins) attributed to Peter Abelard, PL 178.611–618. See in general Maurice Hussey, 'The Petitions of the Paternoster in Mediaeval English Literature', *Medium Aevum* 27.1 (1958), pp. 8–16.

12. *Ennarrationes in Matthaeum*, PL 162.1305–1309; it also appears (falsely) attributed to Bernard of Clairvaux, PL 184.811–818, as a separate 'expositio'; John Beleth, writing between 1160 and 1164, takes a similar line over the interpretation of bread, though not quite having the same courage in moving away from Augustine, in his *Rationale Divinorum Officiorum* 47, PL 202.54.

13. See, for example, Matthieu Rougé, *Doctrine et expérience de l'eucharistie chez Guillaume de Saint-Thierry*, Théologie Historique 111

(Paris: Beauchesne, 1999); and Gary Macy, *The Theologies of the Eucharist in the Early Scholastic Period: A Study of the Sacrament according to the Theologians c.1080–c.1220* (Oxford: Clarendon Press, 1984); for the use of *supersubstantialem* in eucharistic controversy, see the eleventh-century 'Aberdeen' manuscript of Alberic's work in Charles M. Radding and Francis Newton, *Theology, Rhetoric and Politics in Eucharistic Controversy, 1078–1079: Alberic of Monte Cassino against Berengar of Tours* (New York: Columbia University Press, 2003), p. 175.

14. *Glossa Ordinaria* III, *PL* 114.100–103; cf. Zacharias of Besançon, *In Unum ex Quattuor*, *PL* 186.137–141.

15. Texts *PL* 192.1256–1298 (*De Ecclesia*), and 1323–1346 (*De Fide*); see also the important essay, by Jan Michael Joncas, 'A Skein of Sacred Sevens: Hugh of Amiens on Orders and Ordination', in Lizette Larson-Miller (ed.), *Medieval Liturgy: A Book of Essays* (New York and London: Garland, 1997), pp. 85–120.

16. Sigisbert Beck (ed.), *Frowini Abbatis Montis Angelorum: Explanatio Dominicae Orationis*, Corpus Christianorum Continuatio Mediaevalis 134 (Turnhout: Brepols, 1998); see introduction, pp. vii–xxxix; Beck is a monk of Engelberg; on daily bread, see pp. 130ff. (IV.1).

17. *De Oratione, Jejunio et Eleemosyna* 9, *PL* 212.171–205.

18. See *Expositio in caput sextum Evangelii Sancti Matthaei – de oratione dominica*, and *Expositio in Evangelium Sancti Lucae*, in A. C. Peltier (ed.), *Sancti Bonaventurae Opera Omnia*, vol. x (Paris: Vives, 1867), pp. 207–210 (Matthew), 514–520 (Luke); and *Expositio in Regulum Fratrum Minorum* III, *Sancti Bonaventurae Opera Omnia*, vol. xiv, pp. 571–572. On Franciscan use of the prayer, see S. J. P. Van Dijk and J. Hazelden Walker, *The Liturgy of the Papal Court and the Franciscan Order in the Thirteenth Century* (London: Darton, Longman and Todd, 1960), pp. 181–183, 196–198. See also Michael Robson, 'Bonaventura', in Evans, *Medieval Theologians*, pp. 187–200.

19. See *Ennarrationes in Evangelium Matthaei*, and *Ennarrationes in Evangelium Lucae*, in Auguste Borgnet (ed.), *Albertus Magnus: Opera Omnia*, vols. xx and xxiii (Paris: Vives, 1893, 1895), pp. 244–303 (Matthew), and 99–128 (Luke): the exposition of Luke is in a similar style.

20. Text in Erich Seeberg (ed.), *Meister Eckhart: Die Deutschen und Lateinischen Werke*, II: *Die Lateinischen Werke*, vol. v (Stuttgart and Berlin: Kohlhammer, 1936), pp. 103–129.

21. *Homilia* 13, text *PL* 118.800–804; on Tariff penance, see, for example, James Dallen, *The Reconciling Community: The Rite of Penance*, Studies in the Reformed Rites of the Catholic Church (New York: Pueblo, 1986), pp. 100–138, especially pp. 110 ff.

22. *Sermo* 22, *PL* 162.599–604; and *Sermo* 5, ibid. 559.

23. See C. A. Robson, *Maurice of Sully and the Medieval Vernacular*

*Homily, with the Text of Maurice's French Homilies from a Sens Cathedral Chapter MS* (Oxford: Blackwell, 1952), pp. 83–87 (text), 196–197 (notes).

24. *Summa de Arte Praedicandi* 15, *PL* 210.140–143.

25. *Expositio de Oratione Dominica*, *PL* 186.1489–1496.

26. For the sermons, see P. Mandonnet (ed.), *S. Thomae Aquinatis Opuscula Omnia*, vol. iv (Paris: Lethielleux, 1927), pp. 389–411; and for the *Summa Theologiae*, see Kevin O'Rourke (ed.), *St Thomas Aquinas: Summa Theologiae*, vol. xxxix, Latin Text, English translation, Introduction, Notes and Glossary (London: Blackfriars, 1964), pp. 68–75 (text of paraphrase on p. 75, the translation of which is based on one by Gavin Kirk). See also Fergus Kerr, 'Thomas Aquinas', in Evans *Medieval Theologians*, pp. 201–220.

27. Texts in I. M. Hanssens, *Amalarii Episcopi Opera Liturgica Omnia*, vols. i, ii, iii: *Opera Minora*, Studi e Testi 138, 139, 140 (Vatican: Bibliotheca Apostolica, 1948), vol. i, pp. 328–336 (Canonis Missae Interpretatio, 58–66, and 80); vol. ii, pp. 355–359 (Liber Officialis, 28), and vol. iii, 312–313 (Ordinis Missae Expositio, 17); see also O. B. Hardison, Jnr, *Christian Rite and Christian Drama in the Middle Ages: The Origin and Early History of Modern Drama*, (Baltimore: Johns Hopkins University Press, 1969), pp. 71–72; and Mary Shaeffer, 'Latin Mass Commentaries from the Ninth through Twelfth Centuries: Chronology and Theology', in Gerard Austin, OP (ed.), *Fountain of Life: In Memory of Neils K. Rasmunssen, OP* (Washington: Pastoral Press, 1991), pp. 35–49.

28. He quotes Cyprian's *Ep.* 63, and *De Dominica Oratione* 27–28.

29. *De Expositione Missae* 75–83, *PL* 119.66–68.

30. *De Divinis Officiis*, *PL* 101.1265–1269; once attributed to Alcuin, it is now accepted as the work of Remigius.

31. *De Expositione Missae*, *PL* 171.1169–1171.

32. *Tractatus de Sacri Altaris* 19, *PL* 177.1303–1308.

33. *Mitrale* 4, *PL* 213.134–138.

34. *De Sacro Altaris Mysterio* V.17–26, *PL* 217.898–905.

35. *Speculum Ecclesiae* 7, *PL* 177.371–373.

36. *Rationale Divinorum Officiorum* IV.47–48, in A. Davril, OSB, and T. M. Thibodeau, *Guillelmi Durranti Rationale Divinorum Officiorum I–IV*, Corpus Christianorum Continuatio Mediaevalis 140 (Turnhout: Brepols, 1995), pp. 504–579; on the 'Seven Words from the Cross', see André Wilmart, OSB, 'Le Grand Poème Bonaventurien sur les Sept Paroles du Christ en Croix', *Revue Bénédictine* 47 (1953), pp. 264ff. (whole article, pp. 235–278).

37. *Meditatio in Orationem Dominicam*, *PL* 149.569–578.

38. *Speculum Ecclesia: De Nativitate Domini*, *PL* 172.815–823.

39. Théophile Desbonnets, Thaddée Matura, Jean-François Godet and Damien Vorreux (eds), *François d'Assise: Ecrits*, Sources Chrétiennes 285

(Paris: Cerf, 1981), pp. 276–281 (text), 39–40 (introduction, accepting authorship); see Edoardo Fumagalli, *San Francesco: il Canto, il Pater Noster* (Milan: Jaca, 1986), pp. 87–105.

40. Text in Walter Skeat (ed.), *The Gospel According to Saint Matthew in Anglo-Saxon, Northumbrian and Old Mercian Versions* (Cambridge: Cambridge University Press, 1887), p. 55; and J. H. Blunt, *The Annotated Book of Common Prayer* (London: Longmans, 1892), p. 207; I am grateful to Julian Elphick-Smith for assistance here.

41. Oxford Bodleian Library MS Junius 121, fol. 43; I am indebted to Sister Benedicta Ward for providing me with this text; an alternative translation is to be found in S. A. J. Bradley, *Anglo-Saxon Poetry* (London: Dent, 1982), pp. 539–541.

42. See Dorothy Bethurum, *The Homilies of Wulfstan* (Oxford: Clarendon Press, 1957), pp. 166–168 (text), 301–302 (notes): I am grateful to James Priory and Julian Elphick-Smith for providing the translation.

43. Text in Richard Morris, *Old English Homilies and Homiletic Treatises* (London: Trubner, 1868), pp. 54–71 (parallel translation and Old English texts), 311–312 (notes); see also, in general, G. Roust, *Preaching in Medieval England* (Cambridge: Cambridge University Press, 1926), pp. 14, 65, 146, 282–283, 291, 319.

44. Thomas Frederick Simmons, *The Lay Folks Mass Book* (Oxford: Oxford University Press, 1879), pp. 46–47 (texts), 203 and 217 (notes); on French vernacular versions, see Artur Langfors, 'Les traductions du *Pater* en vers français du moyen âge', in *Neuphilologische Mitteilungen* 14 (1912), pp. 35–45.

45. See texts in William Maskell, *Monumenta Ritualia Ecclesiae Anglicanae*, vol. ii (London: Pickering, 1846), pp. 238–239; the texts are from Gonville and Caius College Library, Cambridge, and MS Cotton, Cleopatra, B. vi. fol. 201; some adjustments have been made to the originals in order to clarify for modern English readers, with apologies.

46. See Kenneth Stevenson 'Cranmer's Marriage Vow: Its Place in the Tradition', in Paul Ayris and David Selwyn (eds), *Thomas Cranmer: Churchman and Scholar* (Woodbridge: Boydell Press, 1993), pp. 189–198; see also Stevenson, *Nuptial Blessing*, pp. 77–80.

47. On the 'Amen' tradition in the Gregorian Sacramentary texts, see Chapter 4; see also Jungmann, *Missarum Sollemnia*, vol. iii, p. 214.

48. See Peter Abelard, *Epistula* 10, *PL* 178.335–340; see also Chrysogonus Waddell, 'Peter Abelard's *Letter 10* and Cistercian Liturgical Reform', in John Sommerfeldt (ed.), *Studies in Medieval Cistercian History*, vol. ii, Cistercian Studies Series 24 (Kalamazoo: Cistercian Publications, 1976), pp. 75–86; I am indebted to Brother Duncan, OSB, of Quarr Abbey, for drawing my attention to this.

49. See Bailey, *Sponsors at Baptism and Confirmation*; see also the

'Question and Answer' approach in Bruno, Bishop of Würzburg from 1034, *Commentarium in Orationem Dominicam, Symbolum Apostolorum, et Fidem Athanasii, PL* 142.557–559.

50. See Gerard de Frachet, *Vitae Fratrum Ordinis Praedicatorum* (Louvain: Rechert, 1986), p. 137; I am indebted to Father Pierre-Marie Gy, OP, for drawing my attention to this, and to many other kindnesses on liturgical history.

51. Dante Alighieri, *The Divine Comedy*, II: *Purgatory*, translated with an introduction, notes and commentary by Mark Musa (Harmondsworth: Penguin, 1985), pp. 118–119 (text), 122–123 (notes); see also Peter S. Hawkins, 'Crossing Over: Dante's Purgatorial Threshold', in Nathan Mitchell and John Baldovin (eds), *Rule of Prayer, Rule of Faith: Essays in Honor of Aidan Kavanagh, OSB* (Washington: Pastoral Press, 1996), pp. 140–160, esp. pp. 148f.; on the theme of deliverance from evil in the vernacular litanies, see W. H. Karslake, *The Litany of the English Church* (London: Pickering, 1876), pp. 133–135.

## Chapter 7: The Late Middle Ages, Reformation and Counter-Reformation

1. Dix, *Shape of the Liturgy*, pp. 605–734; but see Kenneth Stevenson, *Gregory Dix: 25 Years On*, Grove Liturgical Study 10 (Bramcote: Grove, 1977), pp. 30–34, for a discussion of Dix's sometimes exaggerated view of the Reformation as no more than 'post-medieval'; and Eamon Duffy, *The Stripping of the Altars* (New Haven: Yale University Press, 1992), pp. 53–87.

2. From a review of David Norton, *A History of the English Bible as Literature* (Cambridge: Cambridge University Press, 2000), *Journal of Theological Studies* 54.1 (2003), p. 293.

3. *Commentarius in Orationem Dominicam, PL* 147.333–340; referred to by Hussey, 'Petitions of the Paternoster', p. 9.

4. See text in J. Wickham Legg, *Tracts on The Mass*, Henry Bradshaw Society 27 (1904), pp. 25–26 (whole text, pp. 19–29); discussed in general by Dix, *Shape of the Liturgy*, pp. 605–608. see Wilmart, 'Le Poème Bonaventurien', esp. pp. 264ff.

5. Cf. 'And we yield unto thee most high praise and hearty thanks for the wonderful grace and virtue declared in all thy saints, who have been the choice vessels of thy grace and the lights of the world in their several generations', in Gordon Donaldson, *The Making of the Scottish Prayer Book of 1637* (Edinburgh: Edinburgh University Press, 1954), p. 190; the text persisted in subsequent Scottish Episcopal liturgies, through 1764 into the Scottish Prayer Book of 1929.

6. See J. W. Tyrer, *Historical Survey of Holy Week: Its Services and*

*Ceremonial*, Alcuin Club Collections 29 (London: Oxford University Press, 1932), p. 142.

7. See L. Toulmin Smith, *York Plays* (Oxford: Clarendon Press, 1885), pp. xxviii–xxx; and G. R. Owst, *Literature and Pulpit in Medieval England* (Oxford: Blackwell, 1961), pp. 486, 537, 542–544; I am indebted to Peter Heath for assistance here.

8. See Charles Smyth, *The Art of Preaching: A Practical Survey of Preaching in the Church of England, 747–1939* (London: SPCK, 1940), pp. 19–98 (for discussion of 'ante-theme', see pp. 22f.); W. O. Ross (ed.), *Middle English Sermons*, Early Text Society (Oxford: Oxford University Press, 1940).

9. For the Sarum Missal, see J. Wickham Legg (ed.), *The Sarum Missal* (Oxford: Clarendon Press, 1916), pp. 216 (before Mass), 224–225 (traditional place before fraction); for the Roman, see *Missalis Romani Editio Princeps*, Bibliotheca 'Ephemerides Liturgicae' Subsidia: Instrumenta Liturgica Quarreriensia Supplementa 3 (Rome: Edizioni Liturgiche, 1996), p. 165 (preparation), pp. 181–182; see also Jungmann, *Missarum Sollemnia*, vol. iii, pp. 213–214.

10. See Jungmann, *Missarum Sollemnia*, vol. iii, pp. 215–216; the Premonstratensian Missal of 1578 directs elevation at the bread-petition; the Synod of Trier, 1549, directs prostration.

11. See Maskell, *Monumenta Ritualia*, vol. ii, pp. 238–239 (British Library, MS Cotton Cleopatra B. vi, and Bodleian, Douce 246); for the 1505 text, see Duffy, *Stripping of the Altars*, see plate facing p. 116, and discussion on p. 81.

12. For earlier vernacular English versions, see Chapter 6: Maskell's collection also includes a more wordy translation (British Library MS Bib. Reg. 5), with 'misdeeds', and a straight translation (St John's, Cambridge, MS 142), with 'debts' (both fourteenth century), *Monumenta Ritualia*, pp. 238–239.

13. See, for example, the York Manual, in *Manuale et Processionale ad Usum Insignis Ecclesiae Eboracensis*, Surtees Society 63 (1874), p. 10, where it comes in what was originally the rite for making catechumens, but is now a constituent part of the baptism rite; see Fisher, *Christian Initiation: Baptism in the Medieval West*, pp. 164–165 (Sarum Manual in English translation).

14. On Erasmus's text, see Carmignac, *Recherches*, pp. 33, 47, 134 and 138 (*supersubstantialem*).

15. For a complete list of Luther's works on the Lord's Prayer, see Carmignac *Recherches*, pp. 166–170; see also 'The Sermon on the Mount: The Sixth Chapter', *Luther's Works*, vol. xxi: *The Sermon on the Mount (Sermons) and the Magnificat* (Saint Louis: Concordia, 1956), pp. 141–148 (preached between November 1530 and March 1532, and published in

1523); 'An Exposition on the Lord's Prayer for Simple Laymen' (1519), ibid., pp. 15–81; 'Personal Prayer Book' (1522), ibid., vol. xlii: *Devotional Writings I* (Philadelphia: Fortress, 1968), pp. 29–38; 'A Simple Way to Pray' (1535), 'Vater Unser' (1539), ibid., vol. liii: *Liturgy and Hymns* (Philadelphia: Fortress, 1965), pp. 193–201, 295–298. For the Large and Small Catechisms, see J. N. Lenker (tr.), *Luther's Large Catechism* (Minneapolis: Augsburg, 1967), pp. 96–123; and *Luther's Small Catechism, with Explanation* (St Louis: Concordia, 1991), pp. 169–196.

16. Marc Lienhard, 'Luther et Calvin, commentateurs du Notre Père', *Revue d'Histoire et de Philosophes Religieuses* 72.1 (1992), pp. 73–88.

17. See above n. 15, 'Vater Unser', p. 296. Carmignac, *Recherches*, p. 170.

18. See texts in Ulrich Leupold (ed.), *Luther's Works*, vol. liii: *Liturgy and Hymns* (Philadelphia: Fortress, 1960), pp. 28 (1523), 65 (1526: Catechizing), 78–80 (1526: eucharist), 99 (1523: Baptism), 108 (1526: Baptism); for Bugenhagen and the Danish ordination rites, see Walter Göbell (ed.), *Die Schleswig-Holsteinische Kirchenordnung von 1542* (Neumünster: Wachholtz, 1986), p. 107 (1537 rite); and Max W. Olsen (ed.), *Den Danske Kirkeordinants af 1539* (Copenhagen: Busck, 1936), pp. 86 (pastor), 128 (superintendent); not in Luther's own 1539 ordination rite, where the Lord's Prayer follows the ordination, and leads into the eucharist, *Luther's Works*, vol. liii, p. 126 and n. 9; see also James F. Puglisi, *The Process of Admission to Ordained Ministry: A Comparative Study*, vol. ii: *The First Lutheran, Reformed, Anglican and Wesleyan Rites* (Collegeville: Liturgical Press, 1998), pp. 4–12, where Puglisi draws attention to the place of the Lord's Prayer, without altogether seeing its central position in the Lutheran rites of baptism and eucharist; on baptism, see J. D. C. Fisher, *Christian Initiation: The Reformation Period*, Alcuin Club Collections 51 (London: SPCK, 1970), pp. 14 (Taufbüchlein 1523), 24 (Taufbüchlein 1526); and Hughes Oliphant Old, *The Shaping of the Reformed Baptismal Rite in the Sixteenth Century* (Grand Rapids: Eerdmans, 1992), pp. 36–37, where Old interprets Luther's use of the prayer as 'acting out the gospel'; for the eucharist, see R. C. D. Jasper and G. J. Cuming (eds), *The Prayers of the Eucharist: Early and Reformed*, 3rd rev. edn (New York: Pueblo, 1987), pp. 193–194 (Formula Missae 1523), 196–197 (Deutsche Messe 1526); for the various other Lutheran eucharistic rites, see Irmgard Pahl (ed.), *Coena Domini*, vol. i: *Die Abendmahlsliturgie der Reformationskirchen im 16./17. Jahrhundert*, Spicilegium Friburgense 29 (Fribourg: Universitätsverlag, 1983), esp. p. 55 (Bugenhagen); details are given of the early shift away from Luther's paraphrase to the liturgical recitation of the prayer in the German and Scandinavian books in S. Widding, *Dansk Messe, Tide- og Psalmesang, 1528–1573*, vol. i: *Messen og Tidesang* (Copenhagen: Levin & Munksgaard, 1932), pp. 145–146; see also Bryan Spinks, *Luther's*

# Notes

*Liturgical Criteria and His Reform of the Mass*, Grove Liturgical Study 30 (Bramcote: Grove, 1982). On Zwingli, see Jasper and Cuming, *Prayers of the Eucharist*, pp. 184 (1523) and 187 (1525).

19. See Fisher, *Christian Initiation: The Reformation Period*, p. 4 (discussing Luther's *Babylonian Captivity* of 1520); see Henry Beveridge (tr.), *John Calvin: Treatises on the Sacraments, Catechism of the Church of Geneva, Forms of Prayer, Confessions of Faith* (Fearn: Reformation Heritage Books, 2002), pp. 70–81 (Geneva Catechism).

20. See Günther Stiller, *Johannes Sebastian Bach and Liturgical Life in Leipzig* (St Louis: Concordia, 1984), pp. 126–127.

21. John Calvin, *Calvin: Institutes of the Christian Religion*, ed. John T. McNeill and Ford Lewis Battles, Library of Christian Classics 21 (Philadelphia: Westminster, 1961), pp. 897–917; the alphabetical margin notes refer to the successive editions, a = 1536, b = 1539, (c = 1543, d= 1550), e = 1559; see also Lienhard, 'Luther et Calvin'; for Bucer see Ford Lewis Battles (tr.), *Institutes of the Christian Religion*, The H. H. Meeter Center for Calvin Studies (Grand Rapids: Eerdmans, 1986), Appendix II, pp. 343–362, and margin notes; see also A. W. Morrison (tr.), *Calvin's Commentaries: A Harmony of the Gospels: Matthew, Mark and Luke*, vol. i (Edinburgh: St Andrew's Press, 1972), pp. 204–213, where Calvin reproduces many of the themes noted in the *Institutes*.

22. For the baptism rite, see Fisher, *Christian Initiation: The Reformation Period*, pp. 116 (1542 Geneva), 122 (Knox 1556); and Old, *The Shaping of the Reformed Baptismal Rite*, pp. 59–60 (Bucer's 1525 Strasbourg rite, with congregational Lord's Prayer), 162 (Farel's 1533 rite), 175 (Geneva 1542), and 218 ('Evangelical Confirmation'); for the eucharist, see Jasper and Cuming, *Prayers of the Eucharist*, outlines at pp. 215 (1542) and 250 (Knox 1556); see also Peter Barth and Dora Scheuner (eds), *Joannis Calvini Opera Selecta*, vol. ii (Munich: Kaiser, 1952), pp. 34–35 (baptism), 45 (eucharist) and 23–25 (intercession paraphrase at Sunday morning service); W. D. Maxwell (ed.), *The Liturgical Portions of the Genevan Service Book* (Edinburgh: Oliver and Boyd, 1931) for comparative tables of the Genevan and Genevan-derived rites, pp. 18, 23 (Sunday Service), 49 (baptism), 51 (eucharist), 54 (marriage, which Calvin included as part of Sunday worship), and text, pp. 91 (Sunday morning service), 101 (discussion of the provenance of Calvin's paraphrase–tradition) and 188–198 (Calvin's and Bucer's texts side by side); for Scottish Reformed practice see George W. Sprott and Thomas Leishman (eds), *The Book of Common Order of the Church of Scotland and the Directory for Public Worship of God Agreed upon by the Assembly of Divines at Westminster* (Edinburgh and London: Blackwood, 1868), pp. 89 (Lord's Prayer, after intercessions), 91–97 (text of intercession-paraphrase based on Lord's Prayer), 145 (baptism); and note on pp. 244–245, which identifies it as coming, not from

Knox's Geneva Book, but from Calvin's; it is omitted in later Genevan and French Reformed books, though it lingered on in Belgian Reformed Churches; see also G. W. Sprott, *The Book of Common Order*, Church Service Society (Edinburgh: Blackwood, 1901), p. 91. See also Bryan D. Spinks, 'Calvin's Baptismal Theology and the Making of the Strasbourg and Genevan Baptismal Liturgies 1540 and 1542', *Scottish Journal of Theology* 48 (1995), pp. 55–78. I am indebted to John Webster for assistance over Calvin.

23. See Theodor Klauser, *A Short History of the Western Liturgy: An Account and Some Reflections* (Oxford: Oxford University Press, 1969), pp. 94–117.

24. Texts in *Catechismus ex decreto Concilii Tridentinum at Parochias* (Turin: Peter Maretti, 1875), pp. 454–534, and John A. McHugh and Charles J. Callan (tr. and notes), *Catechism of the Council of Trent for Parish Priests* (New York: Wagner, 1923), pp. 477–589; on the question of 'on earth as in heaven', see Carmignac, *Recherches*, p. 113.

25. For baptism rite, see, for example, *Rituale Romanum* (Antwerp: Plantiniana, 1826), p. 19; for the mass, see, for example, *Missale Romanum ex decreto Sacrosancti Concilii Tridentini Restitutum* (Antwerp: Plantiniana, 1682), pp. 367–368.

26. See E. Allison Peers (tr.), *Way of Perfection: Saint Teresa of Avila* (London: Sheed and Ward, 1999), pp. 110–186 (chs 27–42) on the Lord's Prayer; discussed in Stevenson, *Abba, Father*, pp. 149–155, and notes on p. 193; see also Rowan Williams, *Teresa of Avila* (London: Geoffrey Chapman, 1991), pp. 78–107; and Jürgen Moltmann, 'Teresa of Avila and Martin Luther: The Turn to the Mysticism of the Cross', *Studies in Religion/Sciences Réligieuses* 13 (1984), pp. 265–278 (quoted in Williams, *Teresa of Avila*, p. 107 n. 14).

27. See *Oeuvres de Saint François de Sales: Édition Complète*, vol. xxvi (Annecy: Monastère de la Visitation, 1932), pp. 377–419 (text of paraphrase) and xix (on the authenticity of the material, for which see also notes at the foot of the text, pp. 377ff.).

28. See texts in Colin Buchanan, *The Lord's Prayer in the Church of England*, Grove Worship Booklet 131 (Bramcote: Grove, 1995), p. 17 (see also pp. 15–20 for the development of the text from 1500–1900); and in Maskell, *Monumenta Ritualia*, vol. ii, p. 239; and in *Miscellaneous Writings and Letters of Thomas Cranmer*, Parker Society (Cambridge: Cambridge University Press, 1846), p. 106, where Cranmer, commenting on 'The King's Book' before its publication, makes it clear that this is not what Christ taught, and we should not alter it!

29. Text in J. Eric Hunt (ed.), *Cranmer's First Litany, 1544 and Merbecke's Book of Common Prayer Noted, 1550* (London: 1939), pp. 104–105; see also Cranmer, *Miscellaneous Writings and Letters of*

*Thomas Cranmer*, pp. 106 and 110 for other comments on the Lord's Prayer by Cranmer; summary text also in G. J. Cuming, *A History of Anglican Liturgy* (London: Macmillan, 1969), p. 359.

30. Texts in F. E. Brightman, *The English Rite*, 2 vols (London: Rivingtons, 1915) as follows: vol. i, pp. 132–133 and 146–147 (Morning Prayer), 156–157 and 162–163 (Evening Prayer), 180–181 (Litany); vol. ii, pp. 640–641 and 696–697/704–707 (Holy Communion), 732–733 (Baptism, 1549), 742–745 (Baptism, 1552), 748–749 and 752–753 (Private Baptism), 772–753 (Baptism for 'those of Riper Years', a service added in 1662), 784–787 (Catechism), 796–797 (Confirmation, only added in 1662), 810–811 (Marriage), 820–821 (Visitation of the Sick), 846–847 (Communion of the Sick, 1549 only), 872–873 (Burial), 882–883 (Thanksgiving after Childbirth), 896–897 (Lenten 'Commination' Service) and 906–908 (For Use at Sea, a service added in 1662).

31. John Dowden, *Further Studies in the Prayer Book* (London: Methuen, 1908), pp. 88–93. (The 1539 Primer read, 'And let us not be led into temptation', Brightman, *English Rite*, vol. ii, p. 786.)

32. Ashley Null, *Thomas Cranmer's Doctrine of Repentance: Renewing the Power to Love* (Oxford: Oxford University Press, 2000), pp. 99–105, 112–115 (quotation from Gardiner, p. 113, from *A Declaration of such true articles as George Ioye, hath gone about to confute as false* (London: Hereford, 1546), fo. 5 r. and v.); I am indebted to Ashley Null for assistance here.

33. See Diarmaid MacCulloch, *Thomas Cranmer: A Life* (New Haven and London: Yale University Press, 1996).

34. Texts in *Expositions and Notes on Sundry Portions of the Holy Scriptures by William Tyndale*, Parker Society (Cambridge: Cambridge University Press, 1849), pp. 80–86 (using yet another version of the prayer, with 'honoured be thy name', p. 80); see also, in general, David Daniell, *William Tyndale: A Biography* (New Haven and London: Yale University Press, 1994); *Sermons by Hugh Latimer*, Parker Society (Cambridge: Cambridge University Press, 1844), pp. 326–446 (where he uses the Prayer Book version, adding his own doxology at the conclusion of the final sermon); *The Writings of John Bradford*, Parker Society (Cambridge: Cambridge University Press, 1848), pp. 119–139 (meditation), 178–184 (paraphrase); and *The Catechism of Thomas Becon*, Parker Society (Cambridge: Cambridge University Press, 1844), pp. 143–198.

35. See Kenneth Stevenson, 'Richard Hooker and the Lord's Prayer: A Chapter in Reformation Controversy', in *Scottish Journal of Theology*, 57.1 (2004) for a discussion of this issue.

36. See W. T. Whitley, *The Works of John Smyth, Fellow of Christ's College (1594–1598)* (Cambridge: Cambridge University Press, 1915), p. 247.

37. See George W. Sprott (ed.), *Scottish Liturgies of the Reign of James VI* (Edinburgh: Edmonston and Douglas, 1871), pp. 21–22 and 63.

38. See Gordon Donaldson, *The Making of the Scottish Prayer Book of 1637*, pp. 131, 133, 135, 200; and also in the Visitation of the Sick, p. 230; it also appears without the doxology in the Litany, p. 144, at the start of the eucharist, p. 183, in the Catechism, p. 219, at Marriage, p. 227, at Burial, p. 238, and at Churching and Commination, pp. 240, 246; Donaldson notes, however, that there were those in Scotland who did not want to see the introduction of the doxology (p. 25); see also doxology, with title, in John Cosin's Private Devotions (1627), in P. G. Stanwood and Daniel O'Connor (eds), *John Cosin: A Collection of Private Devotions* (Oxford: Clarendon Press, 1967), p. 39.

39. See Ian Breward (ed.), *The Westminster Directory*, Grove Liturgical Study 21 (Bramcote: Grove, 1980), p. 18.

40. See above n. 30 for page refs in Brightman, *English Rite*; the doxology was also added in Thanksgiving after Childbirth, and in the Form for Use at Sea (a new service).

41. *Laws* V.35.2, 3, and V.36.3, in John Keble (ed.), *The Works of that Learned and Judicious Divine Mr Richard Hooker*, vol. ii, 7th edn, rev. R. W. Church and F. Paget (Oxford: Clarendon Press, 1888), pp. 154, 157.

42. William Perkins, *An Exposition of the Lord's Prayer* (London: Legatt, 1636), p. 8; see also Bryan D. Spinks, *Two Faces of Elizabethan Anglican Theology: Sacraments and Salvation in the Thought of William Perkins and Richard Hooker*, Drew University Studies in Liturgy 9 (Lanham, MD, and London: Scarecrow Press, 1999).

43. See *The Sermons of Lancelot Andrewes*, vol. v, Library of Anglo-Catholic Theology (Oxford: Parker, 1854); the sermons specifically on the Lord's Prayer are 7–19, pp. 362–476; see also Stevenson, *Abba, Father*, pp. 168–174 and notes on p. 194; see also Nicholas Lossky, *Lancelot Andrewes, the Preacher (1555–1626): The Origins of the Mystical Theology of the Church of England* (Oxford: Clarendon Press, 1991); and T. S. Eliot, *For Lancelot Andrewes: Essays on Style and Order* (London: Faber, 1928), pp. 11–26; these (and other) studies concentrate on the Court Sermons; a proper study of the lesser-known sermons, those on the Lord's Prayer included, is needed.

44. See F. E. Brightman (ed.), *The Preces Privatae of Lancelot Andrewes* (London: Methuen, 1903), p. 284.

45. See R. Heber (ed.), *The Whole Works of the Right Revd Jeremy Taylor*, vol. iii (London: Rivingtons, 1828), pp. 77, 75, 79; and *The Prose Works of Thomas Ken* (London: Rivingtons, 1838), pp. 312–313; see also H. R. McAdoo, *First of its Kind: Jeremy Taylor's Life of Christ: A Study in the Functioning of a Moral Theology* (Norwich: Canterbury Press, 1994).

46. Mary Hobbs, *The Sermons of Henry King (1592–1669), Bishop of*

# Notes

*Chichester* (Aldershot: Scolar Press, 1992), pp. 135–218 (text), and 285–291 (notes); and Thomas Watson, *The Lord's Prayer*, Banner of Truth (Avon: Bath Press, 1965) (first published in 1692 as *A Body of Practical Divinity*).

47. *A Practical Catechism by Henry Hammond*, Library of Anglo-Catholic Theology (Oxford: Parker, 1847), pp. 222 ('prayer of the heart'), 229f. (vain repetitions), 235f. ('daily bread'), and 239f. (doxology).

## Chapter 8: Into Modernity and Beyond

1. See Karl Barth, *Prayer and Preaching* (London: SCM Press, 1964), pp. 35–40; on Barth, see below.

2. See Norman Sykes, *Church and State in England in the Eighteenth Century* (Cambridge: Cambridge University Press, 1934); see also Geoffrey Rowell, Kenneth Stevenson and Rowan Williams (eds), *Love's Redeeming Work: The Anglican Quest for Holiness* (Oxford: Oxford University Press, 2001), pp. 188–191; see John Walsh, 'The Church of England in the "Long" Eighteenth Century', in John Walsh, Colin Hayden and Stephen Taylor (eds), *From Toleration to Tractarianism* (Cambridge: Cambridge University Press, 1993), pp. 1–64.

3. (George Hickes), *A Collection of Meditations and Devotions* (London, 1717), p. 126 (whole text, pp. 126–136).

4. Texts in *The Works of Thomas Wilson*, vol. v, Library of Anglo-Catholic Theology (Oxford: Parker, 1860), pp. 47–49, 13–14, 50–51, 92–95, 120–126, 307–313 (with 'debts' on p. 311 and no doxology), 357–358 (stops after 'Thy Kingdom come'), 365–370, 625–633 (with 'debts'); quotation from p. 47. On the Spirit and the Kingdom, see Gregory of Nyssa and Maximus the Confessor, Chapter 3, and Luther and Calvin, Chapter 7.

5. See *The Works of John Wesley*, vol. i: *Sermons I* (Nashville: Abingdon, 1984), pp. 572–589 (Sermon 26 in the edition, 'Discourse the Sixth' in the series on The Sermon on the Mount), with an appended nine-stanza metrical version, pp. 589–591; sermon also printed in special selections of Wesley's preaching, for which see, for example, *John Wesley: Forty-Four Sermons* (London: Epworth Press, 1952), pp. 269–286; cf. John Wesley, *Explanatory Notes upon the New Testament* (London: Wesleyan-Methodist Book-Room, n.d.) on Matthew 6:9–13, where many other points (apart from 'the language of the heart') made in the sermon are echoed, including the shape of the prayer, and the Spirit and the will. See Tore Meistad's important study, *Martin Luther and John Wesley on the Sermon on the Mount*, Pietist and Wesleyan Studies 10 (Lanham, MD, and London: Scarecrow Press, 1999), esp. pp. 162–169; and H. D. Rack, *Reasonable Enthusiast* (London: Epworth Press, 1989).

6. See A. Elliott Peaston, *The Prayer Book Tradition in the Free Churches* (London: Clarke, 1964), pp. 35–65.

7. See Sermon 5, pp. 579–580, and p. 580 n. 43.

8. See ibid., p. 590 (stanza v).

9. Lectures 30–33, in *The Works of Thomas Secker*, vol. iv (London: 1804), pp. 265–294 (quotations from pp. 273, 283 and 285); the first two lectures deal with the prayer in its two main parts, the third with the doxology.

10. See Horton Davies, *Worship and Theology in England*, vol. iii: *From Watts and Wesley to Maurice, 1690–1850* (Princeton: Princeton University Press, 1961), pp. 23 and 39 (iconography), 81 and 92 (recitation twice questioned), 105 (Baptist practice), and 217 (Samuel Walker); for the 1764 Scottish Liturgy, and 1789 American Prayer Book, see John Dowden, *The Annotated Scottish Communion Office* (Edinburgh: Grant, 1884), p. 17 (where it is introduced with the 1549 adaptation of the Roman formula, 'As our Saviour Christ hath commanded and taught us, we are bold to say'; and it includes the doxology); and Marion Hatchett, *The Making of the First American Book of Common Prayer: 1776–1789* (New York: Seabury, 1982); on the eighteenth-century patristic-liturgical scene, see R. C. D. Jasper, *The Search for an Apostolic Liturgy*, Alcuin Club Pamphlet 18 (London: Mowbrays, 1963), and, in general, Bradshaw, *Search for the Origins*, pp. 73–97.

11. See Carl Braaten (ed.), *Paul Tillich: Perspectives on Nineteenth and Twentieth Century Protestant Theology* (London: SCM Press, 1967), pp. 82–83.

12. See preface in John Keble, *Sermons, Academical and Occasional* (London: Parker, 1847), pp. lxxi–lxxiii; see also John Keble, *Village Sermons on the Baptismal Service* (London: Parker, 1868), collected together and edited by his fellow Tractarian, Edward Pusey.

13. F. D. Maurice, *The Lord's Prayer: Nine Sermons Preached in the Chapel of Lincoln's Inn* (Cambridge: Macmillan, 1861); see also *The Kingdom of Christ*, vol. iii (London: Rivingtons, 1842), pp. 43–51 and 537–538; and *The Prayer Book: Nineteen Sermons Preached in the Chapel of Lincoln's Inn* (London: Macmillan, 1880), p. 54. Among the many studies of Maurice are Alec Vidler, *The Theology of F. D. Maurice* (London: SCM Press, 1948); and Arthur Michael Ramsey, *F. D. Maurice and the Conflicts of Modern Theology* (Cambridge: Cambridge University Press, 1951); see also Stevenson, *Abba, Father*, pp. 127–134 and notes on p. 192.

14. Text of (as yet unedited) sermon transcribed by Elisabeth Glenthøj from the original manuscripts, for which I am most grateful. On Grundtvig in general, the principal work is A. M. Allchin, *N. F. S. Grundtvig: An Introduction to his Life and Work* (Arhus: University Press; London: Darton, Longman and Todd, 1997); see also A. M. Allchin, D. Jasper, J. H.

# Notes

Schjørring and K. Stevenson (eds), *Heritage and Prophecy: Grundtvig and the English-Speaking World* (Århus: University Press; Norwich: Canterbury Press, 1993), particularly Christian Thodberg's essay, 'The Importance of Baptism in Grundtvig's View of Christianity', pp. 133–152 (esp. pp. 139–142 on the Lord's Prayer); Valdemar Leth Ludvigsen, 'Herrens bøn "Fadervor"', in *For Sammenhaengens Skyld: Ord og Motiver I Grundtvigs Salmer og Praedikener* (Århus: University Press, 1977), pp. 158–185; and Kenneth Stevenson, *Handing On: Borderlands of Worship and Tradition* (London: Darton, Longman and Todd, 1996), pp. 83–99, and notes on pp. 139–141. For Grundtvig's metrical versions, see *Grundtvigs Sang-Vaerk*, vols iv and v (Copenhagen: Det Danske Forlag, 1949/1951), vol. iv, nos. 281 (8 stanzas, composed in 1852/3, pp. 372–374), 301 (9 stanzas, composed in 1853, pp. 407–409); vol. v, nos. 35 (12 stanzas, composed in 1855/6, pp. 61–62), 36 (7 stanzas, composed in 1855/6, pp. 62–63), 112 (12 stanzas, composed in 1858, pp. 181–182), 175 (5 stanzas, composed in 1862, pp. 312–313), but see the other hymns mentioning the prayer referred to by Thodberg in the article cited above.

15. See Thodberg, 'The Importance of Baptism', p. 140 for English translation of 'Stol du kun på din Fadervor', in *Grundtvigs Sangvaerk*, vol. iv, no. 337 (4 stanzas, composed in 1855, pp. 439–440); unlike the metrical versions listed in n. 14, this hymn is in the current Danish Hymn Book (no. 553). For the Danish 1912 baptism rite, see *Vejledning i Den Danske Folkekirkes Gudstjenesteordning* (Copenhagen: Haase, 1955), p. 54 (cf. 1895 rite, following older practice, p. 46); Christian Thodberg, 'Dåbsritualets historie', in *Dåb og Brudevielse*, Betaenkning 973 (Copenhagen: Kirkeministeriet, 1983), pp. 33–34 (whole article, pp. 7–42). I am indebted to Christian Thodberg for use of his study of the Danish Baptism rite, *Dåben og Dåbsritualets Historie* (Forelæsningsmanuskript, 1998).

16. Texts in *Metropolitan Tabernacle Pulpit* 24, pp. 133–144 (Matthew 6:13, 'Lead us not into temptation') and 30, 'preached on Wednesday morning, April 30th 1884 By C. H. Spurgeon at Exeter-Hall, Being the Annual Sermon of the Baptist Missionary Society', pp. 241–252 (Matthew 6:10, 'Thy will be done in earth, as it is in heaven'); I am grateful to Andrew Jarvis for identifying these sermons.

17. See R. C. D. Jasper, *Prayer Book Revision in England 1800–1900* (London: SPCK, 1954) esp. pp. 59–73; for the early twentieth-century books, see (England) *The Book of Common Prayer with the Additions and Deviations Proposed in 1928* (Oxford: Oxford University Press; London: SPCK, n.d.); see also *The Book of Common Prayer according to the use of the Protestant Episcopal Church in the United States of America* (Greenwich, CT: Seabury Press, 1928), p. 7 (it is only to be used once at the daily offices); and *The Scottish Book of Common Prayer* (Cambridge: Cambridge University Press, n.d.). On the Church of Scotland, see

*Euchologion or a Book of Common Order* (Edinburgh: Blackwood, 1867).

18. F. H. Chase, *The Lord's Prayer in the Early Church*, Texts and Studies I.3 (Cambridge: Cambridge University Press, 1891).

19. See Evelyn Underhill, *Abba: Meditations based on the Lord's Prayer* (London: Longmans, 1940); see also Stevenson, *Abba, Father*, pp. 121–126, and notes on p. 191; and see, in general, Margaret Cropper, *Evelyn Underhill* (London: Longmans, 1958) and Christopher J. R. Armstrong, *Evelyn Underhill (1875–1941)* (London: Mowbrays, 1975); and also Ann Loades, *Evelyn Underhill*, Fount Christian Thinkers (London: Harper-Collins, 1999).

20. Barth, *Prayer and Preaching*, pp. 24–63; and *The Christian Life* (Edinburgh: T. & T. Clark, 1981), pp. 233–271 (quotation p. 245); the literature on Barth's theology is vast; see Stephen Sykes (ed.), *Karl Barth: Studies in Theological Method* (Oxford: Blackwell, 1979), and T. F. Torrance, *Karl Barth* (Edinburgh: T. & T. Clark, 1990); I am indebted to Peter Forster for assistance here; see also Don Saliers (ed.), *Karl Barth: Prayer. 50th Anniversary Edition with Essays by I. John Hesselink, Daniel L. Migliore, and Donald K. McKim* (Westminster: John Knox Press, 2002).

21. Dietrich Bonhoeffer, *The Cost of Discipleship*, complete edition (London: SCM Press, 1959), pp. 145–150; and *Sanctorum Communio* (London: Collins, 1963), the 1927 doctoral dissertation, which was properly published in German only in 1960; see also Eberhard Bethge (ed.), *Dietrich Bonhoeffer: Letters and Papers from Prison*, enlarged edition (London: SCM Press, 1971); Mary Bosanquet, *The Life and Death of Dietrich Bonhoeffer* (London: Hodder and Stoughton, 1968); and Eberhard Bethge, *Dietrich Bonhoeffer, Theologian, Christian, Contemporary* (London: Collins, 1977). See also David F. Ford, *Self and Salvation: Being Transformed* (Cambridge: Cambridge University Press, 1999), pp. 243–265; I am grateful to David Ford for important insights on Bonhoeffer.

22. From the original German, in E. Bethge *et al.* (eds), *Dietrich Bonhoeffer: Gesammelte Werke*, vol. v (Munich: Chr. Kaiserverlag, 1987), p. 569; earlier Bonhoeffer states of the prayer, 'In ihm ist alles Beten enthalten' (p. 547).

23. Helmut Thielicke, *The Prayer that Spans the World* (London: Clarke, 1965); see note on p. 68 describing these circumstances.

24. Quoted from Gian Paolo Biasin, 'Our Daily Bread–Pane–Brot–Broid–Chleb–Pain–Lechem–Kenyer', in Pietro Frassica (ed.), *Primo Levi as Witness: Proceedings of a Symposium held at Princeton University, April 30–May 2, 1989* (Princeton: Casalini, 1991), pp. 1–20 (quotation from *Gargantua* on p. 1); see also Robert Gordon, *Primo Levi's Ordinary Virtues: From Testimony to Ethics* (Oxford: Oxford University Press, 2001); and Ian Hutchinson, *Primo Levi* (London: Hutchinson, 2002); I am indebted to Ann Loades for assistance here.

# Notes

25. Leonardo Boff, *The Lord's Prayer: The Prayer of Integral Liberation* (Maryhill: Orbis, 1983) English Translation of *O pai-nosso: a oração da libertação integral* (Petropolis: Vozes, 1979); and Stevenson, *Abba, Father*, pp. 135–141 and notes on p. 192; see also, for example, Leonardo Boff, *Saint Francis: A Model for Human Liberation* (London: SCM Press, 1983) and *Trinity and Society* (London: Burns and Oates, 1988); I am grateful to Ann Leonard for assistance with Boff.

26. See Maurizzo Barba, *La riforma conciliare dell' "Ordo Missae": le percorso storico-redazionale dei riti d'ingresso, di offertorio e di communione*, Bibliotheca 'Ephemerides Liturgicae' Subsidia 120 (Rome: Edizioni Liturgiche, 2002), p. 353, which gives an account of a meeting in October 1965 at which the orientalist Alphone Raes, SJ, argued that the embolism should remain; but the following May it was noted that most of the East and all the Reformation churches used the doxology; see also *Missale Romanum ex decreto Sacrosancti Oecumenici Concilii Vaticani Instauratum Auctoritiate Paul PP. VI Promulgatam* (Typis Polyglottis Vaticanis, 1971), p. 472.

27. *The Rites of the Catholic Church as Revised by Decree of the Second Ecumenical Council and Published by Authority of Pope Paul VI*, vol. i (New York: Pueblo, 1976), pp. 87–88 (adult rite), 225 (children rite); cf. *Common Worship: Initiation Services* (London: Church House Publishing, 1998), p. 44.

28. See Carmignac, *Recherches*, pp. 401–436 for the story of the French version.

29. See Colin Buchanan, *Modern Anglican Liturgies: 1958–1968* (Oxford: Oxford University Press, 1968), p. 137: Buchanan, in correspondence with the author, has indicated that the text was introduced by the Chairman of the Liturgical Commission, at the time, Dr Ronald Jasper; and that the members were (understandably) more concerned about other matters than this particular item; see also *The Sacramentary* (New York: Catholic Book Publishing, 1974), pp. 561–562. For a description of these issues from an Anglican Perspective, see Buchanan, *The Lord's Prayer in the Church of England*, pp. 21–39; the inclusion of the doxology was re-debated on the Liturgical Commission, with Kenneth Ross, Vicar of All Saints' Margaret Street, arguing against; in the end a compromise was reached, adopted in 1980 but mercifully abandoned in 2000, where the doxology is separated by a typographical space from the main text of the prayer, to indicate its non-dominical origin (Buchanan, pp. 21–22 n. 20); both the issue and the solution represent a particular form of Anglo-Catholic nit-picking.

30. See Church of England Liturgical Commission, *Modern Liturgical Texts*, pp. 1–3, for the important contribution by Austin Farrer; for texts, see in *Prayers We Have in Common*, 1st edn (London: Geoffrey Chapman,

1970), p. 5 (notes pp. 5–8); enlarged and revised edition (London: Geoffrey Chapman, 1971), p. 5 (notes pp. 5–8); and 2nd rev. edn (London: SPCK, 1975), p. 1 (notes pp. 1–3); reinforced by ICET's successor, the English Liturgical Language Consultation (ELLC), in *Praying Together* (Norwich: Canterbury Press, 1988), p. 1 (notes pp. 1–4).

31. See, for example, *The Book of Common Prayer of the Episcopal Church* (New York: Church Hymnal Corporation/Seabury Press, 1979), e.g. p. 364 (eucharist).

32. See *The Alternative Service Book* (1980) (Oxford: Oxford University Press; London: Mowbrays, 2000), p. 142 (eucharist); subsequent editions printed both the 'modern' and the 'adapted traditional' versions side-by-side; on the evolution of the modern text, see *The Alternative Service Book (1980): A Commentary by the Liturgical Commission* (London: Church Information Office, 1980), pp. 91–93. See also *Common Worship: Services and Prayers for the Church of England* (London: Church House Publishing, 2000), p. 178 (eucharist, where the 'modern' version is printed before the 'adapted traditional'); and see Paul Bradshaw (ed.), *Companion to Common Worship*, vol. i (London: SPCK, 2001), pp. 68–69.

33. See *The Book of Common Order (1979)* (Edinburgh: St Andrew's Press, 1979), p. 11 (Eucharist, First Order), *The Book of Common Order (1994)* (Edinburgh: St Andrew's Press, 1994), pp. 138 (Eucharist, First Order, with modern ecumenical text), 164 (Eucharist, Third Order), 180 (Eucharist, Fifth Order), and inside back cover (no fewer than three texts, the modern ecumenical text, the modified traditional, and the old Scots); *The Methodist Worship Book* (Peterborough: Methodist Publishing House, 1999), p. 14 (Daily Prayer: Morning; modern ecumenical side-by-side with 'modified traditional'), and *passim* (other services); on the Anglican Communion story, see Buchanan, *The Lord's Prayer in the Church of England*, pp. 32–39; see also Colin Buchanan, *Further Anglican Liturgies: 1968–1975* (Bramcote: Grove, 1975) esp. p. 392; and *Latest Anglican Liturgies 1976–1984* (London: SPCK/Grove, 1985), pp. 270–271.

34. *The Catechism of the Catholic Church* (London: Geoffrey Chapman, 1994), pp. 586–610; for the Decree on the Lay/Apostolate, see Austin Flannery, OP (ed.), *Vatican Council II: The Conciliar and Post Conciliar Documents* (Collegeville: Liturgical Press, 1975), pp. 766–798.

35. Alexander Schmemann, *Our Father* (New York: St Vladimir's Seminary Press, 2002); see also his *Introduction to Liturgical Theology* (Portland, ME: American Orthodox Press; Leighton Buzzard: Faith Press, 1966).

# Notes

## Chapter 9: Conclusion

1. Johannes Reuter (Janis Reiters), *Oratio Dominica XL Linguarum* (Rostock: Johannes Keil, 1675); a facsimile of the 1675 edition was printed in 1954 in Copenhagen (Imanta press), edited by B. Jegers, with introductions (pp. 5–22 in Latvian, with summary in German, pp. 23–28); the texts follow (there are in fact forty-two); the commendation by Reiters is on p. 46; an abbreviated version, with twenty-five languages, was published in Riga in 1995, with a larger selection of languages local to Riga, including Latgellian (spoken in south-east Latvia), Lithuanian, and Livonian (a Finno-Ugrian language now spoken by only a few people on the promontory west of Riga facing towards Estonia); it is possible that some of these versions could have appeared in the 1662 edition published in Riga, the place of Reiters' schooling, and part of his pastoral ministry. I am grateful to Janis Vanags, Lutheran Archbishop of Latvia, Anita Jacobsone, his Secretary, and Kirsti Eskelinen, Finnish Ambassador in Riga, for much assistance here.

2. Green, *Matthew, Poet of the Beatitudes*, p. 22, quoting from P. Fussell, *Poetic Metre and Poetic Form* (New York: Random House, 1965), p. 133.

3. Church of England Liturgical Commission, *Modern Liturgical Texts*, p. 1.

4. B. F. Westcott and F. J. A. Hort, *The New Testament in the Original Greek*, vol. ii: *Introduction; Appendix* (London and Cambridge: Macmillan, 1881), p. 320; as Carmignac notes (*Recherches*, p. 114), this is endorsed by Charles Gore, *The Sermon on the Mount* (London: Murray, 1896), p. 124.

5. See the teaching of the twentieth-century Chaldean Catholic Bishop Francis Alichoran, in Claire Mazas and Pierre Scheffer, SJ (eds), *L'Evangile en Araméen: L'enseignement de Jésus au sommet de la montagne*, Spiritualité Orientale 80 (Abbaye de Bellefontaine, 2002), pp. 74–75, 152–165.

6. See, for example, Stephen Sykes, ' "Baptisme doth Represente unto us Oure Profession" ', in *Unashamed Anglicanism* (London: Darton, Longman and Todd, 1995), pp. 3–23; Geoffrey Wainwright, *Doxology: The Praise of God in Worship, Doctrine and Life* (London: Epworth Press, 1980); Aidan Kavanagh, *The Shape of Baptism: The Rite of Christian Initiation*, Studies in the Reformed Rites of the Catholic Church 1 (New York: Pueblo, 1978); and Paul Avis, *Anglicanism and the Christian Church: Theological Resources in Historical Perspective* (Edinburgh: T. & T. Clark, 1989; revised and expanded version 2002).

7. J.-B. Frey, 'Le pater est-il juif ou chrétien?', p. 563.

8. William West, *The Nature, Design, Tendency and Importance of*

*Prayer: Illustrated in Seven Practical Dissertations on the Lord's Prayer* (London: Griffiths, 1758), p. 7.

9. See Prayer D, *Common Worship*, p. 194.

10. See Roland Mushat Frye, 'On Praying "Our Father": The Challenge of Radical Feminist Language for God', in Helen Hull Hitchcock (ed.), *The Politics of Prayer: Feminist Language and The Worship of God* (San Francisco: Ignatius Press, 1991), pp. 209–228; see p. 227, where he cited Origen, *Contra Celsum* 6.65, in *The Ante-Nicene Fathers*, vol. iv (Edinburgh: T. & T. Clark, 1994), p. 603.

11. See Saliers, *Karl Barth: Prayer*, p. x.

12. Schmemann, *Introduction to Liturgical Theology*; Wainwright, *Doxology*; and Aidan Kavanagh, *On Liturgical Theology* (New York: Pueblo, 1984); see also Kenneth Stevenson, 'Lex Orandi and Lex Credendi – Strange Bedfellows?: Some Reflections on Worship and Doctrine', *Scottish Journal of Theology* 39.2 (1986), pp. 225–241; see also Nathan Mitchell, in Mitchell and Baldovin, *Rule of Prayer, Rule of Faith*, pp. vii–xiv.

13. *Living on the Edge: Christians in Bangladesh take a Fresh Look at the Lord's Prayer*, A Five-Week Study Series (London: USPG, 2003).

14. See Terry Eagleton, *Sweet Violence: The Idea of the Tragic* (Oxford: Blackwell, 2003); I am indebted to Martin Kitchen for drawing my attention to this important work: cf. *Being Human: A Christian Understanding of Personhood Illustrated with reference to Power, Money, Sex and Time*, Report of the Doctrine Commission of the General Synod of the Church of England (London: Church House Publishing, 2003).

15. See Daniel W. Hardy, 'Worship and the Formation of a Holy People', in Stephen C. Barton (ed.), *Holiness, Past and Present* (Edinburgh: T. & T. Clark, 2003), pp. 493–496.

16. I am much indebted to insights on tradition in David Brown, *Tradition and Imagination: Revelation and Change* (Oxford: Oxford University Press, 1999); and *Discipleship and Imagination: Christian Tradition and Truth* (Oxford: Oxford University Press, 2000).

17. Jonathan Clark, *Our Shadowed Present: Modernism, Postmodernism and History* (London: Atlantic Books, 2003).

# Select Bibliography

Bailey, D. Sherwin, *Sponsors at Baptism and Confirmation* (London: SPCK, 1952)

Barclay, William, *The Lord's Prayer*, with foreword by George Carey (Berkhamsted: James, 1998)

Barth, Karl, *Prayer: 50th Anniversary Edition*, ed. Don Saliers, with essays by I. John Hesselink, Daniel L. Migliore and Donald K. McKim (Louisville and London: Westminster John Knox Press, 2002)

Boff, Leonardo, *The Lord's Prayer: The Prayer of Integral Liberation* (Maryhill: Orbis, 1983)

Bonhoeffer, Dietrich, *The Cost of Discipleship* Complete Edition (London: SCM Press, 1959)

Bornert, R., *Les Commentaires Byzantins de la Divine Liturgie du VIIe au XVe Siècle*, Archives de l'Orient Chrétien 9 (Paris: Institut Français d'Études Byzantines, 1966)

Botte, B., OSB (ed.), *Ambroise de Milan: Des Sacrements. Des Mystères*, Sources Chrétiennes 25bis (Paris: Cerf, 1994)

Bradshaw, Paul F., and Hoffmann, Lawrence, *The Making of Jewish and Christian Worship* (Notre Dame, IN: University of Notre Dame Press, 1991)

Bradshaw, Paul F., 'The Gospel and the Catechumenate in the Third Century', *Journal of Theological Studies* 50.1 (1999), pp. 143–152

Bradshaw, Paul F., *The Search for the Origins of Christian Worship* (London: SPCK, 1st edn 1992; 2nd rev. edn 2001)

Brightman, F. E., *Liturgies Eastern and Western*, vol. i: *Eastern* (Oxford: Clarendon Press, 1896)

Brightman, F. E., *The English Rite*, 2 vols (London: Rivingtons, 1915)

Brown, Peter, *Augustine of Hippo: A Biography* (London: Faber, 1967)

Brown, R. E., 'The Pater Noster as an Eschatological Prayer', in *New Testament Essays* (New York: Doubleday, 1982), pp. 217–253

Buchanan, Colin, *The Lord's Prayer in the Church of England*, Grove Worship Booklet 131 (Bramcote: Grove, 1995)

Calvin, John, *Calvin: Institutes of the Christian Religion*, ed. John T.

McNeill and Ford Lewis Battles, Library of Christian Classics 21 (Philadelphia: Westminster, 1961)

Carmignac, Jean, '"Fais que nous n'entrons pas dans la tentation"': la portée d'une négation devant un verbe au causatif', *Revue Biblique* 72.2 (1965), pp. 218–226

Carmignac, Jean, *Recherches sur le Notre Père* (Paris: Letouzey, 1969)

Church of England Liturgical Commission, *Modern Liturgical Texts* (London: SPCK, 1968)

Connolly, R. H., and Codrington, H. W., *Two Commentaries on the Jacobite Liturgy*, Text and Translation Society (London: Williams and Norgate, 1913)

Cranmer, Thomas, *Miscellaneous Writings and Letters of Thomas Cranmer*, Parker Society (Cambridge: Cambridge University Press, 1846)

Cullmann, Oscar, *Prayer in the New Testament*, tr. John Bowden (London: SCM Press, 1997)

De Latte, R., 'Saint Augustin et le baptême: étude liturgico-historique du rituel baptismal des adultes chez Saint Augustin', *Questions Liturgiques* 56.4 (1975), pp. 177–224; and 'Saint Augustin et le baptême: étude liturgico-historique du rituel baptismal des enfants chez Saint Augustin', *Questions Liturgiques* 57.1 (1976), pp. 41–55

Denzinger, H., *Ritus Orientalium*, vol. i (Würzburg: Stahl, 1863)

Dix, Gregory, *The Shape of the Liturgy* (London: Dacre, 1945)

Duffy, Eamon, *The Stripping of the Altars* (New Haven: Yale University Press, 1992)

Evans, C. F., *The Lord's Prayer* (London: SPCK, 1963; SCM Press, 1997)

Evans, G. R. (ed.), *The Medieval Theologians* (Oxford: Blackwell, 2001)

Fisher, J. D. C., *Christian Initiation: Baptism in the Medieval West*, Alcuin Club Collections 47 (London: SPCK, 1965)

Fisher, J. D. C., *Christian Initiation: The Reformation Period*, Alcuin Club Collections 51 (London: SPCK, 1970)

Fry, Timothy (ed.), *The Rule of St Benedict in Latin and English with Notes* (Collegeville: Liturgical Press, 1981)

Furberg, Ingemar, *Das Pater Noster in der Messe*, Bibliotheca Theologiae Practicae 21 (Lund: Gleerups, 1968)

Graef, Hilda C. (ed.), *St Gregory of Nyssa: The Lord's Prayer; The Beatitudes*, Ancient Christian Writers 18 (New York: Newman Press, 1954)

Green, H. Benedict, CR, *Matthew, Poet of the Beatitudes*, Journal for the Study of the New Testament Supplement Series 203 (Sheffield: Academic Press, 2001)

Grisbrooke, W. Jardine (ed. and tr.) *The Liturgical Portions of the Apostolic Constitutions: A Text for Students*, Alcuin/GROW Liturgical Study 13–14 (Bramcote: Grove, 1991)

# Select Bibliography

Harmless, William, *Augustine and the Catechumenate* (New York: Pueblo, 1995)

Hussey, Maurice, 'The Petitions of the Paternoster in Mediaeval English Literature', *Medium Aevum* 27.1 (1958), pp. 8–16

Jackson, M. G., 'The Lord's Prayer in St Augustine', in E. A. Livingstone (ed.), *Studia Patristica*, vol. xxvii (Louvain: Peeters, 1993), pp. 311–321

Jasper, R. C. D., and Cuming, G. J. (eds), *The Prayers of the Eucharist: Early and Reformed*, 3rd rev. edn (New York: Pueblo, 1987)

Jeremias, Joachim, *The Prayers of Jesus*, Studies in Biblical Theology (London: SCM Press, 1967)

Johnson, Maxwell, *Liturgy in Early Christian Egypt*, Alcuin/GROW Liturgical Study 33 (Bramcote: Grove, 1995)

Jungmann, Joseph-Andreas, *Missarum Sollemnia*, vol. iii, Théologie Historique 21 (Paris: Aubier, 1954)

Kelly, J. N. D., *Jerome* (London: Duckworth, 1975)

Kelly, J. N. D., *Golden Mouth* (London: Duckworth, 1995)

Lampe, Geoffrey, ' "Our Father" in the Fathers', in Peter Brooks (ed.), *Christian Spirituality: Essays in Honour of Gordon Rupp* (London: SCM Press, 1975), pp. 11–31

Lienhard, Marc, 'Luther et Calvin, commentateurs du Notre Père', *Revue d'Histoire et de Philosophes Religieuses* 72.1 (1992), pp. 73–88

Lohmeyer, Ernst, *The Lord's Prayer*, tr. John Bowden (London: Collins, 1965)

Luther, Martin, *Luther's Works*, vol. xxi: *The Sermon on the Mount (Sermons) and the Magnificat* (Saint Louis: Concordia, 1956); vol. xlii: *Devotional Writings I* (Philadelphia: Fortress, 1968); vol. liii: *Liturgy and Hymns* (Philadelphia: Fortress, 1965)

Luther, Martin, *Luther's Large Catechism*, tr. J. N. Lenker (Minneapolis: Augsburg, 1967)

Luther, Martin, *Luther's Small Catechism, with Explanation* (St Louis: Concordia, 1991)

Luz, Ulrich, *Matthew 1–7: A Commentary*, tr. Wilhelm C. Linss (Edinburgh: T. & T. Clark, 1990)

McAdoo, H. R., *First of its Kind: Jeremy Taylor's Life of Christ: A Study in the Funtioning of a Moral Theology* (Norwich: Canterbury Press, 1994)

Maskell, William, *Monumenta Ritualia Ecclesiae Anglicanae*, vol. ii (London: Pickering, 1846)

Maximus the Confessor, *Selected Writings: Maximus Confessor*, tr. and ed. George C. Berthold, Classics of Western Spirituality (New York: Paulist Press, 1985)

Mazza, Enrico, *Mystagogy: A Theology of Liturgy in the Patristic Age* (New York: Pueblo, 1989)

Meyendorff, P. (ed. and tr.), *St Germanus of Constantinople: On the Divine Liturgy* (Crestwood, NY: St Vladimir's Seminary Press, 1984)

Old, Hughes Oliphant, *The Shaping of the Reformed Baptismal Rite in the Sixteenth Century* (Grand Rapids: Eerdmans, 1992)

Origen, *Prayer: Exhortation to Martyrdom*, tr. John O'Meara, Ancient Christian Writers 19 (London: Longmans, 1954)

Petuchowski, Jakob, and Brocke, Michael (eds), *The Lord's Prayer and Jewish Liturgy* (New York: Seabury, 1978)

Reuter, Johannes (Reiters, Janis), *Oratio Dominica XL Linguarum* (Rostock: Johannes Keil, 1675), facsimile reprint, with introduction and notes, B. Jegers (Copenhagen: Imanta, 1954)

Schmemann, Alexander, *Our Father* (New York: St Vladimir's Seminary Press, 2002)

Simonetti, M., and Moreschini, C. (eds), *Sancti Cypriani Episcopi Opera* (Pars II), Corpus Christianorum Series Latina 3A (Turnhout: Brepols, 1976)

Stanton, Graham N., *A Gospel for a New People: Studies in Matthew's Gospel* (Edinburgh: T. & T. Clark, 1992)

Stevenson, Kenneth, *Nuptial Blessing: A Study of Christian Marriage Rites*, Alcuin Club Collections 64 (London: SPCK, 1982)

Stevenson, Kenneth, *Abba, Father: Understanding and Using the Lord's Prayer* (Norwich: Canterbury Press, 2000)

Stevenson, Kenneth, 'Richard Hooker and the Lord's Prayer: A Chapter in Reformation Controversy', *Scottish Journal of Theology* 57.1 (2004)

Stevenson, Kenneth, 'The Six Homilies of Peter Chrysologus on the Lord's Prayer', in Maxwell E. Johnson and L. Edward Phillips (eds), *Studia Liturgica Diversa: Essays in Honor of Paul F. Bradshaw* (Portland: Pastoral Press, 2004)

Taft, Robert F., SJ, *The Liturgy of the Hours in East and West: The Origins of the Divine Office and its Meaning Today* (Collegeville: Liturgical Press, 1986)

Taft, Robert F., SJ, 'The Lord's Prayer in the Eucharist: When and Why?' *Ecclesia Orans* 14 (1997) pp. 137–155.

Taft, Robert F., SJ, *A History of the Liturgy of St John Chrysostom: The Pre-Communion Rites*, Orientalia Christiana Analecta 261 (Rome: Pontificio Istituto Orientale, 2000)

Taft, Robert F., SJ, *Beyond East and West: Problems in Liturgical Understanding*, 2nd rev. edn, enlarged, Edizioni Orientalia Christiana (Rome: Pontifical Oriental Institute, 2001)

Teresa of Avila, *The Way of Perfection* (tr. E. Allison Peers) (London: Sheed and Ward, 1977)

Underhill, Evelyn, *Abba: Meditations based on the Lord's Prayer* (London: Longmans, 1940)

# Select Bibliography

Vokes, P. E., 'The Lord's Prayer in the First Three Centuries', in F. L. Cross (ed.), *Studia Patristica*, vol. x, Texte und Untersuchungen 107 (Berlin: Akademieverlag, 1970) pp. 253–260

von Stritzky, Maria-Barbara, *Studien zur Überlieferung und Interpretation des Vaterunsers in der frühchristlichen Literatur*, Münsterische Beiträge zur Theologie 57 (Münster: Aschendorff, 1989)

Wainwright, Geoffrey, *Doxology: The Praise of God in Worship, Doctrine and Life* (London: Epworth Press, 1980)

Wesley, John, *The Works of John Wesley*, vol. i: *Sermons I* (Nashville: Abingdon, 1984)

Whitaker, E. C., *Documents of the Baptismal Liturgy* (London: SPCK, 1970)

Williams, Rowan, *Teresa of Avila* (London: Geoffrey Chapman, 1991)

Willis, G. G., 'St Gregory the Great and the Lord's Prayer in the Roman Mass', in *Further Essays in Early Roman Liturgy*, Alcuin Club Collections 50 (London: SPCK, 1968)

Wright, Tom, *The Lord and His Prayer*, Triangle Books (London: SPCK, 1996)

Yarnold, Edward, SJ, *The Awe-Inspiring Rites of Initiation* (Edinburgh: T. & T. Clark, 1994)

# Index of Names

# Index of Subjects